The Cas

or

The Impossi

University of Pennsylvania Press
NEW CULTURAL STUDIES
*Joan DeJean, Carroll Smith-Rosenberg,
and Peter Stallybrass, Editors*

A complete listing of the books
in the series appears at the
back of this volume

The Case of Peter Pan

or

The Impossibility of Children's Fiction

Jacqueline Rose

University of Pennsylvania Press

Philadelphia

First published 1984 by The Macmillan Press Ltd.; reprinted 1985

1993 edition published by the University of Pennsylvania Press by
arrangement with The Macmillan Press Ltd

U.S. Library of Congress Cataloging in Publication Data

Rose, Jacqueline.
  The case of Peter Pan, or The impossibility of children's fiction
  / Jacqueline Rose.
    p.   cm.
  Originally published: London : Macmillan, 1984.
  Includes bibliographical references and index.
  ISBN 0-8122-1435-8
    1. Barrie, J. M. (James Matthew), 1860–1937. Peter Pan.
2. Children's stories–History and criticism. 3. Peter Pan
(Fictitious character) 4. Children—Books and reading. 5. Children
in literature. I. Title. II. Title: Impossibility of children's
fiction.
[PR4074.P33R67 1992]
823'.912—dc20   92-30533
                                                          CIP

Printed in the United States of America

For Eloïse Bennett
who has *grown up—*

Contents

Acknowledgements

I would like to thank Frank Kermode for his supervision of this work in its early stages and for his support and encouragement throughout.

I am also indebted to: Marc Soriano, the Central Research Fund Committee of the University of London, Christina M. Hanson at the Beinecke Rare Book and Manuscript Library of Yale University, the staff at the Enthoven Theatre Collection of the Victoria and Albert Museum, and the House Governors of the Great Ormond Street Hospital for Sick Children for interviews in 1976 and 1982.

The illustrations on pp. 39–40 are based on original drawings by A. H. Watson.

Special personal thanks to Gillian Rose, Colin MacCabe and Greg Bright.

The Return of Peter Pan

'Nothing is a precedent until it is done for the first time.'
Lord Boyd-Carpenter, debating Lord Callaghan's proposal on
rights in *Peter Pan* presented as an Amendment to the Copyright,
Designs and Patent Bill in the English House of Lords, after pas-
sage of the Bill through the House of Commons, 10 March 1988
(The Parliamentary Debates, 1987–88)

'It will be a very different story from the one you've been putting
about'
First mother to Wendy, John and Michael at the end of the lesbian production of *Peter Pan*, Drill Hall Theatre, London, Christmas 1991

In 1987 the Great Ormond Street Hospital for Sick Children in
London, to which James Barrie had assigned copyright in *Peter Pan*,
lost its right to refuse permission in the work. A special amendment
brought to the English House of Lords by ex-Labour Prime Minister James Callaghan, newly elevated to a peerage, restored the
Hospital's share in the royalties but not its control over the interpretation or, as it is legally termed, the 'exploitation' of *Peter Pan*.
As if in response, Peter Pan has since surfaced as a high-flying business executive (Steven Spielberg's 1992 Columbia Tristar film *Hook*)
and as a lesbian in disguise (the 1991 Christmas production put on
by the all-woman theatre group Dramatrix at London's Drill Hall).
It is at least arguable which of these two interpretations – grown
man or lesbian – presents the innocence of childhood with its greatest affront. Either way, both of these versions seem, if not quite for
adults only, certainly for the grown-ups.

Since *The Case of Peter Pan* was first published in 1984, the concept of childhood innocence has been put under multiple strain. Not just by these variations on an old theme which should by definition have resisted them, since the only meaning of *Peter Pan* is the eternal sameness with which it (or he) recurs, but also in the wider culture, in the form of a crisis in the public perception of what, exactly, *is* a relation to a child. The amendment by James Callaghan was not without its ironies since the only reason the Hospital was in such dire need of the money was the systematic assault on the National Health Service which had started with the defeat of his own government by the Conservatives in 1979. It is not, objected another Labour peer, the task of the theatre to subsidise hospitals, but the task of the state to fund them: 'Where exactly is it all leading?' Peter Pan, it seems, always provokes a crisis of precedence because of the tension between his eternal repetition and his status as a 'once and for all'. Hence one refrain of the debate: 'a unique situation'; 'a unique solution to a unique problem'; 'it is only Peter Pan who never grows up and only rights in *Peter Pan* that we are prepared to see continue indefinitely'.

Not for the first time in its history, *Peter Pan* has revealed its fully political dimension: its bizarre appearance in the House of Lords was a symptom of the very ill it was being called on to cure. In the context of the English debate, the fear about setting a precedent concealed a vaguely acknowledged awareness that the case was not aberrant but representative, that charity as opposed to state provision, far from being exceptional, was becoming a norm ('this fast moving technological age where we as a society are asked to be more Christian, more forbearing and more supportive of those who are less fortunate, we may well be asked, not in 300 years or 30 years, but perhaps in three years, to approve something similar'). Conservatism in Britain neglects provision for children in exact proportion as it elevates the principle of the good fairy – 'little people who grant wishes and do good deeds around the world' – into a social law (one version of the child – 'a little person' – doing service for another). Thus *Peter Pan* managed, almost, to force a recognition of one of Conservatism's central and most cynical political and ideological turns.

Quirky but significant, the debate in the English House of Lords showed the extent to which sentimentality about childhood ('My Lords, I must tell my noble friend that one of my greatest friends was Tinkerbell') is the other side of guilt. What are we doing *to* – or not doing *for* – children? While this question appeared in the form of an embarrassment in relation to *Peter Pan*, elsewhere in the culture, but parallel to the developments which led to that debate, it has been taking on a far more disturbing shape. If there is widespread sexual abuse of children, then it is not so much the innocence of childhood as the boundary between adult and child, their status as stable and knowable entities, which starts to shake. Child abuse confronts us with the violence of limits flouted and transgressed. Bodies open where they should remain closed, and a defining space is invaded – the space which conceptually as well as physically is meant to keep children and adults apart.

In response to this discovery – something which can fairly be called one of the traumas of the 1980s – innocence then returns with all the renewed authority of a value literally and brutally under assault. In order to insist on the reality of child sexual abuse (something which can still be fervently and religiously denied), you pay a conceptual price. In one, dominant set of representations, a symbolic shift – partly a re-flexing of old images – has taken place. The child victim is desexualised – necessarily – for there does not seem to be a readily available language in which one can talk of childhood sexuality and insist on the reality of child sexual abuse at the same time. Language itself is made innocent – since children can only be made to talk of abuse with great difficulty, it is essential to believe them when they do (in cases of alleged child sexual abuse, the idea that there might be play, fantasy or ambiguity in language is almost invariably used to discredit the child). It is essential, too, that the child's voice be clear and unequivocal in order to lift the adult burden of disbelief. More important still, if damage to children can be shown to stem from lone abusers, then the wider culture – with its responsibilities, trials and dangers in relation to children – can be absolved. Thus childhood returns to a pre-Freudian state of sexual innocence and families, that is, families without abusers, revert to the ideal. Oddly labile as a concept (contrary to first appearances), innocence stretches its meanings and contracts.

If *Peter Pan* is so relevant in this context – if it indeed gains new significance when seen in the framework of these events – it is because its own myth of innocence has ridden the back of all these trouble spots (of sexuality, language, social policy) concerning the child. In the pages which follow, I argue that *Peter Pan* was only ever innocent to the extent that it told a different story; that Peter's innocence was protested in exact measure to the burden of repression which he had, from the outset, been expected to bear.

What seemed to me to make *Peter Pan* so significant was the way that, as a cultural myth, it undoes itself, or offers the tools for its own undoing, as it goes. There is, wrote Roland Barthes, around the meaning of every myth 'a halo of virtualities where other possible meanings are floating' (Barthes, 1972, p. 132). 'Floating', 'virtuality' – the terms perfectly capture that deceptive aura of inoffensive openness or potentiality which is the hallmark of *Peter Pan*. It is, however, precisely because *Peter Pan* offers virtuality and openness with such insistence that it seems to call attention to the trouble and murkiness not so much hidden underneath as running all along the seams.

Peter Pan is a front – a cover not as concealer but as vehicle – for what is most unsettling and uncertain about the relationship between adult and child. It shows innocence not as a property of childhood but as a portion of adult desire. In this context, the eruptions of the 1980s, as they relate to *Peter Pan* and to childhood more generally, can be read as the return of the repressed. There is nothing like a born again Conservatism (moral majority in the United States), relying as it does on myths of primordial innocence, racial purity, Victorian values – revivalism always sets its sights on purity – for bringing the myth of innocence to a head. Racism has indeed always been one of the subtexts of *Peter Pan* – *Peter Pan* can also be read as one of the great myths of an empire in decline. It is in fact remarkable how often 'Englishness' and childhood innocence appear as mutually reinforcing terms – the House of Lords debate: 'I think if we follow that precedent we will find ourselves in very strange Indian country'; one comment on the controversy over child abuse: 'Unless this is a vastly different country from the one I think I know, I simply do not believe in the avalanche of child abuse presented by [these] figures' (Toner, 1987, p. 21). In the context of the conservative revival and of child sexual abuse, innocence has found itself simultaneously and alternately destabilised and reaffirmed. Perhaps more than ever it has revealed something of its essential *desperation*. But whenever innocence reappears on the cultural agenda, there is always something – I would suggest – to be learnt from *Peter Pan*.

Peter Pan lays bare a basic social and psychic structure – that so-called perversion resides in the house of innocence, alarming not because it is alien to innocence but because it is aleady there. It felt, for instance, both aberrant and strangely unsurprising to watch a

lesbian production of *Peter Pan*. After all, since Peter Pan is tradi-
tionally played by a woman, why not make Peter's resistence to
Wendy's advances the sign of her failure to acknowledge her true
desire? Why not take that life-and-death moment of audience participation – 'clap your hands if you believe in fairies' – at its word?
(Once you see it performed like this it will never be the same again.)
When homophobia receives government sanction, as in Great Britain, where it has been made illegal to promote homosexuality as a
'pretended family relationship' in schools, this production could be
used to make a simple political point. As Wendy, John and Michael,
in flight from their lesbian parents, play at happy families on the
island (Wendy: 'Just you keep quiet about those horrible mummies
back there. Proper families have one mummy and one daddy and
that's how it should be'), the audience is forced to ask which of the
two, 'normality' or 'deviance', is the pretense. Is normality one fantasy like – even if not *quite* like – the rest?

These questions, this unsettling of gender identities, were of
course present from the earliest performances of *Peter Pan*: in
Peter's swaggering effeminacy, in the high camp of Hook. In her
book *Vested Interests*, Marjorie Garber suggests that it is the 'split
vision' of transvestism which has always enchanted in *Peter Pan*:
'Peter Pan and Hook, a dream and nightmare of transvestism . . .
transgression without guilt, pain, penalty, conflict or cost: this is
what Peter Pan – and *Peter Pan* – is all about' (Garber, 1992, p. 184).
Thus, according to one reading, *Peter Pan* turns into the emblem of
a new license, the bearer of culturally repressed meanings which,
even if present from the start of its history, can only be spoken
openly today.

Transgression as enchantment or unadulterated pleasure – this
might be, however, to move the argument, to move *Peter Pan*, on a
little too fast. The psychoanalytic concept of repression suggests
that it is not without reason that the unconscious keeps, or tries to
keep, its most feared and cherished secrets to itself. Repression
would have no meaning if it could simply be lifted without cost. License is always bound, even in the form of defiance, to the law. If
Peter Pan is read today as pure transgression, the risk is that it will
simply reemerge on the other side of its more familiar mythology –
the reverse image of the innocence for which it stood, or seemed to
stand, before. Rather like the symptom in psychoanalysis, what
Peter Pan seems instead to demonstrate is a type of permanent

oscillation (between sugar and spice), not so much litheness of sig-
nification as resilience. It might be that we are witnessing the beginning of the end of *Peter Pan*; but to date *Peter Pan* has shown that
uncanny ability, which Brecht wrote of in relation to theatre in
Weimar Germany, to absorb or take on board exactly what it needs
in order to reproduce itself.

It seems important therefore to place these changes in the interpretation of *Peter Pan* in context, above all in the context of the other
very different meanings which it has been generating more or less at
the same time. Thus, on the other side of its more radical re-read-
ings, *Peter Pan* has become a type of self-diagnosing symptom of a
cultural malady seen as requiring much more limited forms of redress. Here *Peter Pan* appears as deficiency or lost internal object – as
in Dan Kiley's *Peter Pan Syndrome*, best-selling popular psychology
book first published in the United States in 1983, where Peter Pan
represents the alienation of men failing to confront the emotional
realities of the modern world (a failure for which women are finally
accountable and which they are exhorted to look out for and repair);
or in Spielberg's *Hook* where Peter Pan appears as that part of
human-ness which fathers must retrieve if families are to survive
the material onslaught of the modern age (nostalgia about childhood as corporate capitalism's last saving grace).

Spielberg's film is in fact a perfect example of what Roland
Barthes described as 'bourgeois myth' which appeals to a generalised humanity by glossing over social and cultural division, presenting itself as the solution to all ills. This is the very definition and
limit of a sentimental or weak liberalism which sees capitalist culture as reparable or redeemable by human-ness rather than in
need of more radical challenge or critique. Capitalism, or, at least
money, could, however, be said to be the ultimate meaning of Spielberg's *Peter Pan*. Anxiously, all Hollywood watched *Hook*. After a
period of financial over-reaching, it was on *Hook* that the material
future of Hollywood relied:

> Tonight's Hollywood premiere of *Hook*, the updated movie
> version of James Barrie's *Peter Pan*, could not be more crucial for
> the movie industry . . . Hollywood itself can draw a moral from
> *Hook*. Like Banning [Peter Pan's name as adult in the film], it has
> become too greedy, too self-interested. It has made movies that
> have cost too much'. ('Hollywood hangs hopes on *Hook*', Brooks,
> p. 22)

One taboo attached to *Peter Pan* does, however, seem to have been irretrievably broken in the past decade. It brings us to transgression-as-celebration at its most fragile edge or breaking point. 'No one ever touches me', Peter says to Wendy in their famous dialogue at the start of the play. It is because Peter Pan can never be touched that he remains forever disembodied (rather than the other way round), because he surrounds himself with an aura of inpenetrability that his mythical status persists, that he remains eternal child. Children of course touch each other, but more or less innocently. The concept of childhood sexuality in Freud always had its limits in this sense since infantile sexuality was precisely not genital but polymorphous, unfocussed and diffuse. It might not be a coincidence that Peter Pan crosses the barrier of untouchability (both in *Hook* and at the Drill Hall) at the very moment when the permeability of that same barrier revealed by child sexual abuse has engendered one of the decades apparently most unassimilable cultural shocks. Seen in this context, *Peter Pan* appears perhaps less as myth, more as 'sublime object' (the term is coined by the psychoanalytic cultural critic from Ljubljana, Slavoj Zizek), an object sported by the culture which attracts to itself the component of fantasy belonging to all social identities; instead of veiling a hidden reality, it captures and serves to keep in social circulation what is most difficult and potentially unmanageable about subjective desire. But, precisely by touching on the most vulnerable point of identity, it aways contains a potential terror.

If we return to the question of child abuse, we see that it has something to tell which is more, and perhaps even more difficult, than the story of violated and reaffirmed innocence. While it offers one narrative of discovery and legitimate outrage, it also offers another – possibly incompatible with the very concept or logic of narrative – in which any form of certainty about bodies, language and sexuality disappears. On the one hand, there are all the forms of conviction which the discovery of child abuse has fostered and on which it has had to insist and rely. On the other, there has been a systematic undermining of convictions – personal and professional – in every field which the discovery has reached.

Touch a child out of intimacy, play or abuse. We often do not know – children often do not know – the difference. In 1987, Marietta Higgs, the paediatrician from Cleveland in the North of England, was at the centre of the largest controversy in England over child sexual abuse. Between the spring and early summer,

Higgs, together with her co-paediatrician Geoffrey Wyatt, diagnosed abuse in a total of 165 children at Middlesborough General Hospital (at the end of a lengthy legal battle, 26 children from 12 families were deemed wrongly diagnosed, most became the subjects of some state support or intervention, contrary to the impression conveyed by the media that most cases had been cleared by the courts). Higgs was renowned – legally challenged and publicly pilloried – for the clarity or decisiveness with which she removed suspected cases from their homes. And yet in a public lecture she herself stated that abuse is not always experienced as abuse, that the boundary between intrusion and intimacy can be blurred.

How do you read children's bodies? What does an anus which opens at touch tell you (violation or response)? What does it mean to believe in utterances when events pass under silence and the child's speech can serve to deflect and protect as much as reveal? Can something be known if it is not spoken? Can something be known but in the form of a knowledge which cannot be passed on or shared? How can you make compatible psychiatric and social work time (the time for understanding, the time to act)? What do you do when every response provokes another crisis or round of dispute? It was, as Beatrix Campbell put it in *Unofficial Secrets*, her brilliant study of the Cleveland case, 'as disturbing as a murder where there's no motive, no murderer, no clues, no confession . . . the classic case of the crisis that causes' (Campbell, 1988, p. 5) (the crisis, we could rephrase, that throws the idea of cause into crisis).

Allowance should have been made, stated Lord Justice Elizabeth Butler-Sloss in her official government-commissioned inquiry into the Cleveland case, 'for the boundaries of present knowledge and the possibility of the unknown' (Butler-Sloss, 1988, p. 144). Her report can be, and has been, read as evasion: the Commission never passed judgement on whether the children had or had not been abused, the one thing everyone wanted to know. But it can also be read as providing, through that same hesitancy, a brake on the fantasy of knowledge without qualification or flaw. For everyone who approached it, the sexual abuse of children seemed to provoke a crisis of self-authorisation and belief. Social workers stated to the Commission that their conviction in their methods was 'shaken and questioned', doctors that the whole concept of diagnosis had to be redefined ('there was a time when an illness consisted of a defined syndrome of symptoms and signs with definite pathology and a discoverable physical cause'). We have, stated one psychiatrist, 'no reliable norms for interpretation of play with certainty as to its origin and meaning.' There is a possibility that 'we will not know.' Extraordinarily, in a crisis on which everyone had an opinion ('no matter where you went or who you met, people had something to say about it. They had an opinion'), there was nothing, about bodies or language, which could in the final analysis be unequivocally ascertained.

It may be that we need today to approach *Peter Pan* from the angle of this level of disturbance; it may be the rawness of this uncertainty, alongside the openly conservative appeal back to innocence, which is the difference between the early 1980s and today. It is as if innocence (that moment before the trials of knowledge) and unknowing (certainty's loss of pure faith) have both been stretched to the limit, providing a new space for the emergence of the radical and the re-policed meanings which seem today to cluster around *Peter Pan*. But the issue may not finally be just the other, freer, sexualities or the more radical social critique which *Peter Pan's* mythical status has served, with diminishing success, to keep at bay. *Peter Pan* has certainly fulfilled this traditional function of myth, as bearer and veil for a hidden history, as the study that follows makes clear. But what is now in question is less the *content* (which sexuality, normal or deviant, innocent or corrupt?), more the *form* or *frame* through which one approaches a child.

The crisis of child sexual abuse in the 1980s has made it harder and harder to know, when we describe a child and even more our relationship to it, what we are talking about. Or to put it another way, it has forced us to recognise that childhood will not provide us with the answers we need to guarantee a certain knowledge of ourselves. For it is not only childhood, but adulthood itself, which can serve as the last of all myths. As Melanie Klein puts it in her famous *Narrative of a Child Analysis*, growing up is not omniscient conviction but hope, 'the hope to grow up' – the alternative in the mind of the adult neurotic being either to be very young or very old: 'there seems nothing between the two extremes' (Klein, 1961, p. 180).

If we do not know what a child is, then it becomes impossible to invest in their sweet self-evidence, impossible to use the translucent clarity of childhood to deny the anxieties we have about our psychic, sexual and social being in the world. We could say that self-knowingness – that sureness, complacency and promotion of fixed identity on which so much right wing ideology of the last decade

has thrived – has, in the past decade, been increasingly undermined by what has been presented to us by the child. It is an ironic
reversal of the child's status as one of the key modern bearers of all
myth. Today an even more radical uncertainty than before confronts the shifting yet self-perpetuating myth of *Peter Pan*.

Jacqueline Rose, September 1992

BIBLIOGRAPHY

Barthes, Roland. *Mythologies* (New York: Hill and Wang, 1972).
Brooks, Richard. 'Hollywood hangs hopes on *Hook*', *Observer*, 8 December,
    1991.
Butler-Sloss, Lord Justice Elizabeth. *Report of the Inquiry into Child Abuse in
    Cleveland* (London: Her Majesty's Stationery Office, 1988).
Campbell, Beatrix. *Unofficial Secrets: Child Sexual Abuse – The Cleveland Case*
    (London: Virago, 1988).
Garber, Marjorie. *Vested Interests: Cross-Dressing and Cultural Anxiety* (New
    York: Routledge, 1992)
Kiley, Dan. *The Peter Pan Syndrome: Men Who Have Never Grown Up* (New
    York: Dodd and Mead, 1983).
Klein, Melanie. *Narrative of a Child Analysis: The Conduct of the Psycho-Analysis
    of Children as Seen in the Treatment of a Ten-year-old Boy* (New York: Basic
    Books, 1961).
The Parliamentary Papers (Hansard), Fifth Series, Vol. CDXCIV, House of
    Lords Session 1987–88.
Toner, Michael. 'Should a father be afraid to kiss his daughter goodnight?'
    Sunday Express, 28 June, 1987.
Zizek, Slavoj. *The Sublime Object of Ideology* (New York/London: Verso,
    1989).

Introduction

Peter Pan offers us the child – for ever. It gives us the child, but it does not speak *to* the child. In fact so rarely has it spoken to the child throughout its history, that it led me to ask whether there might not be some relation between this all-too-perfect presence of the child and a set of problems, or evasions, in the very concept of children's fiction itself. Children's fiction rests on the idea that there is a child who is simply there to be addressed and that speaking to it might be simple. It is an idea whose innocent generality covers up a multitude of sins. This book will attempt to trace the fantasy which lies behind the concept of children's fiction, and will base its case on *Peter Pan*.

Peter Pan stands in our culture as a monument to the impossibility of its own claims – that it represents the child, speaks to and for children, addresses them as a group which is knowable and exists for the book, much as the book (so the claim runs) exists for them. Where or how such a claim originates in the first place will be one of the questions asked here, but the question will be focused on *Peter Pan* in so far as *Peter Pan* is the text for children which has made that claim most boldly, and which most clearly reveals it as a fraud. *Peter Pan* has never, in any easy way, been a book for children at all, but the question this throws back to us is whether there can be any such thing.

Children's fiction is impossible, not in the sense that it cannot be written (that would be nonsense), but in that it hangs on an impossibility, one which it rarely ventures to speak. This is the impossible relation between adult and child. Children's fiction is clearly about that relation, but it has the remarkable characteristic of being about something which it hardly ever talks of. Children's fiction sets up a world in which the adult comes first

1

(author, maker, giver) and the child comes after (reader, product, receiver), but where neither of them enter the space in between. To say that the child is inside the book – children's books are after all as often as not *about* children – is to fall straight into a trap. It is to confuse the adult's intention to get at the child with the child it portrays. If children's fiction builds an image of the child inside the book, it does so in order to secure the child who is outside the book, the one who does not come so easily within its grasp.

There is, in one sense, no body of literature which rests so openly on an acknowledged difference, a rupture almost, between writer and addressee. Children's fiction sets up the child as an outsider to its own process, and then aims, unashamedly, to take the child *in*.

None of this appears explicitly inside the book itself, which works precisely to the extent that any question of who is talking to whom, and why, is totally erased. We do see something of it in the expanding industry of children's book criticism, but mostly in the form of a disavowal – the best book for children is a book for adult *and* child, or else in the form of a moralism (another version of the same thing) – the best book is the book which does the child most good, that is, the book which secures the reader to its intent and can be absolutely sure of its effects.

Let it be said from the start that it will be no part of this book's contention that what is for the good of the child could somehow be better defined, that we could, if we shifted the terms of the discussion, determine what it is that the child really wants. It will not be an issue here of what the child wants, but of what the adult desires – desires in the very act of construing the child as the object of its speech. Children's fiction draws in the child, it secures, places and frames the child. How often has it been said recently that what is best about writing for children is that the writer can count absolutely on the child's willingness to enter into the book, and *live* the story? (Townsend, 1971, p. 13).

This is to describe children's fiction, quite deliberately, as something of a soliciting, a chase, or even a seduction. *Peter Pan* is certainly all of these. Recently we have been made at least partly aware of this, as J. M. Barrie's story has been told and retold, as the story of a man and five small boys, whom he picked up, stole and possessed (Dunbar, 1970; Birkin, 1979). Barrie eventually adopted the Llewellyn Davies boys around whom he built the story of *Peter Pan*, staking a claim to them which he had already acted out symbolically by drawing them into his tale. But in the case of *Peter Pan*, knowledge of this has taken longer to surface than it did, say, in the case of *Alice*, whose underworld journey was long ago traced to its author's fantasied seduction of a little girl. Charles Lutwidge Dodgson (*alias* Lewis Carroll) wrote his classic for children on condition that the child remain a little girl, held to him by the act of telling the tale. A sexual act which we can easily recognise now, despite (or because of) the innocence and youth of its object. But then, it is argued, Dodgson was a 'schizophrenic', both a mathematician and a writer for children (as if mathematics and verbal play were somehow incompatible), and the worst thing he did was take pictures of little girls (as if the visual image were not the ultimate fetish). *Alice* has been saved as a classic for children, and the question of what we mean by that '*for*' – the question of its more difficult implications – remains unasked.

In the case of *Peter Pan*, the problem is more delicate. Behind *Peter Pan* lies the desire of a man for a little boy (or boys), a fantasy or drama which has only recently caught the public eye.[1] Thus just at the moment when we are accepting the presence of sexuality in children's fiction (which we believed – wrongly – that the Victorians had repressed (Marcus, 1966)), we are asked to recognise it in a form which violates not only the innocence of childhood, not just that of children's fiction, but what we like to think of as normal sexuality itself. There is nothing too disturbing about a man desiring little girls – it is, after all, the desire in which little girls are in the end expected to recognise themselves. And the fact has in any case been relegated to a contingent status as far as *Alice*'s position as a classic for children is concerned. But 'men and little boys' is something else, something in which our very idea of what constitutes normal sexuality is at stake. Children's fiction cannot, I will be arguing, be discussed without touching on this question, but it almost invariably is.

Suppose, therefore, that Peter Pan is a little boy who does not grow up, not because he doesn't want to, but because someone else prefers that he shouldn't. Suppose, therefore, that what is at stake in *Peter Pan* is the adult's desire for the child. I am not using 'desire' here in the sense of an act which is sought after or which must actually take place. It is not relevant, therefore, to insist that nothing ever happened, or that Barrie was innocent of any interest in sex (a point which is often made). I am using desire to refer to a form of investment by the adult in the child, and to the demand made by the adult on the child as the effect of that investment, a demand which fixes the child and then holds it in place. A turning to the child, or a circulating around the child – what is at stake here is not so much something which could be enacted as something which cannot be spoken.

The sexual act which underpins *Peter Pan* is neither act nor fantasy in the sense in which these are normally understood and wrongly opposed to each other. It is an act in which the child is used (and abused) to represent the whole problem of what sexuality is, or can be, and to hold that problem at bay. This is something which, we will see, surfaces constantly throughout the history of *Peter Pan* – it is part of the fabric of the work. But the fact is either not known, or else it is displaced (as with Carroll) onto Barrie himself, and then disavowed (Barrie as the innocent of all innocents).

To call *Peter Pan* a fantasy does not, therefore, absolve us of the sexual question. It focuses it more sharply. At the moment when Barrie was writing *Peter Pan*, Freud was making his most crucial (and in this context least known) discovery that sexuality works above all at the level of fantasy, and that what we take to be our sexual identity is always precarious and can never be assumed. Sexuality persists, for all of us, at the level of the unconscious precisely because it is a question which is never quite settled, a story which can never be brought to a close. Freud is known to have undermined the concept of childhood innocence, but his real challenge is easily lost if we see in the child merely a miniature version of what our sexuality eventually comes to be. The child is sexual, but its sexuality (bisexual, polymorphous, perverse) threatens our own at its very roots. Setting up the child as innocent is not, therefore, repressing its sexuality – it is above all holding off any possible challenge to our own.

The problem is not, therefore, J. M. Barrie's – it is ours. Ours to the extent that we are undoubtedly implicated in the status which *Peter Pan* has acquired as the ultimate fetish of childhood. All Barrie ever did was to write *Peter Pan*, and even that can be disputed, as we will see. But it is we who have recognised *Peter Pan* ('recognised' in both senses of the term), and given it its status. *Peter Pan* has been almost unreservedly acclaimed as a children's classic for the greater part of this century. Its presence in our culture is in fact so diffused that most of the time we do not even notice it. We take it for granted as something which belongs to us and to children, without there being any need for us to ask the question of the relation between the two. Like all children's classics, *Peter Pan* is considered to speak for everyone – adult and child (which in itself neatly disposes of the whole issue of what we mean by fiction for children). The child and the adult are one at that point of pure identity which the best of children's books somehow manage to retrieve. Time and again in its history, *Peter Pan* has been set up as the very emblem of that purity and identity. But this, I would say, has only been possible (and desirable) because it reveals so crudely the travesty on which any such notion rests.

It is, therefore, no part of my intention to analyse Barrie, to try to produce a psychobiography which would diagnose the author so as to set *Peter Pan* free as a myth. *Peter Pan* is a myth, but its status as such rests on the very difficulty which most commentaries refuse to recognise, or else recognise in order to diagnose and remove. *Peter Pan* is a classic in which the problem of the relationship between adult and child is unmistakably at the heart of the matter.

Peter Pan was not originally intended for children. It first appeared inside a novel for adults, J. M. Barrie's *The Little White Bird* (Barrie, 1902), as a story told by the narrator to a little boy whom the narrator was trying to steal. In order for it to become a work for children, it was extracted from its source, transformed into a play, and sent out on its own. *Peter Pan* emerges, therefore, out of an unmistakable act of censorship. The book which it leaves behind is one of the most explicit accounts to date of what it might mean to write fiction for the child. *The Little White Bird* is the story of the difficulty of that process – the difficulty of the relation between adult and child, and a question about the sexuality of each. What is the sexuality of the narrator? What is the origin of the child? What is *going on* between them? Questions which are never quite answered in the book, but which provide the basis for the telling of *Peter Pan*. The rest of *Peter Pan*'s history can then be read as one long attempt to wipe out the residual signs of the disturbance out of which it was produced. *The Little White Bird* is an origin of sorts, but only in the sense that no origin is ever left behind, since it necessarily *persists*. *The Little White Bird* shows what cannot, or must not, be allowed to get into fiction for children, but the problems to which it so eloquently bears witness do not go away. They remain in such a way as to undermine, finally, any simple notion of children's fiction itself.

Thus the result of that first act of censorship was that *Peter Pan* was both never written and, paradoxically, has never ceased to be written. Barrie himself certainly couldn't manage it. He did not write the play until twenty-four years after its first production. The publication had nothing to do with children, since it was the only children's text in a volume of collected plays (this was the main publication although in the same year it was printed on its own). The story from *The Little White Bird* was eventually published separately, but it cannot be described as a book for children. It was released onto the fine art collector's market, at a time when a whole new market for children's books was developing, a market which it completely by-passed and to which it never belonged. Barrie persistently refused to write a narrative version of the play, and, when he did, it was a failure, almost incomprehensible, and later had to be completely rewritten along the lines of a new state educational policy on language in the early part of the century (Barrie, 1915). During this time Barrie authorised *Peter Pan* to a number of different writers, which means that its status as a classic for children depends at least as much on them as it does on Barrie himself. Barrie may well be the source of the play, but this constant dispersion of *Peter Pan* challenges any straightforward idea of origin or source. Above all it should caution us against the idea that things can simply be traced back to their beginning, since, in the case of *Peter Pan*, what followed is at least as important as what came before.

What has followed has been a total mystification of all these forms of difficulty and confusion. Barrie *is Peter Pan*, despite the fact that he could not write it. *Peter Pan* is a classic for children, despite the fact that they could not read it – either because it was too expensive, or because it was virtually impossible to read. Nowhere has it been recognised that there might be a problem of writing, of address, and of language, in the history of *Peter Pan*. *Peter Pan*'s dispersion – the fact that it is everywhere and nowhere at one and the same time – has been taken as the sign of its cultural value. Its own ethereal nature merely sanctions the eternal youth and innocence of the child it portrays, and for which it is most renowned.

The sexual disavowal is, therefore, a political disavowal. A disavowal of the material differences which are concealed behind the category of *all* children to which Peter Pan is meant to make its appeal. That *all* speaks volumes of a further set of evasions: not just why are we speaking to the child, and what is our investment in that process; but to which child are we speaking? For, as *Peter Pan* very clearly demonstrates, if we are talking to one group of children, then the chances are that we will not be speaking to another. More likely, the very idea of speaking to *all* children serves to close off a set of cultural divisions, divisions in which not only children, but we ourselves, are necessarily caught.

There is no children's book market which does not, on closer scrutiny, crumble under just such a set of divisions – of class, culture and literacy – divisions which undermine any generalised concept of the child. And there is no language for children which can be described independently of divisions in the institution of schooling, the institution out of which modern childhood has more or less been produced (Ariès, 1960). How language is spoken – both by and to the child – is subject to strictures which need to be located inside the institution where language is systematically taught. The clash between *Peter Pan*'s status as a cultural myth and as a children's book is nowhere clearer than at the point of its confrontation with educational policy of the state.

When *Peter Pan* was written, educational policy on language was directed towards a rigorous separation of the forms of language to be taught in different sectors of the state schools. A whole new concept of 'synthetic' language was developed in the public elementary schools. It was a language to be based on the impressions of the visible world, as opposed to the classical and literary language which was simultaneously being taught in the secondary schools. This is a division which still affects the way in which we use language today, but it is rarely discussed in relation to children's writing. Recently there has been attention paid to class difference in children's books, but this has been posed exclusively in terms of values, to be identified and then avoided in subsequent children's books. *Peter Pan* is no exception to this, and it can certainly be assessed in this way. But when *Peter Pan* is rewritten in order for it to be accepted into the state schools, class difference can be seen to operate at a more fundamental level – that of the base components of the language which the child is actually allowed to speak.

This is an issue which relates to our understanding of literature as a whole – the fact that language has an institutional history which determines how it is written, spoken and understood. But it is a history which most literary criticism, in its concern to identify creativity and individual expression, makes every effort to ignore. In the case of children's fiction, however, the problem comes much closer, since the child belongs to the very institution through which language is being produced. The failure to discuss the importance of educational policy on language for children's writing is, therefore, the more conspicuous evasion.

The material and sexual aspects of *Peter Pan* have been the vanishing-points of its history. They are there, however, and they can be exposed. But what we have been given instead is a glorification of the child. This suggests not only a refusal to acknowledge difficulties and contradictions in relation to childhood; it implies that we *use* the image of the child to deny those same difficulties in relation to ourselves.

Peter Pan comes at the end of a long history, one which can be traced back to the beginnings of children's fiction. Literature for children first became an independent commercial venture in England in the mid- to late-eighteenth century, at a time when conceptualisation of childhood was dominated by the philosophical writings of Locke and Rousseau. This is a fact which is known, but its implications for thinking about children's fiction have not been fully recognised. It is assumed that children's fiction has grown away from this moment, whereas in fact children's fiction has constantly returned to this moment, repeated it, and reproduced its fundamental conception of the child. Children's fiction has never completely severed its links with a philosophy which sets up the child as a pure point of origin in relation to language, sexuality and the state.

The earliest children's writers took from Locke the idea of an education based on the child's direct and unproblematic access to objects of the real world, an education which would by-pass the imperfections of language (Newbery, 1744, 1756; Watts, 1782). They took from Rousseau the idea that it is sexuality which most totally sabotages the child's correct use of language and its exact knowledge of the world. One of the earliest extended narratives for children, Thomas Day's *The History of Sandford and Merton* (Day, 1783–9), was based directly on Rousseau's *Emile* (Rousseau (1762) 1763). It shared with Rousseau's tract a conviction that both sexuality and social inequality were realities that the child somehow be used to circumvent. The child is rendered innocent of all the contradictions which flaw our interaction with the world. Above all, for both Locke and Rousseau, the child can be seen, observed and known in exactly the same way as the world can be grasped by a rational understanding.

Children's fiction emerges, therefore, out of a conception of both the child and the world as knowable in a direct and unmediated way, a conception which places the innocence of the child and a primary state of language and/or culture in a close and mutually dependent relation. It is a conception which has affected children's writing and the way that we think about it to this day. We can see it, in differing forms, in such apparently diverse types of writing as the fairy tale and the adventure story for boys. Andrew Lang published his fairy tales in the nineteenth century as the uncontaminated record of our cultural infancy (Lang, 1899) to which, it was assumed, the child had a direct and privileged access (an idea whose purely mythical nature was pointed out by Tolkien long ago (Tolkien (1938) 1947)). And the boy's adventure story, which came into its own in the mid to late nineteenth century with writers such as Marryat, Kingston, Henty and Stevenson, was always part of an exploratory and colonialist venture which assumed that discovering or seeing the world was the same thing as controlling it. Both types of writing are present in *Peter Pan* which condenses a whole history of children's fiction into its form. They can also be seen in the works of Alan Garner who is considered by many to be one of the most innovatory writers today. But what I want to stress in both cases is the idea which they share of a primitive or lost state to which the child has special access. The child is, if you like, something of a pioneer who restores these worlds to us, and gives them back to us with a facility or directness which ensures that our own relationship to them is, finally, safe.

I am not, of course, talking here of the child's own experience of the book which, despite all the attempts which have been made, I consider more or less impossible to gauge. What I am describing is how these different forms of writing, in their long and continuing association with childhood, have been thought about *for* children. Again, Freud's concept of the unconscious can be seen as a challenge to this association, for it not only undermines our idea of sexuality; it equally questions the idea of mastery which lies behind the notion that the world is something to which we simply have access, or that language is something which we can control. And yet for all the apparent shifts in the way that childhood and children's writing is discussed, what always seems to return in the analysis, in one form or another, is this idea of mastery, which means by implication securing the child's rationality, its control of sexuality or of language (or both).

Thus, for example, even when a troubling of sexuality is recognised in the fairy tale (Bettelheim, 1976), it is something contained by the cohesion of the narrative, transcended on the path to reality, and resolved in the name of a psychological and sexual identity, which ensures in the end that we can master not only the world, but also ourselves. And although addressed to a very different context of children's writing, a similar demand can be seen in the recent appeal to the coherence of realist writing in children's fiction, against the disintegration of the adult novel form, which can lead such a well-known children's writer as John Rowe Townsend to say without inhibition 'I came to the child because I see in him the last refuge from a literature gone berserk and ready for suicide' (quoting Isaac Bashevis Singer, Townsend, 1971, p. 12).

Peter Pan was written at the time of Freud, and the status which it has been given seems to testify above all to our inability to recognise the dislocation which he operated on our conception of childhood. Not just in the sense of what childhood is supposed to be, but, more crucially, as a challenge to why, in terms of our own relationship to language and sexuality, we attempt to construct an image of the child at all.

What we constantly see in discussion of children's fiction is how the child can be used to hold off a panic, a threat to our assumption that language is something which can simply be organised and cohered, and that sexuality, while it cannot be removed, will eventually take on the forms in which we prefer to recognise and acknowledge each other. Childhood also serves as a term of universal social reference which conceals all the historical divisions and difficulties of which children, no less than ourselves, form a part.

There is no child behind the category 'children's fiction', other than the one which the category itself sets in place, the one which it needs to believe is there for its own purposes. These purposes are often perverse and mostly dishonest, not wilfully, but of necessity, given that addressing the child must touch on all of these difficulties, none of which it dares speak. *Peter Pan* is sometimes scoffed at today for the excessive and cloying nature of its innocence. It is in fact one of the most fragmented and troubled works in the history of children's fiction to date. *Peter Pan* is peculiar, and yet not peculiar, in so far as it recapitulates a whole history of children's fiction which has not yet come to an end. My objective in exposing the difficulties of its history will be to make some contribution to the dismantling of what I see as the ongoing sexual and political mystification of the child.

1

Peter Pan and Freud
Who is talking and to whom?

We have been reading the wrong Freud to children.

We do not realise that Freud was first brought up against the unconscious when asking how we remember ourselves as a child. The unconscious is not an object, something to be laid hold of and retrieved. It is the term which Freud used to describe the complex ways in which our very idea of ourselves as children is produced. In 1897, two French psychologists, V. and C. Henri, published a monograph of adult recollections of childhood and were baffled by a number of apparently meaningless memories. Freud found their very 'innocence . . . mysterious' (Freud, SE, III, 1899, p. 306).[1] Setting himself to analyse one of his earliest recollections, he found that the event he remembered had never taken place. The importance of the memory was not, however, any the less for that. For what it revealed was the unresolved conflicts affecting the way in which he was thinking about himself *now*. The most crucial aspect of psychoanalysis for discussing children's fiction is its insistence that childhood is something in which we continue to be implicated and which is never simply left behind. Childhood persists – this is the opposite, note, from the reductive idea of a regression to childhood most often associated with Freud. It persists as something which we endlessly rework in our attempt to build an image of our own history. When we think about childhood, it is above all our investment in doing so which counts. The very ambiguity of the term 'children's fiction' – fiction the child produces or fiction given to the child? – is striking for the way in which it leaves the adult completely out of the picture.

Childhood is not an object, any more than the unconscious,

although this is often how they are both understood. The idea that childhood is something separate which can be scrutinised and assessed is the other side of the illusion which makes of childhood something which we have simply ceased to be. In most discussions of children's fiction which make their appeal to Freud, childhood is part of a strict developmental sequence at the end of which stands the cohered and rational consciousness of the adult mind. Children may, on occasions, be disturbed, but they do not disturb us as long as that sequence (and that development) can be ensured. Children are no threat to our identity because they are, so to speak, 'on their way' (the journey metaphor is a recurrent one). Their difference stands purely as the sign of just how far we have progressed.

We have been reading the wrong Freud to children, because this is the most reductive, even if it is the most prevalent, reading of Freud. It is reductive to the extent that it holds off the challenge, which is present in Freud's own work, to the very notions of identity, development and subjective cohesion which this conception of childhood is so often used to sustain.

When Freud analysed that first memory and laid out – not so much what it might mean as the processes of transformation which lay between the original event and what he chose to recall – he was demonstrating the divisions and distortions which are characteristic of our psychic life. Later he would formulate these processes more precisely in relation to dreams, jokes and slips of the tongue – phenomena which could not be dismissed as neurotic, but which revealed an essential continuity between the disturbances of Freud's patients and the psychic mechanisms of normal adult life. What Freud had discovered in that first recollection was that there are aspects of our psychic life which *escape* our conscious control. Childhood amnesia or partial recollection of childhood has nothing to do with a gradual cohering of the mind as we get older and our ability to remember improves. Instead it reveals that there are aspects of our childhood which one part of our mind, a part over which we precisely do not have control, would rather forget.

That moment was the starting-point for two sets of questions which would be closely related throughout Freud's work, and which are crucial to any consideration of fiction for the child: the question of the unconscious – its constant pull against our seeming identity (the unconscious is not the site of some irrational truth, its truth is merely this repeated slippage); the question of childhood – its threat to the idea that we have neatly picked up and resolved everything that came before on the way to where we are now. The issue of childhood sexuality is subordinate to these two questions. For it is relatively easy to acknowledge in the child a sexuality different from our own, if we can see this sexuality as something which is simply grown out of (rather like a set of clothes). In fact, Freud uncovered in the sexual life of children the same perverse sexuality that analysis revealed in the symptoms of his patients and which was expressed indirectly in their dreams. By stating that this perverse sexuality was in fact quite normal to the extent that it could be located in the sexual life of the child, and by insisting, furthermore, that it was only spoken in the form of a symptom because it was a form of sexuality which had to be so totally repressed elsewhere, Freud effected a break in our conception of both sexuality and childhood from which we do not seem to have recovered. The neurotic simply bears witness to the effects of what is always at some level an impossible task – the task of cohering the fragmented, component and perverse sexuality of the child. The fact that Freud used a myth to describe how this ordering is meant to take place (the myth of Oedipus) should alert us to the fictional nature of this process, which is at best precarious, and never complete.

In discussions of fantasy in children's writing, it is, however, always this notion of an ultimate identity which is involved. Bettelheim, in the book which has become the model for this type of analysis (Bettelheim, 1976), discusses the fairy tale in terms of the function it can serve in 'fortifying' (the word is his) the child's personality and resolving its Oedipal drama (this is the *use* of enchantment). Bettelheim's work is distinguished by its attention to the complexity of unconscious process for both adult and child; but the concept of mastery – with its associated meaning of coherence in psychic and sexual life – is none the less the central term through which this complexity is conceived and by means of which it is finally resolved. The unconscious does not therefore challenge the human ego, its seeming coherence and identity; the unconscious 'enriches' the ego, and, much as a quantity of energy or a current, it can be transferred into the ego where it becomes neutralised and safe. 'The human personality', writes Bettelheim, 'is indivisible' (1976, p. 118). The purpose of the fairy tale is to allow the child that early instability or instance of disruption in order to ensure that any such instability will, in the last analysis, be more effectively removed. Thus, although this account fully recognises in the fairy tale the difficulty of the unconscious fantasies of the child, it does so only to the extent that the form of their appearance is also the mode of their resolution (the ordering of the narrative and the end of the story).

The issue is not, therefore, just that of the sexuality of the child; it is, more crucially, that of how our subjectivity is divided in relation to itself. In his book *Philosophy and the Young Child* (Matthews, 1980), Gareth Matthews criticises Jean Piaget, the educational psychologist, for being unable to grasp that, in relation to its dream, the child is in two places at once (Matthews, 1980, pp. 48–55). Piaget wants to transform this division into two stages of a sequence – at first the child thinks that he is both in the bed and actually on the other side of the room, but eventually he will realise that the dream, and that other part of himself, are both safely inside his head. The child becomes a unified subject, and the idea that the dream might suggest otherwise is dismissed as an error of logic. It is, however, the very meaning of the unconscious to undermine exactly this unity, and it is not by chance that Freud first formulated how it does so in relation to the interpretation of dreams.

In the Preface to the fourth edition of his major work on sexuality (*Three Essays on the Theory of Sexuality*, Freud, SE, vii, 1905, Preface (1920) p. 133, PF, 7, pp. 42–3), Freud stated that the concept of the unconscious had been easily assimilated into common knowledge, as compared with the total resistance that he had met with in relation to the sexual life of the child. He was wrong. For it can be argued that the concept of the unconscious has been refused at exactly that point where it throws into question the idea of our subjectivity as something which we can fully know, or that ultimately can be cohered. Childhood sexuality was in this sense *easier* to acknowledge. It could, eventually, become an object of curiosity and investigation, something to be mastered – the very meaning of sexual development as it is commonly understood.

Freud, it must be recognised, was at least partly responsible for this. His own investigation of childhood was in many ways inconsistent and contradictory. But there is one movement in his discussion of childhood sexuality which makes it clear that the issue of sexuality cannot be separated from that of the unconscious without losing sight of what is central to the importance of each. In 1915, he added to the second of the *Three Essays on the Theory of Sexuality* on infantile sexuality, a section entitled 'The Sexual Researches of Childhood' (Freud, SE, vii, 1905, pp. 195–7, PF, 7, pp. 112–15). In this section he described how infantile sexuality starts to turn on a number of questions which the child sets itself, questions about its own origin (the birth of children) and its sexual identity (the difference between the sexes) which the child will eventually have to resolve. By describing the child's development in terms of a *query*, Freud moves it out of the realm of an almost biological sequence, and into that of fantasy and representation where things are not so clear. In one sense both these questions can be answered – children are born of parents, and the difference between the sexes is there for all to see. But equally they cannot be answered – behind the question about origins is the idea of a moment when the child did not exist, and behind the question about difference is the recognition that the child's sexual identity rests solely in its differentiation from something (or someone) which it is not. There is a level, therefore, at which both these questions undermine the very identity which they simultaneously put in place. We answer them *for* the child at the cost of deceiving ourselves.

Deception is, however, for Freud, in the very order of language. When we speak, we take up a position of identity and certainty in language, a position whose largely fictional nature only the occasional slip, and at times the joke, is allowed to reveal. Deception is what characterises human utterances since language can be used to say the opposite of what is true (this is no doubt why, for Locke, the lie is the ultimate monstrosity in the child (Locke, 1693, pp. 153–4)).[2] Language is not something which we simply use to communicate, as everything in psychoanalytic practice makes clear. Psychoanalysis directs its attention to what cannot be spoken in what is actually being said. It starts from the assumption that there is a difficulty in language, that in speaking to others we might be speaking against ourselves, or at least against that part of ourselves which would rather remain unspoken. This includes, necessarily, speaking *to* children, answering their questions and telling them tales. But the problem of language – the idea that language might *be* a problem – is the dimension of psychoanalysis which has been most rigorously avoided in discussions of fiction for the child.

How we think about children – what it might mean to address them, to speak to them and write them down – is, therefore, directly implicated in this question of language. Our relationship to language is no more fixed and stable than our relationship to childhood itself. We use language to identify ourselves and objects in the world. But the pronoun 'I', which apparently gives us that identity, only has as its meaning whoever happens to be using it at the time; and it is no simple term of unity or cohesion, as the processes of the dream, our ability to lie, or merely to deceive ourselves, all too clearly demonstrate. Objects are defined in language, but the relation between the linguistic term and its referent is arbitrary (this was for Locke the 'imperfection' of words (Locke, 1700, pp. 280–9)); and the meaning of one word can only be fixed with reference to another, in a process which finally has us going round in circles (the chase through the dictionary from one entry to the next to find out what a word *really* means). Freud located all these difficulties in his attempt to negotiate the complex, overdetermined and contradictory meanings of symptoms, dreams and jokes. But they came up first, and most forcefully, in response to the question he started by asking – the question of how we produce our image of the child.

In one of Freud's most famous case histories – the case of 'The Wolf Man' (Freud, SE, xvii (1914) 1918, PF, 9) – he attempted to identify the exact meaning of a childhood event, as if it were a single point of significance which could resolve the patient's past and remove his present symptoms together. As in the case of those earlier memories (Freud, SE, iii, 1899) – which was where it had all started – he discovered that there was no single event, that possibly nothing had ever happened, but that the multiple associations and images uncovered in the course of the analysis belonged to the still continuing history of his patient. Freud thought that the 'Wolf Man' had *seen* something – his parents engaged in a sexual act which would answer for him the question of generations. But what flashed up in the analysis over and over again was more like a piece of staging, a theatrical performance which represented for the patient the question of sexual difference and origins which he was still attempting to answer for himself. What Freud uncovered in that analysis is that there is no straightforward answer to the question, no single meaning to an event, and no childhood which is simply over and done with. For

Freud, neither childhood nor meaning can be pinned down – they shift, and our own identity with them.

The discussion of children's fiction often takes the form of a re-run of the debate between Freud and Jung. Alan Garner, for example, is a Jungian, and he builds Jung's philosophy quite openly into his writing for children. Jung has in fact been much better received than Freud in relation to children's fiction (cf. for example Cook, 1969), which might seem surprising given Jung's self-confessed lack of interest in individual childhood. Jung's interest was in the history of the *race*, and he saw the unconscious as the repository of a set of myths and symbols which our culture has destroyed (Jung, 1959, Part 1). The appeal to Jung, in relation to children's writing, is therefore in direct line with that mystification which places the child at the origin of all human history (I will be discussing this in the next chapter). But there is more to it than this. The dispute between Freud and Jung is not just about childhood. It is, more crucially, about this question of language, about whether meaning is something stable which can be directly interpreted and fixed.

For Freud, the often contradictory and inconsistent ways that childhood appears in analysis, undermines any notion of a straightforward sequence and throws into crisis our relationship to meaning itself. Meaning is not simply there – it is built up, it can be determined by totally contradictory associations, and can emerge long after the event which apparently gives it form. For Jung, on the other hand, if childhood appears after the fact, then it is a fantasy which indicates that the patient is going backwards and running away from the tasks of real life. For Jung, distortion, overdetermination, repetition (the terms which Freud uses to characterise our relationship to the unconscious) are the signs of an almost moral evasion. Meaning is no more divided than subjectivity itself (hence his central term 'individuation'). Jung's main concern is to restore the original meaning of the symbol or archetype, a meaning which is fixed for all time. Interpreting it serves to establish both our psychic and our historical continuity. Meaning is something which can be grasped according to a strict chronology which leads from the infancy of the race directly to the apotheosis of mankind.

The idea that symbols simply *speak* is one with which Freud is most often associated. For Freud, it is thought, what they speak is sexual, for Jung mythical, but in terms of the concept of language and meaning which is involved, there is not much to choose between them. In both cases, the symbol contains a hidden meaning to which we possess the key. Although Freud did at times use this method, he introduces his own method for interpreting dreams (Freud, SE, IV–V, 1900, pp. 96–100, PF, 4, pp. 170–3) by castigating this type of symbolic reading as useless, and it is a concept of meaning which everything else in his work undercuts. But it remains the form of interpretation – where one thing straightforwardly *equals* another – which seems to predominate in the analysis of children's writing. We see this frequently in symbolic interpretations of fairy tales (the wolf in *Little Red Riding Hood is* the Oedipal father),[3] and, in another guise, in biographical readings of children's books (behind *Peter Pan* is Barrie and nothing else). What is striking about this type of interpretation is the way that it by-passes any problem of language, any question of how meaning is constructed, of how it builds up and shifts. Instead it presupposes a type of original innocence of meaning which the act of criticism can retrieve – the very notion of how meaning (and childhood) operate which Freud himself had had to discard.

It seems to me that it is no coincidence that symbolism and biography are the two forms of 'Freudian' analysis which are most commonly associated with children's fiction (which is why someone like Matthews, in his discussion of fantasy, dismisses Freud more or less out of hand (Matthews, 1980, p. 82)). I consider these forms of analysis to be the 'worst' of Freud, not least because of the other, more difficult, aspects of Freud's work on childhood and language which they avoid. Both presuppose a pure point of origin lurking behind the text which we, as adults and critics, can trace. This is, of course, the ultimate fantasy of much literary criticism which tries to uncover the true and primary meaning of a work. But in the analysis of children's fiction, the child seems to become implicated in the process. It is as if the child serves to sanction that concept of a pure origin because the child is seen as just such an origin in itself. The child is there, and the original meaning is there – they *reinforce* each other. Thus a strange complicity can be seen between the archaic status of the fairy tale, for example, and the idea of the child as the true, unconscious recipient of its meaning ('the child understands this intuitively, though he does not "know" it explicitly' (Bettelheim, 1976, p. 179)); or in the case of biographical criticism, the idea of the child behind the writer (Barrie as eternal child) supports a form of analysis which allows us to take the work back to its beginning and to stop it there (Dunbar, 1971; Birkin, 1979).[4]

We need to ask why interpreting children's fiction – reading it *for* the child – seems to be untouched by the idea that language itself might be unstable, and that our relationship to it is never safe. We need to ask why we appear to straddle our present division in language across the present of the book and its past – that original meaning which we can uncover by so totally *knowing* the child.

In the discussion of children's fiction, I repeatedly come across the most emphatic of refusals or demands: that there should be no disturbance at the level of language, no challenge to our own sexuality, no threat to our status as critics, and no question of our relation to the child. These demands are all impossible; they carry a weight that no individual child could be expected to support. The fact that they are impossible is nowhere clearer than in the case of *Peter Pan*.

*   *   *

If a book exists which contains more knowledge and more love of children, we do not know it.

Review of J. M. Barrie's *The Little White Bird*, *Times Literary Supplement*, 14 November 1902.

Writing for children is an act of love. It is a way of 'knowing' the child. Loving the child and knowing the child – the idea is one of an innocent attachment, all the more effective for the casual ease with which it binds the child to its purpose. Love and knowledge can both be used with reference to the child – in 1902 at least – with no hint of the sexuality at play. Today we might recognise the sexuality contained in the first, but we are perhaps still no more likely to notice the disturbance conveyed by the very certainty of the second.

The Little White Bird, to which this quotation from the *Times Literary Supplement* refers, was not written for children. It was written by J. M. Barrie as a novel for adults and published in 1902. Most of the book, however, is told by the narrator as a story to a little boy who is addressed inside the book; and one of the stories which the narrator tells to this child is the story of *Peter Pan*. *The Little White Bird* is not often discussed in relation to *Peter Pan*, and when it is, it is mainly in terms of the biographical information which it provides about J. M. Barrie.[5] *The Little White Bird*, it is said, reveals Barrie's longing for and adoration of a child who is identified as George Llewellyn Davies, one of the five Llewellyn Davies boys whom Barrie finally adopted. Placing the child thus firmly outside the limits of the text, however, absolves us of the need to ask what might be happening to the child who is contained, equally firmly, within it.

'Telling tales to children' – the formulation jars, since telling tales is something which children are meant to do *to*, or *against*, each other. It also carries the idea of deception and dishonesty, as if something is told as a tale to the extent that it is not true. Adults do not tell *tales* to children, they tell *stories*. Even if the story is a fantasy, its truth is none the less guaranteed by the simple and unquestioned communication which passes between the adult and child.

The idea that there could be a problem at just that level of communication, a troubling of intention and address, is not one which is often entertained in discussion of children's fiction. In fact one effect of the increasing attention being paid to the content and meanings of children's books seems to be that this issue is hardly ever raised. The history of *Peter Pan*, however, has so visibly hung on a set of repeated (and largely failed) attempts to remove this problem of address from the area of what properly constitutes children's fiction, that it starts to look like a case of censorship. The history of *Peter Pan* suggests, if anything, that children's fiction relies, for its continuity and untroubled existence, on the fact that this issue is normally ruled out of bounds.

Linguistics has a term for this whole area of potential trouble and confusion. It is the term 'enunciation' which does not refer to what is being said, but asks who speaks and to whom, and why, by implication, they are speaking (Benveniste (1956) (1958) 1966). 'Enunciation' exists as a term in linguistics solely to differentiate this question from the content of any individual utterance. When we speak, there is an 'I' behind the statement, who is never the same as the person or thing to which we refer, even when (or especially when) we are speaking about ourselves (that 'about' in itself reveals the distance between these two moments of an apparent identity). 'Enunciation' is the term for that division in language which speaking to anyone (including children) necessarily reveals. It marks a potential dislocation at the heart of any utterance (that same dislocation which Freud identified at its most insistent in the gap between the dreamer and the message of his or her dream). Above all, it undermines the idea of language as a simple tool of communication by allowing us to ask what might be the relationship – of procurement or desire – which holds between the one who speaks and what he or she offers as the innocence of their statement.

We cannot think about *Peter Pan* – its endless rewritings, its confusion of address, and the adoration which it has received as if it were itself a child – without thinking about this problem of what lies behind or produces the very act of speech. It has emerged constantly in the history of *Peter Pan* only to be ignored, forgotten or repressed. *The Little White Bird*, for example, speaks of this problem and of virtually nothing else. What matters in this book is the way that the child is placed in the story, and why (although the question may seem gratuitous) he is there at all.

The Little White Bird tells the story of a bachelor clubman who anonymously befriends a courting couple, and then, after their marriage, becomes friend and story-teller to their child. One of these stories is the story of Peter Pan who lives in Kensington Gardens – where the narrator and the little boy, David, take their walks – and of his encounter with a little girl, Maimie Mannering, who meets him when she breaks the rules and stays in the Gardens overnight. Around this story is wrapped that of the narrator's relationship to the little boy to whom he tells it, which is in turn interspersed with his own memories and fantasies, and which ends when David leaves for school. This structure of stories within stories ('en abîme') makes *The Little White Bird* a story about story-telling itself, and of the child's vital place in that process.

This is a fuller extract from the *Times Literary Supplement*'s review of 1902:

> The book is all Barrie-ness; whimsical, sentimental, profound, ridiculous Barrie-ness; utterly impossible, yet absolutely real, a fairy tower built on the eternal truth. To say what happens in it is to stultify one's praise for one of the most charming books ever written. A middle-aged and bachelor clubman, who becomes so enamoured of someone else's baby that he kidnaps

him, perambulator and all, into Kensington-gardens, and there wheels him about, dexterously dodging the anxious mother, for half a day – who squabbles openly and unashamedly in public places with Irene the nurse (the daughter of his own club-waiter) about her cap and his own moral influence – such a man is as impossible as his St. Bernard dog, who turns a while into a human being, or as Peter Pan, half baby, half bird, who dwells on the island in the Serpentine and plays his pipe at the fairies' ball in the gardens. The clubman, it is true, is careful to warn us that he is whimsical; but we heed him not. The most whimsical of bachelors would never do such things; but it does not matter. . . . the smallest details of his adored David, his braces and behaviour in the bath, are not too trivial to dwell on; and all the while it is clear that the details are but symbols, that the man's whole mind is given to developing and revealing the best that is in himself, lest any speck of contamination should fall on the boy who was not his son . . . In fine, here is an exquisite piece of work. To analyse its merits and defects – its fun, its pathos, its character-drawing, or its sentimentality, its improbability, its lack of cohesion – would be to vivisect a fairy. (*Times Literary Supplement*, 14 November 1902, p. 339)

In *The Little White Bird*, talking to the child is, therefore, an act of love, but it is also a claim on the child, a demand made on the child as a means of holding it fast. The child, David, does not belong to the narrator, but to another couple with whom the narrator is vicariously involved (he spends most of his time following them and watching them). The narrator is trying to steal the child, to get at the mother and replace the father. His involvement with the child is, therefore, anything but innocent. In fact it can be traced back to an unconsummated sexual desire for which David is the substitute and replacement. This is not, it should be stressed, an 'analysis' of the book – the motives and the past history are all given by the narrator himself. It is no doubt the easy slippage between description and diagnosis which has, more recently, made this book such a biographical landmine in relation to Barrie himself. But the effect of locating this disturbance in Barrie is, paradoxically, that his communication with the child is seen as all the more unproblematic and complete: Barrie wrote *Peter Pan* as part of his interaction with the Llewellyn Davies boys, but about the work itself very little needs to be said. This is to ignore, however, the disturbance, the difficulty, and above all the impossible questions – about origins and sexual difference – which circulate between the narrator and child in *The Little White Bird*, and which lead straight into (one could almost say *engender*) the story of Peter Pan.

The Little White Bird starts with the narrator telling David the story of the child's own origins. The time of the narrative spans the courtship of David's parents, and David's birth, up to the present relationship between David and the narrator whose end brings the book to a close. David is, therefore, implicated in the story at a number of different levels, each with their own form of ambiguity. The story is told *to* him, but since it goes back to before his beginning, he has to disappear in order for it to be told: 'As I enter the club room you are to conceive of David vanishing into nothingness' (Barrie, 1902, p. 11). This child is produced inside the story and the story stands in for him when he leaves. He is, therefore, multiply caught up in, possessed and owned by the story. This is an impossible position which effectively sets David up as a total object of desire (the 'be-all and end-all' of the story). Like any other object of such an absolute investment, there is a sense in which David does not exist:

> 'It doesn't make me littler does it?' he asked anxiously, and then, with a terrible misgiving: 'It doesn't make me too little, does it father?' by which he hoped that it would not do for him altogether. (Barrie, 1902, p. 10)

The child's place in the story which is told to him, and about him, is therefore highly equivocal. At one point in the narrative, when the narrator is about to reconcile David's parents during their courtship (an event which is after all crucial if David is to be born), David reappears, interrupts the story and hesitates before he allows it to take its course. Being a witness at your own birth is, it would seem, rather like being present at your own funeral.

In *The Little White Bird*, the question of origins, of sexuality and of death are all presented as inherent to the very process of writing. Writing the book in itself seems to be nothing more than a constant return to these points of difficulty around which it gravitates and stalls. In the end, the book is presented as a substitute, not only for David who leaves to go to school (this in itself is described as an act of abduction by the schoolmaster,

Pilkington), but also for a dead child, Timothy. This child was already a fantasy of the narrator's, invented by him in a dialogue with David's real father on the night when David was born. Later in the story, the narrator pretends that Timothy has died in order to pass on his clothes to David, when he follows David's mother to a pawnshop and realises that she is in financial need. The child, Timothy, is therefore a pure fantasy who dies. This may seem to be a contradiction in terms, but it touches on the nerve of what it might mean to talk of a child who could last for ever. As *The Little White Bird* so clearly demonstrates, there are only two ways of making sure of this – having the child die early or, alternatively, writing the child down. The narrator of *The Little White Bird*, in his total worship (love? knowledge?) of the child, does both – worship of course always carries with it this ambiguity that what is being worshipped is never really there. The narrator produces the book when David is about to leave him and his mother gives birth to a second child: 'When in the fulness of time, she held her baby on high implying that she had done a big thing, I was to hold up the book' (Barrie, 1902, pp. 290–1).

The sexuality of *The Little White Bird* operates in a similar mode of difficulty and confusion. What is important at this level is not what, sexually, the narrator can or cannot do (I consider this to be of no interest), but what it is, in the very process of writing, that cannot be *conceived*, in both senses of the term. Much of the early part of the story is taken up with David's life as a bird before he was born (this is told as David's own recollection). In *The Little White Bird*, all children are birds before they are born, which means first that they can be produced out of thin air (the title of the book refers to the fantasied child, Timothy), and secondly that the narrator can claim true ownership of David on the grounds that he saw him before anyone else: 'The first time I ever saw David was on a Sword behind the Baby's walk. He was then a misselthrush' (Barrie, 1902, p. 22).

Together with this disavowal of origins, or conception, goes a corresponding refusal of sexual difference. *The Little White Bird* starts with the narrator rejecting all communication with David's mother (his voyeurism is the obverse of this rejection), and it ends when, despite the narrator's insisting to David that the new child will be a boy, she gives birth to a girl. At the few points in the book when the narrator seems to be talking to a child who is outside the text, this child is clearly a boy: 'Girls can't really play cricket, and when you are watching their futile efforts, you make funny sounds at them . . . You are a solitary boy while all this is taking place' (Barrie, 1902, pp. 133, 135). This over-insistence on the presence and value of the male child also appears in the way that children's literature, in the more familiar sense of the term, is used in *The Little White Bird*. Towards the end of the book, the narrator tells David and his friend, Oliver, a shipwreck story (he calls them 'wrecked island' stories), drawing quite explicitly on that branch of children's literature which had, in the previous fifty years, specifically been designated as literature for boys (the story is presented as a parody of the *genre*). In this book, however, landing the children on the island is used by the narrator to abrogate the threat of their departure when they are about to leave for school. Literature for children is, therefore, a way of colonising (or wrecking) the child; and it is emphatically literature for boys only.

The story of *Peter Pan* is told in the middle of *The Little White Bird* as part of this interaction, its refusals and its demands. This is no doubt what makes for its unquestioning (and largely unquestioned) innocence.

What, therefore, do we mean by talking to, or addressing, the child – what are we asking *of* the child in doing just that? The very strangeness of *The Little White Bird* – its present absence behind the classic which we know – suggests that the only story we can ever tell the child is the story of the child's (and our) coming-to-be. 'Coming-to-be' is a story which we repeat continually to ourselves. It is there, not just in *The Little White Bird* but in the form of most narratives which we expect to set up a problem and then bring it to a successful resolution. It is present in the sexual query – where do babies come from? – which the adult is asked by the child; and, in another form, in the philosophical puzzle of what happened 'before the beginning' to which there is no satisfactory reply.[6] What is most significant about *The Little White Bird* is the way in which this same query is expressed as a question which the adult sends *back* to the child. Put at its crudest, the narrator of *The Little White Bird* cannot answer the question of sexuality, of origins and difference, so he turns to a little boy instead: where did he come from and what was the sexuality in that? or could it have happened in some other way which would remove the problem altogether? Peter Pan is a little boy who flies away because he does not want to grow up (this remains in the play and in most of the versions which we know today), but the island to which he flies is the place from which unborn babies are dispatched by birds (that bit has been dropped). The sexual query which lies behind the telling of the story to the child surfaces right in the middle of it.

The sexuality of *The Little White Bird* is not, therefore, just that of a man and a little boy, although the possessiveness, the 'adoration' (the word is that of the *Times Literary Supplement* in 1902), or even 'teasing' of the child (*Observer*, 1979 (Lewis, 1979)), all suggest that too in their way. The sexuality which matters is both more and less explicit than this. It is sexuality in the form of its repeated disavowal, a relentless return to the question of origins and sexual difference which is focused time and again on the child. The child is there, purely and simply, to bear the weight of that impossible question.

The story of *Peter Pan* which is given in *The Little White Bird* has never, strictly speaking, been distributed as a book for children, even with the surrounding narrative cut out. *Peter Pan in Kensington Gardens*, with illustrations by Arthur Rackham (Barrie, 1906), has always hovered on the edge of the children's book market as something of an art book – a collector's item destined less and less to be read and more and more to be cherished and preserved. This ambiguity merely reproduces at another level the confusions of intention and address which we have seen internally to *The Little White Bird* in the chapters which have been removed. Thus the question of the distribution of *Peter Pan* (the child outside the text) and the question of how it symbolises its relationship to the child inside the text can be seen as related (the commercial history is discussed more fully in Chapter 4).

It could also be, however, that this Peter Pan story is not so well known because of the residual forms of disturbance which are present in the narrative itself. Peter Pan is a 'Betwixt-and-Between' who hovers between the island of birds and the nursery – the two places which offer the two different versions of where babies come from (the 'stork' and the 'true-life' version of the same story). When he hesitates too long, he is locked out of the nursery, which is why he endlessly returns to the same place – the play *starts* here. But what this story indicates far more explicitly than any of the versions to follow is the difficulty of Peter Pan's relationship to the child, and the anxiety and disturbance in that.

Peter Pan's task in Kensington Gardens is to bury the dead children who break the rules by staying in the Gardens over night. His own favourite birds are the house-swallows, which, unlike all the other birds, are not unborn children, but children who were born and then died. One child, Maimie Mannering – forerunner of Wendy – gains access to Peter by transgressing the rules and staying in the Gardens after 'Lock-Out' time. As will be the case with Wendy, their interaction partly takes the form of a courtship which cannot finally be fulfilled (Maimie leaves, as Wendy will leave the Neverland, when she hears how Peter Pan was barred from the nursery). But unlike Wendy, who becomes the very model of normality, Maimie is a 'strange' girl – an 'ordinary' girl in the daytime when she looks up to, and imitates, her brother (like little girls should), but 'terrible at night' when she charges him with an imaginary goat and terrifies him out of his wits (like little girls should not) (Barrie, 1902, pp. 189–90). The encounter with Peter starts with this, because Maimie only stays in the Gardens when her brother, Tony, backs down in fear from his original pledge to do so himself. Peter therefore meets Maimie instead of Tony, the little girl instead of the little boy, but things could (indeed, *should*) have been different. The encounter between Peter and Maimie also ends with this. When Maimie goes home, she sends back to Peter, in a magic incantation, her night-time goat which he turns into a real goat and rides. Thus Peter Pan touches, or belongs, on the edge of the difference between boys and girls, and of their fears, just as he does on the death of the child. His story, which makes up the central chapters of *The Little White Bird*, ends with these lines:

> But how strange for parents, when they hurry into the Gardens looking for their lost one, to find the sweetest little tombstone instead. I do hope that Peter is not too ready with his spade. It is all rather sad. (Barrie, 1902, p. 226)

In subsequent versions of *Peter Pan* all these elements are rearranged in ways which I will go on to discuss now. But there is a sense in which their very openness here already makes them innocent. For as a set of themes and references in a narrative about children, the whole problem of address, out of which they were produced, starts to fade. They become, more simply, a story which is told, as opposed to something whose difficulty, and challenge to us, lies in the process of its telling.

Turning the story of Peter Pan into a play – the form in which it was first a success and is perhaps still best known today – carries out this transformation before it does anything else. There is no one who tells the story in a play since everyone speaks their own lines. A play is performed before one's eyes, and the immediacy and visibility of the performance gives it a ring of authenticity which is even harder to challenge than that of a story being told. Staging something always relies for its effect on the impression that it is happening then and there. As a play, *Peter Pan* is above all famous for the moment when Peter Pan turns to the audience and asks it if it believes in fairies. This is merely an extreme version of the demand of any play that, at least for the duration of its performance, the audience should believe that it is true.

And yet the term 'staging' carries its own ambiguity, which is why Freud used it to describe the unconscious, whose truth lies solely in its challenge to what we conventionally recognise as real. The dreaming child in Piaget's example saw himself on the other side of the room, taking part in a scenario in which he both did, and did not, recognise himself. Once again it is the process of dreaming, and not just its content, which poses the real threat to the idea that there is a straightforward continuity to our psychic life. For Freud, the very immediacy of the visual image forces us to think again.

Setting the child up as a spectacle, shining a light on it and giving it up to our gaze – there is something in this which also needs to be questioned. It reenacts in another form that strange and overinsistent focus on the child which we saw in *The Little White Bird*. It also links up with a history of the visual image in relation to the child, in which *Peter Pan* has its part. Barrie, like Lewis Carroll, took photographs of children. In Barrie's case they were little boys, in Carroll's they were for the most part, but not exclusively, little girls (Gernsheim, 1949, see, for example Greville MacDonald, plate 31, and Cyril Bickersteth, plate 55). Barrie's collection, *The Boy Castaways of Black Lake Island* (Beinecke, 1901)[7] consists of thirty-six photographs of the Llewel-lyn Davies boys, and the rudiments of an adventure narrative. Together with *The Little White Bird*, it almost constitutes a second source book for *Peter Pan*. Only two copies of it were ever produced, one of which Arthur Llewellyn Davies, the boys' father, promptly mislaid on a train. The rarity, the exclusive and precious nature of this work has contributed to its status as one of the ultimate records of Barrie's personal history. It is as if it has been moved sideways into the fetishism of the document so we do not need to think about the fetishism in the gaze.

A photograph offers itself as something innocent and authentic which speaks for itself – merely capturing the moment it records. Its immediacy belies the technique, the framing, the pose, all of which make the photograph possible (terms of artifice and calculation which are cancelled out by the natural and effortless feel of the best pictures). The innocence of the photograph as a record or document seems to vouch for the innocence of our pleasure in looking, and no more so perhaps than when what we are looking at is a child. This might explain why it was such a scandal when a number of Graham Ovenden's photographs of Victorian street urchins were discovered to be fakes (Ovenden, 1972; Linklater, 1978); for it exposed too sharply that what was represented by the photograph was not the desire to recapture a moment of history, but rather that same history at the service of the desire to look at the child (in this case little girls).

The Boy Castaways of Black Lake Island is made up almost exclusively of photographs of little boys. The book comprises thirty-six captioned photographs, a preface and a series of chapter headings with no text. The book is dedicated to 'our mother in cordial recognition of her efforts to elevate us above the brutes'. The preface is the only extended piece of writing in the book:

> I have been requested by my brothers to write a few words of introduction to this little volume, and I comply with pleasure, though well aware that others may be better acquitted for the task. The strange happenings here set forth with a *currente calamo* are expansions of a note-book kept by me while we were on the island, but I have thought fit, in exercise of my prerogative as general editor, to omit certain observations with regard to *flaura, fauna*, etc., which, however valuable to myself and to others of scientific bent, would probably have but a limited interest to the lay mind. I have also in this edition excluded a chapter on *strata* as caviare to the general.
>
> The date on which we were wrecked was this year on August 1, 1901, and I have still therefore a vivid recollection of that strange and terrible summer, when we suffered experiences such as have probably never before been experienced by three brothers. At this time, the eldest, George, was eight and a

month, Jack was approaching his seventh *lustrum*, and I was a good bit past four. Perhaps a few words about my companions will not be deemed out of place.

George was a fine, fearless youth, and had now been a term at Wilkinson's. He was modest withal. His chief fault was wanting to do all the shooting, and carrying the arrows inside his shirt with that selfish object. Jack is also as brave as a lion, but he also has many faults (see pp. 25–29), and he has a weakness, perhaps pardonable, for a pretty face (bless them!). Of Peter, I prefer to say nothing, hoping that the tale, as it is unwound, will show that he was a boy of deeds rather than words, which was another of Jack's blemishes (see p. 41, also pp. 93 and 117). In conclusion, I should say that the work was in the first instance compiled as a record simply, at which we could whet our memories, and that it is now published for Michael's benefit. If it teaches him by example lessons in fortitude and manly endurance we shall consider that we were not wrecked in vain.

Peter Llewellyn Davies.(Beinecke, 1901, Preface, pp. vii–ix)

The voice of this is unmistakably the voice of the narrator of *The Little White Bird* when he was both recreating the boys' adventure story and parodying the didacticism of its tone. It is also clearly the voice of an adult who offers the document as instruction for the boy, Michael, as well as a record of his childhood (proof, indeed, that he once was a child). But this question of voice is not restricted to the preface – it is evoked by the photographs themselves. For, in exactly the same way as the adult reveals himself here in the writing, the innocence of the photographs (the idyllic romping, the adventure) calls up the question of who – that is, which adult – is taking them? Where, we ask, is the creator of these pictures, the very transparency of the image (boys presented to us so unequivocally at play, that is, *their* play and *their* story) uneasily evoking the necessary presence of the one who is watching (in this case, as we know, Barrie himself). Capturing a moment has, therefore, two meanings – the record of a past history which is lost (reconstituted so fully by Andrew Birkin in *J. M. Barrie and the Lost Boys* (Birkin, 1979)), and the seizing of the child by an image which, as the very condition of its effectivity, leaves outside its frame the look of the adult who creates it.

What are we doing, therefore, when we put the child on the stage? This is not as uncalled for a question as it might seem.

Barrie was a highly successful playwright when *Peter Pan* was first performed as a play in 1904, and it had been billed as his new theatrical extravaganza. The audience was made up of London's theatre-going élite, and there was hardly a child among them (Mackail, 1941, p. 366; Green, 1954, p. 85; Birkin, 1979, p. 116). Calling *Peter Pan* a play for children, we have to ask not only what we think we are doing when we put the child on the stage, but also what we are doing when we assume, as we have for more than three-quarters of a century, that the child belongs in the audience.

The 1904–5 production script of *Peter Pan* (Beinecke, 1904–5B) and the 1905 script for Act I are prefaced with 'A Note. On the Acting of a Fairy Play'. This note emphatically places the child on the stage, but it never once refers to any children in the audience. What distinguishes a fairy play from a realistic drama is the fact that all its characters are children: 'this applies to the so-called adults of the story as well as to the young people' (Beinecke, 1904–5B, p. i). I think that this has to mean by implication that children are not real. But they are the authors of the play which was 'written by a child in *deadly* earnestness' (my italics), and they are also behind the scenes: 'The scenic artist is another child in league with them' (Beinecke, 1904–5B, p. i). The whole performance and its staging is, therefore, given up to the child; but what about the child in the audience?

Barrie's note in fact indicates that stage space, in and of itself, redistributes in another form the divisions which lie behind any act of representation. There is an off-stage to the play, where Barrie's note puts the child as 'scenic artist', but where the child in the audience cannot go, and which it is not allowed to see without risking the collapse of the whole stage illusion. And there is a barrier in the theatre between the stage and the audience, which the audience, for much the same reason, is not allowed to cross. The distinction between a pantomime and a real children's play (a distinction sometimes used mistakenly in relation to *Peter Pan*, see Chapter 4 below) is often made on this basis – what distinguishes a real play for children is that the child does not go on the stage and join in. The child is there precisely to watch what is happening, to query only up to the point of the limits on either side of the stage, and to recognise itself in the scenario which unfolds before its eyes. But that recognition also has its limits. The actors are mostly adults, and, as likely as not, there will be an adult with the child in the audience, watching the child at least as much as what is going on on stage. If we want to call *Peter Pan* a play for children, therefore, we should start by recognising our place in its history and performance, and the complexity of the relations which once again lie behind the transparency of the term.[8]

Spectacle of childhood for *us*, or play for *children*? The question goes beyond the issue of trying to determine how many children might have seen *Peter Pan* (millions by now), or whether or not they said they liked it (for that you will find evidence either way).

When *Peter Pan* becomes a play, the first thing to notice is the way that this question of how a space of representation is being constituted for the child has been forced to the outer limits of its performance. *Peter Pan* takes the difficulties of *The Little White Bird* – of the adult–child relationship, and of how and why a story is told to the child – and either cuts them out completely, or reduces them to mere child's-play. From this point on in *Peter Pan*'s history we will see all these difficulties surfacing constantly in different forms, and just as constantly being suppressed. It is, however, the very definition of suppression – according to Freud at least – that it never really works, especially perhaps when what is being got rid of are all the queries, at the level of sexuality and language, which Freudian psychoanalysis was uncovering at exactly the same time that *Peter Pan* was being promoted and reproduced. As Freud himself puts it in another context: 'the distortion of a text resembles a murder: the difficulty is not in perpetrating the deed, but in getting rid of its traces' (Freud, SE, xxiii (1934–8) 1939, p. 43).

Roger Lancelyn Green has pointed out that *Peter Pan* is the perfect adventure story (Green, 1954, p. 31). A little boy breaks into a nursery and takes the children away to an island of redskins and pirates, where they act out the adventures which they normally read in books, before safely returning home. In *Peter Pan*, these adventures, with all their risk and danger, come true, but their threat is contained, first by Peter Pan himself who comes from the island to which he takes the children, and who has already been through the whole thing several times before, and secondly by the nursery which is the start and the finishing point of the whole story. This structure – of an exploration which is finally held in place by the world which we recognise and know as real – is one which is frequently used in children's fiction to this day. It is central to the early works of Alan Garner (Garner, 1965,

1967), and it forms the basis of Maurice Sendak's most famous book (*Where The Wild Things Are*, Sendak, 1967).[9]

Bringing the children home is one of the most striking things which happens in *Peter Pan* as a play. The child is put back in the nursery (the central battle was about this in *The Little White Bird*), and the act of telling stories is given to the little girl, Wendy. It is because of the stories which Wendy knows that she is invited to the island to tell stories to the lost boys. Mothers tell stories to their children, and nothing could be safer than that. As a play, therefore, *Peter Pan* assigns the act of telling stories to its socially recognisable context. The difficult relationship between the narrator and the boy child of *The Little White Bird* is turned into a relationship between a mother and her child. Hook is the male villain, but he so recognisably belongs to literary and theatrical convention that the sexual problem is dissolved. The success of *Peter Pan*, then, would stem from the way in which it brings together adventure fantasy and the recognisable domestic scene.

None of this, however, really works. Staging always carries with it something of the question of how things are done, as well as for whom, and by whom, they are produced, the question which the child first asks when confronted with the family drama. No nursery is ever *just* safe, and in *Peter Pan* it is the repository of much of the disturbance which was present in *The Little White Bird*. The play opens with the Darling children (the name of the family) playing at mothers and fathers, acting out the history of their own birth and stopping the game when there is one of them whom they do not wish to be born: 'Michael. Am I not to be born at all?' (Beinecke, 1904–5B, Act I, p. 5). Peter Pan, like the child in the audience, watches from outside. This is the one performance in which he cannot play a part. The play therefore opens with the question of the child's place in the most familiar, and primary, of family scenes. It is a question which is repeatedly posed in the play, and it shows up in the most unlikely of places. On the island, Wendy tells the story of growing up and of life back in the nursery (this is unheard of in the adventure stories of Marryat, Kingston and Henty, and in any case she had been invited to tell *Cinderella*). It is when Peter Pan challenges her story as untrue, and tells her that, like him, she will not be able to go home, that the whole island sequence breaks up and the children rush to depart. This leads to the final confrontation between Peter Pan and Hook, and then between Peter and Wendy after he has taken her back to the nursery. Barrie did not know how to end the play and the difficulty appears to have revolved around the two relationships – between Peter and Hook and between Peter and Wendy – in which the sexual difficulty had only seemingly been neutered.

There are in fact two conflicts in *Peter Pan*, that between the nursery and the Never Land (originally the Never Never Never Land), and that waged by Peter Pan against both. Thus Peter Pan attacks the family scene in the home underground and precipitates its break-up, but this is in turn attacked by Hook and the pirates who are waging war on Peter. Peter Pan, having differentiated himself from the children, is left behind and it is the children who are captured. Putting it crudely, we can say that this was not what Hook was after since his object was Peter himself. This produces a series of structural confusions and panics which spread across the different arenas of the spectacle – thus Hook tries to get at Peter and fails, Tinkerbell swallows the poison in order to save Peter, Peter comes *off* stage in order to get the children in the audience to save Tinkerbell (the famous episode), and then goes off to save the children which leads to the battle with Hook. The fight between Peter and Hook has a clear logic in relation to the family drama – part of a retaliation fantasy, the completion of the Oedipal circuit for John and Michael with Peter Pan exactly the 'avenger' (Mr Darling and Hook almost invariably double in performance) – but it has the secondary effect of bringing Peter, who had been left behind, back up against the maternal nursery. Peter's battle with Hook, therefore, leads to his accidentally siding with the nursery, and the difficulties of the final act can then be read in terms of the need to re-differentiate him.

In point of fact it is too easy to give an Oedipal reading of *Peter Pan*. The father, Mr Darling, is humiliated – he plays a joke on Nana the nurse (the Newfoundland dog) which falls flat and then challenges the family: 'Am I master in this house or is she?' (Beinecke, 1904–5B, Act I, p. 13). The children fly off and he crawls into the kennel out of shame. On the island, the children meet their father in another form, symbolically murder him through Peter Pan and return home. Whereupon Mr Darling crawls out of the kennel and the children can grow up.

It is equally easy to describe the difficulties which Barrie had in writing, and especially in ending *Peter Pan*, in terms of the magic elusiveness of the play and the mystery of the eternal boy child: 'no real beginning and no real end . . . obviously a little piece of immortality' (Noyes, *The Bookman*, December 1911, p. 132); 'there was behind this willingness to change a feeling that [this finale] was rather out of keeping with the character of Peter himself who, as is the case with creations of genius, was beginning to develop an independent personality of his own' (Green, 1954, p. 65). The drama of the performance – the fact that the actors were all sworn to secrecy and that no one knew how the play was going to end (Green, 1954, p. 72) – can then be seen as appropriate to something which defies description, understanding and even representation, an intangible factor which can only add to the essential mystique of the play.

I see these responses as related, because of their shared resistance to the idea of any trouble or disturbance in the play: whether that of the difficulty which always persists from any Oedipal 'resolution',[10] or whether that of Barrie's own confusion which seems to have manifested itself in an almost physical inability to write the play down. The problem of the ending can easily be exaggerated (for instance, revisions and major editing, right up to and even after the first performance, were a regular feature of pantomime production). On the other hand, looking through the different production scripts, programmes, reviews and the various endings which they offer of the play, it is clear that the particular forms of hesitancy, at the level of writing and performance, belong in different ways to those questions about origins, sexuality and death which the play tries, unsuccessfully, to bring to a resolution.

The main problem is Peter Pan himself. How can he be got rid of or 'resolved' given that it is the very definition of the child who does not grow up that he will always remain and constantly returns to the same place? Peter Pan is *stuck*, and the play with him. In all versions, Peter fails to answer the sexual query which Wendy puts to him when he invites her back to the island: 'But what as, Peter, what as?', she asks, to which he replies 'Your son' (not the reply she wanted); and his failure merely underlines the fact that the play cannot assimilate him to the 'normality' which it has constructed all around him. But in the earliest versions of *Peter Pan*, this sexuality is far more explicit. There is a seduction attempt on the part of Tiger-Lily which is subsequently cut out. Furthermore, Peter recognises that Tinkerbell, Wendy and Tiger-Lily all want the same thing which he cannot understand:

Peter. Now then, what is it you *want*?
Tiger-Lily. Want to be your squaw.
Peter. Is that what you want, Wendy?
Wendy. I suppose it is, Peter.
Peter. Is that what you want, Tink?
    Bells answer.
Peter. You all three want that. Very well – that's really wishing
    to be my mother.
              (Beinecke, 1904–5B, Act ii, scene iii, p. 26)

There is also the other side of this sexual refusal, Hook's desire for
Peter, which in the earliest versions brings him hot on Peter Pan's
tail and right into Kensington Gardens (Beinecke, 1904, Typescript i, Act iii, scene vi).

The effect of all of this is that *Peter Pan* constantly slides into
moments of excess (disavowal always has something of the
overstatement about it), as the insistence on motherhood (Wendy
as a mother to Peter as opposed to anything else) starts to go over
the top. The best example is 'The Beautiful Mothers Scene'
(Beinecke, 1904, Act iii, scene ii) which was performed for part of
the first run of the play, in which the assorted mothers of London
rush onto the stage to lay claim to the lost boys and are subjected
to various tests of true maternity (the scene was mercifully cut
during the first run). But the same insistence can be seen in scenes
which are still performed today, such as the front-scene of the final
act in which the pirate, Starkey, has been taken prisoner by the
Redskins and is left to watch over their babies (an unlikely
combination, but one which has its logic here).

As was the case with *The Little White Bird*, there is an anxiety
about sexuality and birth which goes hand in hand with this
all-too-cloying innocence, sweetness and light (the last act is
called 'Home Sweet Home'). In one of the earliest versions of the
play's ending, Peter reacts with distress when Wendy claims as her
own a baby who appears under a pile of leaves in Kensington
Gardens where they are living together (Beinecke, 1904, Typescript i, Act iii, scene vi). That distress is most obvious in Barrie's
Afterthought, the ending of the play which was only performed once
in 1908 (Beinecke, 1908B–D and Barrie, 1957).[11] Peter Pan returns
to the nursery after many years and finds Wendy a grown woman
with a child. Faced with the 'living proof' of the irreducible
difference between them (the fact of growing up and of passing

time), Peter goes to Wendy's daughter, Jane, with a dagger (the resistance is already there in the title of the piece – conception as something which can only be *thought* of, if indeed it *can* be thought of, *after*). This version copes with the crisis by having the child wake up and address Peter Pan with exactly the same words that Wendy had used in the opening scene of the play which then sets off the whole cycle again. This in itself shows how repetition, in the sense of doing the same thing over and over again, serves above all to ward off something with which it is impossible to deal.

Between the lines of *Peter Pan*, we can see not only the question of origins (mothers and fathers), and of sexuality (boys and girls), but also the reference to death which is latent to the other two. An autographed addition to the second draft of the 1908 ending gives us the term around which *Peter Pan* endlessly circulates:

> Don't be anxious, Nana. This is how I planned it; if he ever came back. (You see – I think now – that Peter is only a sort of dead baby – he is the baby of all the people who never had one.) (Beinecke, 1908C, words in parenthesis are an autograph addition in Barrie's hand facing page 21)

There is no way of talking about sexuality and origins without raising this as an issue; but in a play for children it can, finally, have no place. The end of *Peter Pan*, as it is best known, removes most of this. Peter Pan takes the children home and then returns to the island, where Wendy visits him once a year to do the annual spring-clean. The island is domesticated, Wendy will grow up, and Peter Pan is sent back to where he came from (the ultimate clean-up job we could say).

Peter Pan has, therefore, come into its own by the successive repudiation of those questions which every child has the right to ask despite the fact – or perhaps precisely because – they are virtually impossible to answer; questions out of which *Peter Pan* was itself produced and without which Peter Pan's innocence becomes not only lost as we know it, but also without meaning. They are there, however, in the various trouble spots which remain in the play, but perhaps even more in the demand that we continue to make on the child that it should recognise itself in that scenario – both in the place of the child spectator (which is also that of Peter Pan at the window), and in the happy family scene which is so miraculously reconstituted before its eyes. *Peter Pan* plays itself out with all the innocence of the symptom – which speaks what it intends, and exactly the opposite, at one and the same time.

In 1926, J. M. Barrie published a short story in an anthology for children, *The Treasure Ship*, edited by Cynthia Asquith (Barrie, 1926(a)), called 'The Blot on Peter Pan' (he originally called it 'The Truth about Peter Pan' but changed the title for publication). In this story, the narrator tells a group of children about how he based *Peter Pan* on his relationship with a little boy, Neil. Although written specifically with reference to the play, it has not been heard of since that first publication in 1926 (Roger Lancelyn Green refers to it as a 'scrap of ephemera' (Green, 1954, p. 119)). The story is a type of child's version of *The Little White Bird* which reintroduces the relationship between the writer and child which was cut out of *Peter Pan*, and gives back something of its difficulty. In this story, writing *for* the child is an act of rivalry *with* the child – the 'truth' about, or 'blot' on Peter Pan is his cockiness for vying with the narrator and trying to outdo him as a writer. On the opening night of *Peter Pan*, Neil produces his own play, in his own special language, and has it performed as an opening piece when the playright is out of the theatre:

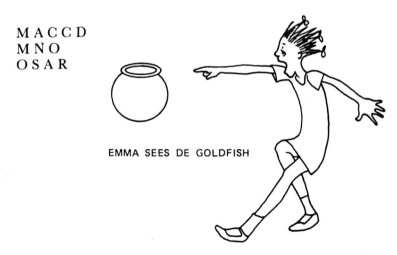

M A C C D
M N O
O S A R

EMMA SEES DE GOLDFISH

This was a problem in three lines and a glass bowl that I had given to some youthful onlookers at that luckless Monday's rehearsal and it stumped them as it had stumped me when propounded to me once by a friend. I see it also stumps you, but debase yourselves sufficiently and you will find it reads:

Emma sees de Goldfish
'Em no goldfish,
Oh ess A are Goldfish.

You follow? I agree with you that 'tis but a tiny joke, and at once it passed out of all our minds save one. That mind was the awful mind of Neil. Though none was in the secret but his Nannie it was suddenly revealed to him how plays are written; quick as a lucky one may jump through a paper hoop and come out on the other side a clown, he had gained access through that friend of mine to a language which he could read, write and spell. (Barrie, 1926(a), pp. 92–3)

The child's own play and its own language – not in the sense of some spontaneous and unspoilt form of expression which speaks for itself (another mystification), but a language which cannot simply be read, and which challenges our own. Neil's play is a rebus or puzzle (Freud, perhaps not coincidentally, used the model of the rebus for his method of interpreting dreams (Freud, SE, iv–v, 1900, pp. 277–8, PF, 4, pp. 381–2). It breaks up the page and demands a special type of attention, inserting its difficulty into the otherwise perfect communication between the adult and child.

Playing with language – in this sense of undercutting its transparency and ease – is something else which has, for the most part, been pushed to the outer limits of children's writing. Edward Lear and Lewis Carroll are the best-known nineteenth-century exceptions, but Lear is covered by the fact that he wrote poetry (specifically designated as nonsense (Lear, 1846)); and Carroll's multiple use of the pun in *Alice* is generally recognised as something unique which tends to be related more to the eccentricity, or even madness, of the author than it is to the linguistic jests and verbal play of the child.[12] Alan Garner, in a completely different way, has recently turned his attention to language, and I will go on to discuss that now. But this other side of language, as it appears here in this mostly forgotten story as an explicit challenge or threat to adult forms of speech, has largely been kept out of children's fiction in much the same way as the adult–child relationship implicit in telling stories has been dropped from *Peter Pan*. The two problems are in fact different forms of the question with which I started this chapter – that of our relationship to childhood and to language, and the way in which we constantly gloss over what is most uncomfortable, and yet insistent, in both.

It should be clear by now that what is important about *Peter Pan* is the very partial nature of the success with which it removes this problem from our view. But, if none of this is normally allowed into children's fiction, then what – we can legitimately ask – have children been given in its place?

2

Rousseau and Alan Garner
Innocence of the child and of the word

'Now if he'd read rocks, instead of books, it might have been a different story, you see.'

Alan Garner, *The Stone Book*, 1976, p. 44.

Let there be no other book but the world . . . The boy that reads does not think, nor gain instruction, he only learns a parcel of words.

Jean Jacques Rousseau, *Emile*, 1762, translated by Nugent, *Emilius*, 1763, vol. I, p. 237.

In the first volume of Alan Garner's four-volume *Stone Quartet* (Garner, 1976–8), Mary asks her father, a stonemason, for a book so that she can learn to read. His reply is to take her to Engine Vein, a crevice in the rocks where the miners' railroad runs, and to send her down into the caves beneath to explore. What Mary finds is her father's mason mark on the wall of a cave and a daubed bull. It was 'the most secret place she had ever seen' – a place where her father's past and her present history were written, and where everything else converged. When Mary comes out of the cave: 'The sky seemed a different place. All things led to the bull and the mark and the hand in the cave' (Garner, 1976, p. 54). Her father takes her home and gives her a book made of stone. This book 'unlike a book you can open' which 'only has one story', contains 'all the stories of the world' (Garner, 1976, pp. 58, 61).

Garner often sends his characters down into the earth. In his first book, *The Weirdstone of Brisingamen* (Garner, 1960), the only path of escape for Colin and Susan, the two central characters, from the evil morthbrood is through the old mine-workings beneath Alderly Edge. They are guided by the dwarf, Fenodyree, who takes them along a disused path which had been shown to him long ago by his father: 'The way is hidden, but my father taught me well . . . the road may no longer be as I was taught, and we may lose ourselves for ever. But it is our only chance, if chance it be, and we must take it' (Garner, 1960, p. 129). The only way out is, therefore, to go back (or down) in place and time. Discovering the hidden depths is also a way of reliving a past history which – in the earlier mythical tales at least – it is up to the child's intervention to recover. Garner, like Rousseau two centuries before him, places on the child's shoulders the responsibility for saving humankind from the degeneracy of modern society.

For Garner, this is to be achieved through myth; for Rousseau, through something which, in various and complicated ways, he defines as 'nature'. It might, therefore, seem strange to argue for their similarity. But there is a continuity in children's fiction which runs from Rousseau up to and beyond *Peter Pan* to Alan Garner, in which the child is constantly set up as the site of a lost truth and/or moment in history, which it can therefore be used to retrieve. Rousseau turned this cult of childhood (the term comes from George Boas (Boas, 1966)) into an educational treatise, but, as has often been pointed out, *Emile* already took the form of a fictional narrative or romance. It was only one step to turn this concept of childhood into the idea of fiction for children which would send the child itself off on this investigatory journey back into our own past.

The purpose of literature for children in Garner, and the purpose of education in Rousseau, are remarkably close. Literature is the repository of a privileged experience and sensibility at risk in the outside world where these values are being crushed under the weight of cultural decay. This is a conception of literature which has important implications for how we think about childhood. It also dominates much aesthetic theory in general, and one of the things which I will be discussing in this chapter is how this type of aesthetic, which sets up literature as something which can save us from what is most socially and culturally degenerate, is in the process of gravitating down to the nursery (the quotation from Townsend on p. 10 already makes this clear). In Garner's work, this notion of cultural decay produces two related assumptions. First, that the child – if we get to him or her soon enough (or keep away long enough) – is where this sensibility is still to be found (childhood is therefore defined as something which exists outside the culture in which it is produced). Secondly, that writing for children can contribute to prolonging or preserving – not only for the child but also for us – values which are constantly on the verge of collapse. The child, therefore, is innocent and can restore that innocence to us. In Garner's earlier books, this always involved a moment of discovery when the child realises that he or she is being addressed by the forces of a mythical past which the child is being asked both to relive and to repair. In the later books, especially in *The Stone Quartet*, the terms have shifted. The child is placed in a rural community of ironsmiths, stonemasons and agricultural labour. Here – in moments of recognition uncontaminated by industry or literacy – the child reads off from the land, the earth and the sky, its own truth and a nature which would otherwise perish.

For Rousseau, education has this same function of giving back to culture the nature which it has destroyed. Rousseau's imaginary pupil, Emile, is to be educated in the country away from the vices (social and sexual) and the discord (civil and political) of city life. Rousseau's project is, however, based on an acknowledged paradox. Given the cultural degeneracy which he sees all around him, the recreation of natural man can only be a highly artificial process. Nature is not something which can be retrieved, it has to be *added*.[1]

On the other hand, by attempting to do this through the child, Rousseau, like Garner, sets up childhood as a primitive state where 'nature' is still to be found if only one gets to it in time. For Rousseau, human action is something which by definition deforms: 'Everything is perfect, coming from the hands of the Creator; every thing degenerates in the hands of man' (Rousseau (1762) 1763, I, p. 1) (these are the first lines of *Emile*). Education can only be justified first by the fact that a child left to its own devices would perish (this may seem obvious but it is important if you are arguing for a self-sufficient natural state), and secondly, because without education the child would be even more totally disfigured by social institutions. Nature is a *quality* in the child which must be cultivated like a plant: 'Plants are fashioned by culture and men by education' (Rousseau (1762) 1763, I, p. 3).

In Rousseau, education preserves nature in the child, and it recovers nature through the child. In much the same way, literature for Garner gives back to children, and to us, something innocent and precious which we have destroyed: 'When men turned from the sun and the earth, and corrupted the air with the smoke of furnaces, it was poison to the lios-aflar' (Garner, 1960, p. 186; the 'lios-aflar' are the mythical forces of good). Whether Alan Garner is a children's writer or not (something which increasingly is being questioned (Philip, 1981, Preface, pp. 7–10)) seems to me irrelevant in the face of this obvious relation between his preoccupation with childhood and the desire to get back to the beginnings of our own mythical and cultural history since the child is so clearly in the service of this desire.

In *The Stone Book*, when Mary is asking her father about the different religions in the village ('Church and Chapel'), he breaks open a stone and hands it to her. His answer to her question is another question: 'Tell me how these flakes were put together, and what they are . . . And who made them into pebbles on a hill, and where that was a rock and when' (Garner, 1976, p. 31). For Mary's father, the history that matters is not one of present cultural divisions, but natural history, in which objects can be dissected and read. Inside the stone is a sea-urchin, and the knowledge which it offers is radically different from that which is provided by the Church: 'And I'm asking parsons, if it was Noah's flood, where was the urchin before? How long do stones take to grow? And how do urchins get in stones?' (Garner, 1976, p. 32).

The idea that you can read the true history of the world from objects, and out of the earth, is a recurrent one in Garner's books. In the earliest works, these objects were magic and their history mythical, like the 'tear' which Susan wears in *The Weirdstone of Brisingamen* which turns out to be the lost stone which is vital for the survival of the mythical race; or the bracelet in the sequel, *The Moon of Gomrath* (Garner, 1963), whose inscription becomes decipherable in moments of crisis as it turns into a magic sign which wards off the forces of evil. The child's relationship to the world of myth passes directly through these objects. It is because the children are in touch with objects, and have something of their *feel*, that they are given access to a mythical past. In the later books, these objects are the familiar objects of labour and the land, but they hold exactly the same resonance of historical origin. In *Granny Reardun*, the third book of the *Stone Quartet* (Garner, 1977), it is acceptable for Joseph to become an ironsmith, instead of a stonemason like his grandfather, because the work of the ironsmith is the more primitive form of work: 'That's aback, that is! That's aback of behind!' (Garner, 1977, p. 50). The ironsmith comes before the stonemason, and produces the bricksetter's trowel which makes his grandfather's work possible. Between them, iron, flint and stone take us back to the beginning of creation (before Noah's Ark). The knowledge they offer, which is the only knowledge that matters, can be read directly from their surfaces.

By setting this knowledge against that of the written word, Garner places himself firmly in the philosophical tradition which goes straight back to Rousseau. Apart from everything else that this philosophy attempts to sidestep, one of its central concerns is to retrieve a form of language or expression which would be uncontaminated by the intrusion of the verbal sign. Objects speak directly, and verbal language is something to be avoided for as long as possible: 'Of what use is it to have their heads filled with a catalogue of signs, which convey no representation to them? By learning the things signified, would they not become masters of the signs' (Rousseau (1762) 1763, i, p. 133). The linguistic sign is superfluous and misleading: 'To what purpose all these representations . . . the representation engrosses the boy's attention, and makes him forget the thing represented' (Rousseau (1762) 1763, i, pp. 237, 241). Objects, therefore, come first, and language is seen as something of a flaw on the world, a way of marking it out, which breaks up the essential continuity of nature and damages our relationship to it.

In a similar way, Locke argued that words were imperfect, since they could not accurately reflect the essences of substances (Locke, 1700, pp. 284–7). Locke's idea of a pictorial language to teach children to read was used as an advertisement by Newbery for one of the earliest children's books, *A Little Lottery Book for Children, containing a new method for playing them into a knowledge of the letters* (Newbery, 1756). But Locke's proposal should not just be seen as reflecting a new liberalism in relation to the child (pleasure in reading). It was inseparable from a deep suspicion of written language, and a desire to hold the written word as closely as possible to the immediacy of the visual image. In relation to children's fiction, Locke is most famous for his favourable remarks on the use of fables in the education of children (Locke, 1693), Rousseau for his recommendation of *Robinson Crusoe* in

Emile. But what tends to be forgotten is their mutual dislike of the written word which, in Rousseau's case, can accurately be described as an aversion: 'I have an aversion to books; they only instruct us to talk beyond our knowledge' (Rousseau (1762) 1763, I, p. 266).

We need to stop here and ask what this hostility towards the written word implies for childhood, and through that for children's literature itself. First of all, there is the obvious paradox that Locke and Rousseau should be seen as the founding fathers of children's fiction in England given their shared suspicion of writing. But more important than this is the conception of childhood which lies behind this attitude to language and the written word, a conception which links back crucially to the concerns of the previous chapter. For, in this preoccupation with an ideal form of language in relation to childhood, the child clearly serves as a means of getting round what is felt as most problematic and unstable about language itself.

Both Locke and Rousseau were alert to what would now be called the 'arbitrary' nature of the linguistic sign (de Saussure (1915) 1972; Benveniste (1939) 1966). They recognise, in different ways, that there is no natural relation between the linguistic sign and the thing to which it refers. But they wish to by-pass this aspect of language *through* the child. Language is imperfect (Locke) or degenerate (Rousseau), which implies the possibility of some perfect, or original and uncontaminated form of expression. For Rousseau, this is quite explicit. Language has gradually progressed into a set of abstractions, and has lost touch with the object, or sentiment, which it was originally intended to express. Its degradation exactly matches the decay which accompanies social advance. In *Emile*, therefore, the child is being asked not only to retrieve a lost state of nature, but also to take language back to its pure and uncontaminated source in the objects of the immediate world. Hence the constant stress throughout *Emile* on the purity of the visual sign:

By neglecting the use of signs which address the imagination, we have lost the most energetical of all languages. The impression of speech is always weak, and we convey our sentiments to the heart far better by the eye than by the ear. (Rousseau (1762) 1763, II, pp. 111–12)

Whether it is a case of physical gesture and expression, or of pointing out objects in the real world, what matters is that signs should immediately *speak*.

In Rousseau's *Emile*, it is clear that this stress on an uncontaminated language is intended to avoid the divisions of language and sexuality discussed in the previous chapter. Rousseau is well aware that his concept of a language in which signs immediately refer to present objects or sensations will founder once there is any question of the relationship between different ideas. For him, comparison and imitation are twin vices: the first because it refers purely to the relation between terms, the second because it allows for the possibility of deception. Comparison is for Rousseau the basis for rational thought, and ultimately it cannot be avoided. But like every other advance, he also sees it as a degeneration. For Rousseau, this problem relates directly to the recognition of sexual difference. In his *Second Discourse* (*A Discourse upon the Origin and Foundation of the Inequality among Mankind*) (Rousseau (1754) 1761), Rousseau describes the new object which stimulates the first comparison as a member of the opposite sex (Rousseau (1754) 1761, pp. 111–12).

In *Emile*, sexual passion is constantly associated with a deformation of language (rhetoric, metaphor and figures of speech in general). The objective is to preserve Emile from both for as long as possible: 'his language would be plain . . . he deals but little in figurative discourse because his passions are seldom enflamed . . . Our pupil will be still more plain and uniform in his discourse; for as his passions have not yet been excited, he will not mix their language with his' (Rousseau (1762) 1763, pp. 289–90, 202).

It is quite remarkable to watch Rousseau descending into a more and more indirect form of expression, and finally into silence, when he is attempting to explain sexuality to Emile (Rousseau (1762) 1763, ii, p. 116). Sexuality produces figures of speech and it also *requires* them; it stands at the opposite pole from the linguistic purity which Rousseau is otherwise trying to promote in the child. This clash between plain speaking and sexual metaphor is one which can still be seen in relation to children's writing today. Neil Philip, for example, in his book on Alan Garner praises the directness of his language, at the same time as he commends Garner's refusal actually to talk about sex in *Red Shift* (Garner, 1973)[2] (Philip, 1981, p. 107). At this level, sexuality seems to pose problems for any theory of language based on the idea that things can be simply and unequivocally referred to. More important, however, is the way that sexuality is associated in Rousseau with a degeneracy of language, and how both are opposed to an earlier purity of the sign.

Rousseau's preoccupation with an original form of language, therefore, goes hand in hand with his interest in nature and the child. Innocence of the child and of the word – the concepts seem to draw on, or attract, each other. Together they form something of a holy alliance which runs right through children's fiction to this day. The writing of Alan Garner is, I would argue, merely the most recent version of this. It has an almost identical conception of a language once pure and an uncorrupted culture or primitive state. If the child can still be in touch with that purity, then writing for children is the closest that we, as adults, can get to it today.

Garner has always been interested in early forms of language. Hence his use of dialect which, in the first books, he associates directly with myth (note that the idea that dialect comes *earlier* is a myth in itself – dialect is simply a form of language which has been differentiated from Received Pronunciation, which is, equally, a dialect). The later works, however, are marked by an even more explicit emphasis on direct knowledge and expression which, as we have seen, Garner opposes to the written word. This is clear not just in the theme of the story, but also in the way that *The Stone Quartet* is written, in its reduction of narrative commentary and in the increasing use of dialogue. Speech becomes direct; it is not reported, but *captured* – the rhythm of the spoken language vouching for the truth of the writing. The stress on voice, rhythm and speech then reproduces itself directly in the responses of the critics: 'His words are absolutes. There is no qualification, no hesitation, only the clear edge of necessary speech' (Philip, 1981, p. 18), 'a simplicity which engages everyone who can hear the voices of the characters on the page' (Meek, 1978b, p. 1081).

Rousseau also opposed the obtrusiveness and aridity of written culture to the purity and immediacy of the spoken word. In the hierarchy between different forms of language, therefore, the visual sign is opposed to the word, but written culture is a further contamination of what is spoken. Although his statements on the language of children are often contradictory,[3] it is clear that he takes his model for this primordial and sensuous language from the earliest speech of the child: 'This language is not articulate, but accented, sonorous, intelligible' (Rousseau (1762) 1763, I, p. 53).

A number of oppositions are starting to emerge which have been crucial in determining how children's fiction has been written since the eighteenth century and how it is still thought about to this day. The opposition between the child and the adult ('the instinctual life of the child and the cerebral life of the adult' (Philip, 1981, p. 153)), between oral and written culture, between innocence and decay. These are structural oppositions in the strictest sense, in that each term only has meaning in relation to the one to which it is opposed. They do not reflect an essential truth about the child (although the way in which childhood attracts the idea of 'essential truth' makes this very difficult to grasp); instead they produce a certain conception of childhood which simply carries the weight of one half of the contradictions which we experience in relation to ourselves.[4] What is important about Rousseau is the way in which he so clearly gives us the negative terms against which this concept of childhood has been built – the arbitrary nature of language, the divisions of sexuality, and civil discord. We can assume, therefore, that wherever childhood purity, or the idea of a primitive culture, is being promoted in one type of discourse, the excluded term of the opposition will be operating somewhere very close at hand.

There are important political repercussions which follow from this concept of childhood innocence. Childhood is seen as the place where an older form of culture is preserved (nature or oral tradition), but the effect of this in turn is that this same form of culture is *infantilised*. At this level, children's fiction has a set of long-established links with the colonialism which identified the new world with the infantile state of man. Along the lines of what is almost a semantic slippage, the child is assumed to have some special relation to a world which – in our eyes at least – was only born when we found it. It is no coincidence that the one book which Rousseau recommends for children in *Emile* is *Robinson Crusoe* (Defoe, 1719). The child, he writes, should 'personate Robinson himself' (Rousseau (1762) 1763, I, p. 268) (we can forget for the moment that imitation was meant to be a bad thing), reproducing his actions and his direct relationship to the land. But Crusoe did not only work on the land, cataloguing his activities in a language which was meant to be the exact record of his experiences. He also built a colony.[5]

The connection between colonialism and the concept of childhood which I have been examining here has had a decisive influence on the development of children's fiction. I want to pick out now some of the most decisive points of that influence. We can see it first in the early full-length narrative fiction for children, Thomas Day's *The History of Sandford and Merton* (Day, 1783–9), which was based directly on *Emile*.[6] The book is important for the way in which it shows how the central terms of Rousseau's discussion of childhood get redistributed in the production of fiction for the child. Day's book turns the opposition between degeneracy and innocence into a division between the classes. Thomas Merton belongs to the gentry, Harry Sandford is a farmer's son. Merton is indolent, Sandford industrious. The book opens when Merton is brought over from Jamaica by his father, and handed over to the vicar, Mr Barlow, who has been responsible for Sandford's education. The objective of the story is to bring the classes together, and to put right the degeneracies of Merton's previous genteel education by setting him to work on the land. *The History of Sandford and Merton*, therefore, reproduces Rousseau's concept of an outdoor education for boys, but this time in the form of a narrative which is intended for children.

Day's book is designed to encourage children to read, and it has somehow to get round Rousseau's dislike of the written word. It does this by making reading characteristic of the industrious class, who use books to teach themselves self-sufficiency and skills. Learning to read is not superfluous or decadent. In fact, far from being seen as a second-order language, it is explicitly opposed to the obsession with image and spectacle typical of the gentry. The opposition between classes is, therefore, an opposition between theories of the sign; but it is reading which inherits the idea of a direct knowledge of the real world. Reading can repair degeneracy precisely because it puts the gentry into contact with the land. It is only through reading stories about distant and primitive communities, where survival depends on physical adaptation and skill, that Merton is brought to recognise the necessity of labour. In *Sandford and Merton*, the dominant image is that of the shipwreck, which will later become so central to one whole section of children's fiction (literature for boys). Faced with the prospect of finding himself at sea, stranded, and left to his own devices (the connection to Crusoe is obvious), Thomas Merton admits that he might have to work:

But, said Mr. Barlow, is a man sure to be always in England, or some country where he can purchase bread?

Tommy. I believe so, sir.

Mr. B. Why, are there not countries in the world where there are no inhabitants, and where no corn is raised?

T. Certainly, sir . . . But then a man need not go to them; he may stay at home.

Mr. B. Then he must not pass the seas in a ship.

T. Why so, sir?

Mr. B. Because the ship may happen to be wrecked.

(Day, 1783–9, i, p. 101)

In one of the first stories read by the children in the book – The Gentleman and the Basketmaker – a judge decrees that a gentleman and basketmaker should be sent to a distant country to see how each of them can survive. In this primitive society 'inhabited by a rude and savage kind of men, who lived in huts, were strangers to riches, and got their living by fishing' (Day, 1783–9, i, p. 47), the basketmaker survives because of his industry, and the gentleman is reduced to being his servant. Furthermore, the success of the basketmaker is related to his ability to communicate in *signs*: 'the poor man who had been always accustomed to hardships and dangers from his infancy, made signs to the people' (Day, 1783–9, i, p. 37); while the gentleman becomes impotent amongst 'a barbarous people whose language he did not understand' (Day, 1783–9, i, p. 47). In Day's book, therefore, the idea of a primordial language has been relegated to the industrious class who, because they understand and can speak it, become identified with this primitive state of man.[7] The child's education will be complete when he recognises himself in the place of this identification, casts off the trappings of culture and goes back to the origins of work. All Rousseau's terms are there – nature, purity and immediacy of expression. But they have been reorganised, and are now assigned to the colonies of the civilised world. The obvious respect in which each of these qualities are held cannot conceal the ethnocentrism which lies behind this realignment.

The opposition between oral and written culture can be seen to belong to a colonialism which it invariably reproduces even when appearing to challenge it. Valuing primitive culture does not mean that it is being represented as anything other than a purely residual state, as Day's book makes clear. Furthermore, the idealisation of this earlier culture, and of the industrious class with which it is identified, is finally impossible to sustain. At the end of the book, Merton and Sandford are separated and Merton goes back to his own class (the differences between classes of children win out over the use of childhood as a universal category). In *Sandford and Merton*, we can see emerging the rudiments of the more familiar adventure story: a colonial fantasy about the primitive and the child (the primitive *as* child), and a belief in childhood as something which is able to by-pass the imperfections of the civilised world. *Sandford and Merton* in fact suggests that the child is serving to mediate, or resolve, a fundamental contradiction – that of seeing modern society as degenerate while still wishing to preserve its superiority over an otherwise idealised primitive state.

Sandford and Merton also gives us the other side of the children's story, the adult discourse which, from this point on, will increasingly be reduced, as children's fiction attempts to sever its links with the pedagogy out of which it was first produced. The central narrative of *Sandford and Merton* is framed by a dialogue between Mr Merton and Mr Barlow ('not one word of which any child will understand' (Day, 1783–9, I, Preface, p. vi)), which states that the purpose of education is to avoid, or at least to reduce, sexual degeneracy in the future life of the child:

> Alas! sir, it seems to me, that this will unavoidably happen, in spite of all our endeavours. Let us then not lose the important moment of human life, when it is possible to flatter ourselves with some hope of success in giving good impressions; they may succeed; they may either preserve a young man from gross immorality, or may have a tendency to reform him, when the first ardour of youth is past. If we neglect this aweful moment . . . it appears to me like launching a vessel into the midst of a storm, without a compass and without a pilot. (Day, 1783–9, I, p. 34)

What we get in the story itself is, of course, the shipwreck without the sex – which it is designed, precisely, to hold off.

In Rousseau's *Essay on the Origins of Language* (Rousseau (1718) 1969), he attributed civilisation's advance from its pure origin to a geographical accident which tipped the world's axis, upset its equilibrium and led to the differentiation of zones. He then charts different stages of language directly onto the distinct forms of civilisation which resulted from the loss of what had once been a perfect state of equilibrium. In *Emile*, the transition from the natural state to the state of civilisation, which Rousseau wants to redress through the child, is described as just such a loss of equilibrium: '[civilisation] breaks that kind of equilibrium which nature had established between [men]' (Rousseau (1762) 1763, I, p. 361). Rousseau is therefore working with two related concepts of origin – geographical and historical – in so far as the earlier state of nature is identified with a different distribution of the resources of the world.

Rousseau's conception of language in the *Essay* is a complex one which sometimes contradicts the points he makes about language in *Emile* (for example, the origins of language in the *Essay* are figurative and stem from the desire to arouse passion and sympathy, whereas passion and figurative speech were associated with a degeneracy of language in *Emile*). I will not go into the details of this here. But this way of bringing geography and history together in relation to a concept of origin has been central in the development of children's fiction. The first half of Volume II of *Sandford and Merton* is taken up almost entirely with documentary reports of the life of the Laplanders, Greenlanders and Kamschatka communities. They are presented as ideal and autonomous social units, whose physical exertions and lack of class division exactly reflect the intemperate nature of their climate. In so far as this perfection is given the status of an earlier state of man, so the geographical focus also carries an historical weight. 'Geography and history': at its simplest the idea is one of going somewhere else in order to get back to our own past. But already we can note that seeing these distant communities as one stage of our own historical development is a way of subordinating them to us. The colonialism of this early children's book does not, therefore, belong solely to the content of the stories; it is inscribed into the very pedagogic format of the book.

One of the most famous debates in the history of children's fiction is known as the 'Peter Parley–Felix Summerly' debate. Harvey Darton, in *Children's Books in England* (Darton (1932), 1982), devotes a chapter to this controversy (Darton (1932), 1982, pp. 219–51). The *Peter Parley* books originated in America with Samuel Griswold Goodrich in 1827.[8] They were explicitly didactic. *Tales of Peter Parley about America* starts by quoting the United States Act of Congress 'for the Encouragement of Learning, by securing the copies of Maps, Charts and Books' (Goodrich (1827), 1977, p. 11). The *Peter Parley* books were designed to teach history on the basis of geography, the idea being that the different stages of civilisation could be read directly from the different zones of the earth, especially from different parts of America (basically, the Indians versus the rest (Goodrich, 1837, pp. 118–30)). Felix Summerly (*alias* Sir Henry Cole) hated the stories, and produced *The Home Treasury* (Summerly, 1843–5), a collection of nursery and fairy tales, against their conception of children's writing. In his preface to the first volume of the series, *Traditional Nursery Songs of England* (Summerly, 1843), he addresses 'mothers, sisters, kind-hearted aunts, and even fathers, who are . . . alive to the importance of cultivating children's natural keenness for rhyme, rhythm, melody, and instinctive love for fun' (Summerly, 1843, Preface, pp. iii–iv).

The opposition is clear. Didacticism against pleasure, narrative against rhyme, true stories against fantasy. It is one which often occurs in contemporary discussion of children's fiction. If fairy tales are pleasurable, they are useless since, unlike didactic stories, they do not teach children about the real world. This might be one of the reasons why Bettelheim felt obliged to argue for fantasy in terms of the almost educational *use* to which it could be put and the contribution which it makes to the child's mastery of the real world.

On the other hand, in the nineteenth century this opposition is also one between America and England, between something which was seen as a cultural importation[9] and an attempt, in the face of this, to revive the English national heritage for the child. The clash between didacticism and fantasy breaks down on the shared concern about cultural origins which characterises both sides of the debate. The only difference, at this level, was that in the still 'childlike' state of American civilisation, history could be read directly off the land (history *based* on geography), whereas if you were after the cultural origins of England, then you had to dig for them.

The 'Peter Parley–Felix Summerly' debate encapsulates most of the terms of that conception of childhood which, I have been arguing, can be traced back to Rousseau. Only, these terms are now being divided up into two distinct notions of what is the correct form of writing for children. Melody and natural lore on the one hand (Summerly), primitive history and direct observation on the other (Parley). What they have in common is a shared stress on something past or lost which both sides see as *owing* to the child. But precisely because of this shared concern, a number of assumptions about their opposition, their relation to children, and the history of children's fiction, start to become problematic.

First, the emphasis on geography and territory, which is central to the didactic stories, also appears internally to the collection and production of fairy tales to which it is normally opposed. Annie Keary's *Heroes of Asgard* (Keary, 1857) is a collection of mythical stories told in response to a child's questions about a map representing the Saxon conception of the world. Although these stories are defined as *real*, that is as non-didactic, stories ('unlike a sham tale with chemistry in it' (Keary, 1857, Introductory conversation, p. 4)), telling them is still related to the idea of educating the child. The stories are, therefore, grounded by a notion of world history, and are part of the process of learning.

Secondly, the assumed connection between children and fairy tales becomes problematic once we recognise the link between the interest in the fairy tale and a preoccupation with cultural infancy and national heritage. As already mentioned, Tolkien made the observation about children and fairy tales in 1938 (Tolkien (1938) 1947), although he shares the concern with and – in his legends of the Middle Earth (Tolkien (1954–5) 1968) – has been instrumental in producing his own mythology for the English. The association of children with the fairy tale has taken different forms at different moments of history. In the seventeenth century, for example, before the development of children's fiction as a commercial venture in the sense that I am describing here, fairy tales were seen as suitable for children mainly at the point when they were downgraded from the French aristocratic salons in which they had originally circulated (d'Aulnoy (1696–9) 1953; Perrault (1697) 1967).[10] But in the nineteenth century, fairy tales are associated with children as the effect of this repeated identification of cultural infancy and childhood. In the Preface to *The Blue Fairy Book* (Lang, 1899), Andrew Lang makes this explicit: 'The children to whom and for whom they were told represent the young age of man' (Lang, 1899, Preface, p. xi). Andrew Lang and Joseph Jacobs, who also collected fairy tales in the late nineteenth century (Jacobs (1890, 1894) 1968), were both members of the Folklore Society. Their interest in philology and national culture ('a book of English Fairy Tales which English children will listen to' (Jacobs (1890) 1968, Preface, p. 2) is something they have in common with – among others – the brothers Grimm, Tolkien and Alan Garner.

Thirdly, the emergence of the boy's adventure story in the second half of the nineteenth century cannot be seen as a decisive break in the way that it is often described:

> Once juvenile fiction, shorn largely of instruction, got a hold, a new class of juvenile literature was bound to be developed. Hence the 'boy's book': that is, the boy's *tale*, not the boy's story-book nor the boyish book, but the whole synoptic literary composition the basis of which is fictitious romance. (Darton (1932) 1982, p. 246)

The division – which falls somewhere between Marryat and Kingston, or Ballantyne – is based on the rejection by these later writers of explicit moralism, and their stated intention to write *real* boys' stories of excitement and romance. A writer like G. A. Henty (Henty, 1871) represents a further stage when the new adventure story has become a 'piece of manufactured goods' (Darton (1932) 1982, p. 303). But in so far as it rests on the presence or absence of explicit didacticism, the division is problematic, for it conceals the continuity – both politically and in terms of narrative structure – of these later adventure stories with the works of Thomas Day and Peter Parley. Exploration, discovery and adventure – terms which could be accurately used with reference to *Peter Pan* and, in a different way, in relation to Alan Garner – do not signal the beginning of a new liberal conception of children's writing. They are the inheritors of a fully colonialist concept of development, and a highly specific and limited conception of the child.

In the earlier adventure stories, this continuity is clear. *Masterman Ready or The Wreck of the Pacific* (Marryat (1841–2) 1878) – shipwrecks are the most recurrent feature of this tradition of writing – tells the story of the Seagrove family who are on their way to Sydney to take possession of new farmlands when their ship is wrecked. The story is about how they survive on the island where they land, their fights with the savages and their cultivation of the land. The question which starts the story (and which it then proceeds to answer) is the one asked by the young Seagrove of the ship's captain, Masterman Ready: 'Were you ever shipwrecked on an island like Robinson Crusoe?' (Marryat (1841–2) 1878, p. 3). In his Preface to the book, Marryat explains that he refused to write a sequel to *The Swiss Family Robinson* (Wyss, 1818), as his children had requested, because of its inaccurate information about the 'animal and vegetable productions of the island on which the family had been wrecked' (Marryat (1841–2) 1878, Preface, p. v). His objective was to correct this and to stimulate children 'to seek for information' (Marryat (1841–2) 1878, Preface, p. vi). The fictitious romance for boys thus completes the transition into narrative of that conception of the world in which discovering, or seeing, the world is equivalent to controlling, or subduing, it. Latent to this, as we have so frequently seen, is an equation between infancy, savagery and the territory of colonial lands: 'what a parallel there is between a colony and her mother-country and a child and its parent' (Marryat (1841–2) 1878, p. 140), 'when a child is first born, William, it acts by instinct only, the reasoning powers are not yet developed; as we grow up, our reason becomes every day more matured, and gains the mastery over our instinct, which decreases in proportion' (Marryat, 1878, p. 362).

Much of this recurs in both Kingston and Henty. In *The Three Midshipmen* (Kingston, 1862) and *Out on the Pampas* (Henty, 1871), there is the same starting-point of a voyage, whose more explicit colonial objectives (civilising of the savage in Kingston, defeat of the Indians in Henty) carries a myth of self-improvement which is directly linked – in Henty at least – to the growth of the child. The book starts with the father wondering what to 'make of the boys' (Henty, 1871, p. 1); it ends when the settlement of the Pampas is sufficiently developed to allow them to be gentlemen off its income or traders off its estate. Once again, the empirical knowledge – cultivation of ginger, vanilla, bean, flax, hemp and coffee, and the identification of fauna (specimens of which are sent to the British Museum) – are both the means to material aggrandisement as well as instruction for the children. The fact that this relationship between labour and learning is so fully incorporated into the narrative gives this book a stronger continuity with *Robinson Crusoe* than the earlier story by Marryat whose didacticism at this level is most strongly stated in the Preface.

In Kingston's book, childhood is given the same privilege of exploration (the book starts with the heroes as three schoolboys), the same connotation of savagery (the savages are described as the 'long neglected children of Ham' (Kingston, 1871, p. 209)) and the same objective of growth through which both of these are related (the savage accepts the values of civilisation and the boys' adventures chart their passage to maturity). What all three books have in common (Marryat, Kingston, Henty) are the parallel oppositions which they establish – and which appear more natural and inevitable precisely as the stories become more 'real' – between the child and the adult, and between savagery and the civilised state; oppositions which can be traced back through the works of Thomas Day and Peter Parley to Rousseau. The terms in which childhood is understood are fundamentally the same, and I would say that they have not shifted greatly in the way that children's fiction is still mostly discussed today.

What I have been describing so far makes no claim to be a complete history of children's fiction. My objective is not to cover the field, but rather to pick out, in a deliberately selective way, some of the recurring points of definition of the child, and of writing for children, which seem to predominate in our culture. Before going on to look at the more recent manifestations of this in discussions of children's books, we should note again the way in which Alan Garner inherits both sides of the division between adventure story and fairy tale, forms whose proximity I have been arguing for in this chapter. What Garner does is take to its furthest extreme the relationship of both these forms to childhood. His stories are island adventures, called myth or fairy, and sent underground (in the earlier books, the struggle over the preservation of folklore was invariably fought in territorial terms). Garner assimilates the two traditions, and reaffirms their link with a concept of an origin which is recoverable through the child. The ease with which he appears to do so might explain something of his extraordinary acclaim.

There has, however, been one fairly consistent progression in children's writing. I would call it an increasing 'narrativisation' of children's fiction, and a gradual dropping of the conspicuous narrating voice – that voice which in the very earliest books revealed itself as so explicitly didactic and repressive. Children's books in the late eighteenth century were *only* justified by the presence of the adult, who laid out for that other adult presumed to be buying the book exactly what he or she was doing. Children's fiction started with a division between two different types of language and modes of address, but this division has progressively been removed, as the adult intention has more and more been absorbed into the story and, apparently, rendered invisible.

One effect of this is that children's fiction has tended to inherit a very specific aesthetic theory, in which showing is better than telling: the ideal work lets the characters and events speak for themselves. This is a 'realist' aesthetic which shares with Rousseau's theory of language the desire for a natural form of expression which seems to be produced automatically and without mediation out of that to which it refers. What it denies precisely is language – the fact that language does not simply reflect the world but is active in its constitution of the world. And this rejection of language as process, its *activity*, means that what is also being refused is the idea that there is someone present inside the utterance ordering it, or disordering it, as the case may be. For, as we saw with Rousseau, once you recognise language, then you also have to acknowledge its potential (Freud would say essential) disorder.

It is no coincidence that the development of children's fiction has followed that of the novel which has been the main repository, in adult writing, of this theory of representation. But what seems to have happened in recent discussions of children's books is that, in response to the breakdown of this aesthetic in the modern adult novel, writers have been arguing with increasing vehemence for its preservation in writing intended for the child. 'Preservation' in the dual sense that children's writing should not be *contaminated* by this development, and that it should also become the place where the earlier form of novel writing can actually be *saved*:

Children's writing is a large and apparently self-containable genre, as it never was before. It is independent of the current adult novel. On the face of it, you wouldn't therefore expect its burgeoning richness. Could it be, ironically, that precisely because the adult novel is so weak in this country, some talents have been drawn into the children's field and flourished? (Townsend, quoting Brian Jackson, director of Advisory Centre for Education, *Use of English*, Spring 1970 (Townsend, 1971, p. 11))

It is a good bet that both *Alice* and *The Wizard* will be around for many centuries after *Tiny Alice* and *The American Dream* – even that monstrous, million-punned labyrynthine dream of H. C. Earwicker's – have been forgotten by everybody except the collectors and students of twentieth century curiosa. (Martin Gardner in Egoff *et al.*, 1969, p. 155)

– note that *Alice* is the model of sanity when compared with Norman Mailer and James Joyce.

Increasingly, children's writing is being talked about in terms of 'tradition' (*The Nesbit Tradition*, Crouch, 1972), 'culture' ('Books are no longer necessary for culture . . . To combat this view is one of the most challenging cultural enterprises of this century' (Trease (1949) 1964, p. 176)), and 'trust' ('Our trust will in the end repose upon our masterpieces', Quiller-Couch, quoted in Eyre, 1971, p. i). Although these may seem to be neutral enough terms (nothing but the best for our children we might say), once again they carry a very specific ideology of writing and its function. The equivalent position in relation to adult fiction would be that of F. R. Leavis who set out to establish the 'great tradition' of English novel writers (Leavis, 1948), writers who express 'an ideal civilised sensibility' (Leavis, 1948, p. 16) and who speak for 'life and growth amid all this mass of destruction and disintegration' (Leavis quoting D. H. Lawrence, Leavis, 1948, p. 26). As with the above writers on children's fiction, literature becomes the chief battleground in the attempt to preserve our culture from imminent decay. But equally, this literature refers to a specific form of writing – the nineteenth-century novel which makes twentieth century writing (notably that of James Joyce) a particular target (note how *The Nesbit Tradition* (Crouch, 1972) echoes Leavis's title). Furthermore, in Leavis's case, the concern to preserve literary tradition is unequivocally part of an anxiety about the damage to cultural values produced by the spread of mass literacy and culture (Leavis, 1930)[11] (this will be crucial to Chapters 4 and 5 which discuss the children's book market in terms of changes in literacy and the educational policy of the state).

My point here is not to pass judgement on the relative moral or aesthetic virtues of these different forms of writing – this would be to accept the very terms which I am trying to question. What I want to stress, rather, is the recurrence of a set of terms (cultural preservation/decay) and the remarkable consistency with which one particular aesthetic is being laid on the child, and associated

with children. It is an aesthetic which takes its reference from the
nineteenth-century novel: 'sustained and developed narrative,
honestly observed and consistent characterisation . . . the qualities mature readers look for in a novel' (Crouch, 1972, pp. 8,
229), and which measure the success of a book according to its
ability to convince us that it is no such thing: 'The fact that it is
possible to argue about her as if she were a real person indicates a
fine achievement of characterisation' (Townsend, 1965, p. 147).
When this criticism refers to twentieth-century writing, it returns
it to this same aesthetic judgement by insisting, for example, that
objects should only be represented if they can be unambiguously
placed in the context of the narrative: 'the displacement of
furniture does indeed have some relevance to the internal world of
the novel' (Hildick on Joyce in relation to children's writing
(Hildick (1970) 1974, p. 67)). Nothing must obtrude, and no word
must be spoken, in excess of those which are absolutely necessary
to convince the child that the world in which he or she is being
asked to participate is, unquestionably, real. The world of the
children's novel (the word 'novel' in itself indicates that children's
fiction has 'grown up' or 'come into its own') is 'recognisably the
real world' (Townsend, 1965, p. 146).

There is a related assumption that children's fiction has
become more progressive *for* children in direct proportion to its
advance into this type of writing. This is because the development
of narrative in children's books has gone hand in hand with an
apparent reduction in its pedagogic function and an increasing
stress on the child's own pleasure. However, given the way that
this form of narrative is almost always described in terms of its
ability to secure the *identification* of the child with the story, and the
corresponding emphasis on a threatened cultural inheritance
which we have seen so often before, the idea that narrative is
progressive *per se* seems to me to be highly questionable.

The writing that is currently being promoted for children is that
form of writing which asks its reader to enter into the story and to
take its world as real, without questioning how that world has
been constituted, or where, or who, it comes from. Even if it is not
the intention, it is the effect of writing which presents itself as
'realistic' that the premises on which it has been built go largely
unnoticed, because it appears so accurately to reflect the world as
it is known to be. In relation to this type of writing, children are
valued because of the ease with which they slip into the book and

live out the story: 'Above all, [the child] has the ability, which in adults is eroded or entirely lost, to identify himself with the characters of the story' (Townsend, quoting Scott O'Dell, *Psychology Today*, January 1968 (Townsend, 1971, p. 160)). What is more, at moments it is even argued that there is something in the very nature of childhood which *facilitates* this form of representation: 'In the natural way of things, children are relatively uncomplicated, and in presenting them fictionally no great distortion or suppression – no artistic dishonesty – is required' (Hildick (1970) 1974, p. 9). Children become the natural object *par excellence*, which can be effortlessly captured by writing, with no distortion or intrusion from language or, indeed, anything else. Innocence of the child and of the word ('no dishonesty', 'no distortion') – yet again the child is enthroned as the guarantee of our safety in language.

Once it is viewed in these terms, children's fiction starts to return to the arena of pedagogy and learning which it was meant to have left behind (one could of course argue that this process had always been more apparent than real). It is not just that children's writing is seen as the repository of a literary tradition under threat of disintegration in the adult world. It is also that narrative fiction starts to be assigned a supreme status in the process of education itself. Fiction is of 'paramount importance in the whole educational and civilising process' (Hildick (1970) 1974, p. 163). It is one of the 'main agents of socialisation' (Applebee, 1978, p. 53), and it should be used as the basis of educational technique (Hildick (1970) 1974, p. 163). Fiction becomes a central tool in the education of the child, and it should be taught to the child according to a notion of competence or skill. This may well be correct – the idea that narrative is the most efficient way of imparting information, and of making absolutely sure that the child takes it in. But, if this is the case, it is precisely because narrative secures the identification of the child with something to which it does not necessarily belong. And it does so without the child being given the chance to notice, let alone question, the smoothness and ease of that process.

Increasingly, the terms of 'capacity', 'competence' and 'behavioural repertory' are used to refer to the way the child acquires the ability to identify with narrative. The acquisition of fictional competence is laid out according to stages which echo, in their idea of an assured progression (heaps, sequences, primitive narrative, unfocused and focused chains, narrative proper (Applebee, 1978)), that march into rationality which dominates one particular conception of the development of the child. In the end, this concept of narrative links up with the idea of childhood development as just such a sequence of straightforward stages which was the idea that I started by questioning in the first chapter of this book. It is the equivalent, at the level of narrative, of Piaget's idea of a gradual acquisition of motor and sensory coordination in the child. The implication is that one thing leads unequivocally to another – in the story and in the child who is reading it (the two belong absolutely together). Applebee, for example, in his book on *The Child's Concept of Story* (Applebee, 1978), makes it clear that the analysis of the conventions of narrative writing in terms of such a rational sequence enables us to dispense with the concept of the unconscious: 'Rather than accepting such stories [fantasies] as expressions of unconscious wishes and desires, it seems more likely that they are simple explorations of this special story world itself' (Applebee, 1978, pp. 80–1). And he quotes Bettelheim to support his concept of fantasy as 'the best way of understanding what the specific consequences of some action might be' (Applebee, 1978, p. 119). Fantasy is, therefore, first rationalised by being removed from the domain of the unconscious, and then assimilated to the idea of narrative cohesion, of fictional identification, and of story. The fact that Piaget (who repudiates the concept of the unconscious) and Bettelheim (who accepts it)[12] should be brought together here to support the idea that language can be so totally ordered and cohered, merely confirms that – in relation to children's fiction – the challenge of the unconscious to this very notion of identity in language has been lost.

This way of talking about fantasy seems to reflect something of a pattern. Far from it being the case that realism and fantasy belong at opposite poles of the spectrum of children's writing, they are finally united by this concern to preserve a certain type of narrative form. The distinction between fantasy and realism ('Books of fantasy appear to be declining in numbers, quality, and readership. Books about "real life" are on the increase' (Egoff *et al.*, 1969, p. 446), 'with the current dominance of social realism in children's fiction, such fantasies may seem not quite the thing' (Greenland, 1982, p. 791)), between aesthetic as opposed to social concerns (the entire *New Statesman* debate on children's fiction in

1980 was conducted in terms of this opposition),[13] is finally untenable in the face of the shared emphasis of response on the coherence of a specific form of writing.

Folk and fairy tale are 'akin' to the Victorian novel for their realism of character, and the non-obtrusiveness of the narrative voice (Buchan (1931) 1973). They can be set against modern adult writing because they give back the rudiments of a type of fiction which that writing has all but destroyed. Above all, they are the supreme embodiments of a 'sense of story': 'Myth, legend, fairy-tale are alive in their own right, endlessly reprinted, endlessly fertile in their influence. Modern children's fiction is permeated by a sense of story' (Townsend, 1971, p. 12) (Townsend is tracing this 'sense' to before the novel, but it is still unequivocally opposed to the decadence of modernism). Fantasy, therefore, belongs to the conventions of narrative, just as the preoccupation with realistic writing is a fully aesthetic and moral concern: 'It is the power of a work of fiction to draw the reader into this process of identification that gives that work its quality – moral as well as aesthetic' (Hildick (1970) 1974, p. 8).

Realism in children's writing cannot be opposed to what is 'literary' or truly 'aesthetic', once it is seen that realism does not refer just to the content of what is described, but to a way of presenting it to the reader. Realism is a fully literary convention – one which is being asserted with increasing urgency in relation to fiction for the child. This may seem a long way off from Garner's (and Rousseau's) emphasis on the degeneracy of what is literate and the purity of the spoken word, but in fact they are very close. Realism – in the sense in which we have seen it defined here for children – is that form of writing which attempts to reduce to an absolute minimum our awareness of the language in which a story is written in order that we will take it for real (the very meaning of 'identification'). To this extent, it shares with the other theories of language which I have looked at in this chapter a conviction that the best form of expression is that which most innocently ('no dishonesty', 'no distortion') reflects the objects of the real world.

When *Peter Pan* was being written, this concept of language had been challenged not just by Freud, but also by a shift in the adult novel which started to turn its attention to the throes of the written word. Meanwhile, children's fiction held out, and *Peter Pan* passed through unscathed (the most innocent object of all).

3

Peter Pan and Literature for the Child
Confusion of tongues

> . . . the author seems to be herself as irrational and abandoned
> in her irrationality as a child.
>
> Wallace Hildick on Enid Blyton in *Children and Fiction*
> (Hildick (1970) 1974, p. 139)

> 'John,' Wendy said falteringly, 'perhaps we don't remember
> the old life as well as we thought we did.' A chill fell upon them;
> and serve them right.
>
> J. M. Barrie, *Peter and Wendy* (Barrie, 1911, p. 245)

J. M. Barrie's *Peter and Wendy* was published in 1911. It was the
only attempt which Barrie ever made to write *Peter Pan* as a
narrative for children. Peter Pan was a children's *classic* before it
was a children's *book*. Barrie himself seems to have been in no
hurry to close up the gap between the two: 'Mr. Barrie has often
been asked to write a short narrative or libretto of his immortal
child's play and has as often refused' (*The Bookman*, January 1907,
p. 161).[1]
While Barrie hesitated, others moved in, with pictures and
images from the play (Herford, 1907; O'Connor and Woodward,
1907), or mementoes and biographies of *Peter Pan* (O'Connor,
1907; Drennan, 1909). All these versions seemed to hover
somewhere between the play and the written word (alphabets,
picture books, keepsakes). It is as if those who produced them
were also unsure as to what a story of *Peter Pan* – that is, a story to
be read or told – might be. And when Barrie produced his own
version in 1911, the other writers did not stop. If anything they

66

seem to have redoubled their efforts, and increased their output, in a way which smacks of something more than the vast commercial appetite which *Peter Pan* undoubtedly stimulated, and which it was part of, right from the beginning of its history.

J. M. Barrie's *Peter Pan* was retold before he had written it, and then rewritten after he had told it. By 1911, *Peter Pan* had already become such a universally acclaimed cultural phenomenon that Barrie himself could only intervene back into its history from outside. The paradox is that Barrie's attempt to reclaim *Peter Pan* – reluctant, we must assume, given the hesitations – failed. *Peter Pan* went on without him. I would go further and suggest that *Peter Pan* could *only* go on without him, because it had come to signify an innocence, or simplicity, which every line of Barrie's 1911 text belies.

'All children, except one, grow up' – these are the first lines of the 1911 story. Who is speaking and what is their place in the story? Are they fully rational and are they an adult or child? (cf. the opening quotation by Wallace Hildick on p. 66). An adult – clearly – since the speaker has the hindsight of one who is no longer a child, who can qualify 'children' with the 'all' of a total wisdom (linguistics calls the 'all' a pronominal *totaliser*), and who thus places at the safe distance of the third person the group which he goes on to describe: 'They soon know that they will grow up, and the way Wendy knew was this. One day when she was two years old she was playing in a garden, and she plucked another flower and ran with it to her mother.' The narrator introduces you to 'all' children, picks one out – Wendy – and tells you her story. It is already a story which carries a considerable weight (that of 'all' children), but it is light enough ('playing in a garden' as the very image of lightness and ease). Furthermore, the 'one day' stands as the convention of story-telling itself (one knowable and utterly unspecified day, compare 'Once upon a time'), even if this convention does come a little late on the page.

The passage continues: 'I suppose she must have looked rather delightful, for Mrs. Darling put her hand to her heart and cried, "Oh, why can't you remain like this for ever!" ' This line is deceitful. The obvious tragedy – Mrs Darling's exclamation and regret (the hallmark of *Peter Pan* as we know it) – conceals something far more aberrant, which is the appearance of another voice on the page. The 'I suppose' inserts the narrator with an apparent disclaimer – his position is one of uncertainty or mere supposition. But for all its casualness, this 'I suppose' marks the presence of the narrator more forcefully than anything that has gone before. Who is this 'I', who can only *suppose* the delight of Wendy's *looks*, but can so utterly penetrate her *thoughts*: 'This was all that passed between them on the subject, but henceforth Wendy knew that she must grow up.' It is the voice of someone who once was as Wendy, and who appeals to the reader on the basis of that identification: 'You always know after you are two. Two is the beginning of the end' (all quotations, Barrie, 1911, p. 1).

This is, therefore, a narrator who can only read the thoughts of his characters because of an acknowledged relationship to them. The passage charts that relationship – it discovers, maps and predicts it. But it is not the relationship of a character in the story who knows because he participates (Wendy or her mother), nor that of the omniscient narrator who knows precisely because he does not participate (the all-knowing from above). It is the relationship of a narrator who himself belongs on the edge of what he offers us as the *trauma* of growth – given three times over in the passage in a crescendo of insistence and anxiety: 'grow up', 'will grow up', 'must grow up'. By the end of the passage, there is no clear distinction between the narrator and the child he describes: 'You always know after you are two.' The child is an adult because it has reached the point of no return ('Two is the beginning of the end'); the adult is a child because of its total identification with the child at that moment (the shift from simple past tense to a continuous present and the 'you' which replaces the 'they').

But if the adult is a child, then it is the narrating voice itself which takes up the position of the one and only child who does not grow up – the exception of the opening line: 'All children, *except one*, grow up' (my italics). In the process of language, in the slippage from 'all' to 'they' to 'you', J. M. Barrie's 1911 version of *Peter Pan* undermines the certainty which should properly distinguish the narrating adult from the child.

The narrator of a children's book does not *have* to take on the voice of an adult. Enid Blyton, for example, usually does, but E. Nesbit, in *The Story of the Treasure Seekers*, written in 1899 (Nesbit, 1899), writes the narrative from the position of one of the children in the story. The child sets the reader the enigma of discovering which one is speaking: 'It is one of us that tells this story – but I shall not tell you which: only at the very end perhaps I will. While the story is going on you may be trying to guess, only I bet you don't' (Nesbit, 1899, p. 4). The rule which Enid Blyton breaks in the passage referred to by Wallace Hildick in *Children and Fiction* in the opening quotation to this chapter, and which Barrie's text constantly violates, is not, therefore, a rule which states that the adult must never speak in the voice of a child. It is a more subtle rule than this, which demands that the narrator be adult *or* child, one or the other. It does not really matter, provided that it knows, with absolutely no equivocation, *which* it is, and that it uses that knowledge to hold the two instances safely apart on the page. In the following passage, for example, it is clear that Enid Blyton has let something slip:

> Julian called out to Edgar. 'You shut up! You're not funny, only jolly silly!'
> 'Georgie-porgie,' began Edgar again, a silly smile on his wide red face. (Blyton, *Five Run Away Together*, 1944, p. 17)

The 'silly' has spread across from Julian's response onto the narrator's 'external' description of Edgar – hence Enid Blyton as 'abandoned in her irrationality as a child' (Hildick, 1974, p. 139).

One could multiply the instances from Enid Blyton's writing. The following passage, for example, has been criticised for its blatant class values and prejudice (Dixon, 1977, pp. 59–66):

> Two people came slowly along the beach. Dick looked at them out of half-closed eyes. A boy and a man – and what a ragamuffin the boy looked! . . . 'What a pair!' said Dick to Julian. 'I hope they don't come near us. I feel as if I can smell them from here.' . . . An unpleasant, unwashed kind of smell came to the children's noses. Pooh! (Blyton, *Five Fall into an Adventure*, 1950, p. 23)

Formally this example is very like the first. Dick expresses a judgement; the narrator confirms and joins in: 'Pooh!' But this device – of sharing in the feelings of her characters – is a basic narrative convention which Enid Blyton often employs: 'Anne went to the little room she shared with George. How good it was to be back again at Kirrin! What fun they would have these holidays with George and dear old Timmy!' (Blyton, 1944, p. 15). The passage moves from the external description of Anne to the child's own excitement of pleasure, but the difference of this passage from the first two is that the transition is smooth since the more child-like comment is given in the form of what can be read as Anne's own reflections. In the other examples, the change from one voice to another jars and calls attention to itself. It is this jarring which draws the epithet 'irrational' and, with it, the criticism of the values expressed. What characterises the two passages singled out for criticism from Enid Blyton's writing, therefore, is something which appears as a momentary loss of narrative *control*.

Writers for children must know who they are. They must know and understand children, otherwise they would not be able to write for them in the first place. But they must also know who *they* (as adults) are, otherwise that first knowledge might put their identity as writers at risk. What is at stake here is a fully literary demand for a cohesion of writing. It is a demand which rests on the formal distinction between narrator and characters, and then holds fast to that distinction to hold off a potential breakdown of literary language itself. The ethics of literature act as a defence mechanism against a possible confusion of tongues.[2]

What all these examples suggest is that, in the case of children's fiction, the question of form turns into a question of limits, of irrationality and lost control, of how far the narrator can go before he or she loses his or her identity, and hence the right to speak, or write, for a child. Writing for children rests on that limit, the edge which the opening passage of Barrie's 1911 text gives effectively as a trauma in process. The demand for better and more cohesive writing in children's fiction, described in the previous chapter, carries with it a plea that certain psychic barriers should go undisturbed, the most important of which is the barrier between adult and child. When children's fiction touches on that barrier, it becomes not experiment (the formal play of a modern adult novel which runs the gamut of its characters' points of view), but *molestation*. Thus the writer for children must keep his or her narrative hands clean and stay in his or her proper place.

Getting too close, or going too far – J. M. Barrie's 1911 *Peter and Wendy* risks both. Whether that is at the level of the story's explicit content (which is more fully elaborated than in the play: 'Mrs. Darling dreamt that the Neverland had come too near' (Barrie,

1911, p. 15)); or else at the level of common narrative decency, whose rules it so constantly flouts:

> That was the story, and they were as pleased with it as the fair narrator herself. Everything just as it should be, you see. Off we skip like the most heartless things in the world, which is what children are, but so attractive; and we have an entirely selfish time; then when we have need of special attention we nobly return for it confident we shall be embraced instead of smacked. (Barrie, 1911, p. 166)

The passage pronounces on 'what children are', but it becomes a child taking pleasure in itself as it makes the observation. This passage is, if anything, more aberrant than the first. For not only does it slide from one pronoun, or pronoun position, to another – 'you' to 'they' ('what children are') to 'we'; but its own child-like confidence and certainty is interrupted by the qualifiers of a distinctly adult judgement – 'an entirely *selfish* time', 'we *nobly* return'. This in addition to the fact that the whole of Peter Pan's tragedy hangs on the fact that he precisely could *not* (either 'nobly' or 'selfishly') return. Thus the voices of the passage contradict each other, and are in turn contradicted by the rest of the narrative which, for Peter Pan at least, tells a different story.

In *The Little White Bird*, the narrator fought over his relationship to the child; telling the child stories was, rather like a possession order, something which had to be contested. The place of the child in the process was always uncertain, since it was never clear whether the narrator told stories in order to hold on to the child, or whether he held on to the child in order to tell stories. The book seemed to turn on the act of narration itself, with all that this implied of an identity never quite sure of itself which had to be claimed and reclaimed. The child was first the focus of that identity, and only secondly the subject of the story; or, more precisely, he was the subject of the story *on condition* that he allowed himself to serve as that focus. Thus the narrator asked the child for the right to speak, whether, indeed, he could speak – in the dual sense of a legal claim and an almost physical capacity. A precarious positioning of adult and child around the question of how to tell a story, and to whom to tell a story – *The Little White Bird* was addressed partly to the adult reader (an adult novel) and partly to the child (David inside the book).

Only by removing all of this could *Peter Pan* become a play for children, although even here, if we look closely, it is arguable that it ever was. *Peter Pan* was taken off the page and worked into a spectacle which gleamed with the overbright innocence characteristic of any act of representation proclaiming its purity to the world. But, as the 1911 *Peter and Wendy* reveals, behind the image of the boy who would not grow up, the problem of the relationship between the adult and child persisted in the form of a question which strikes at the very roots of language:

> On these magic shores, children at play are for ever beaching their coracles. We too have been there; we can still hear the sound of the surf, though we shall land no more.
>
> Of all delectable islands, the Neverland is the snuggest and the most compact; not large and sprawly, you know, with tedious distances between one adventure and another, but nicely crammed. (Barrie, 1911, p. 10)

In this passage, we can ask not only whether it is an adult or child who is speaking, but also from where they are speaking: on the island or off it, joining in the story or able to tell it solely because of their position outside? Thus the issue of narrative position in language takes on the physical quality of location or place. When the children fly off to the Neverland, it is not just their parents whom they leave staring in panic at the window, but also the narrator, whose panic in language reveals the deeper meaning of what it means to be left behind.

Barrie's 1911 text is remarkable for the way that it exposes this problem of identity in language. It runs counter to almost every criterion of acceptability laid down by the writers on children's fiction which I discussed in the previous chapter. Those criteria sought for purity of language (language as the unmediated reflection of the real world) and clarity in its organisation (no confusion between the narrator and the characters, between the speaker and what he or she describes). In both these cases, a line is drawn so as to circumvent gaps in the linguistic order of things in such a way that the writer's identity in language is secured. Writing for children becomes a battleground where the slightest challenge to that identity has to be put down. What seems to be required of children's writing is something in the nature of a linguistic saving of face.

There is a game which children play in which each child asserts supremacy ('I'm the King of the Castle') and is tumbled by the next ('Get down you dirty rascal'). It rests entirely on a principle of rotation. The central position is declared and challenged at one and the same time; it can only be claimed by one child because it circulates among all the rest. Language operates according to a similar principle. The 'I' shifts from person to person, and is only ever momentarily arrested by the one who speaks. The 'I' has a meaning solely by belonging to a system which includes all the other terms ('you'/'he'/'she'/'it') against which it is set. Like the game of the children, language works on the basis of an antagonism between terms. What Barrie's *Peter and Wendy* demonstrates too clearly for comfort is that language is not innocence (word and thing), but rather a taking of sides (one word against the other). In *Peter and Wendy*, the line between the narrator and his characters is not neat and/or invisible; it is marked out as a division, not to say opposition, or even war:

> Even now we venture into that familiar nursery only because its lawful occupants are on their way home; we are merely hurrying on in advance of them to see that their beds are properly aired and that Mr. and Mrs. Darling do not go out for the evening. We are no more than servants. Why on earth should their beds be properly aired, seeing that they left them in such a thankless hurry? . . .
>
> One thing that I should like to do immensely, and that is to tell her, in the way authors have, that the children are coming back, that indeed they will be here on Thursday week. That would spoil so completely the surprise to which Wendy and John and Michael are looking forward. (Barrie, 1911, pp. 234–45)

This is the sequence of the return home. The narrator veers in and out of the story as servant, author and child. He turns on his characters and comments on his own place:

> I had meant to say extraordinarily nice things about her; but I despise her and not one of them will I say now.

> as we are here we may as well stay and look on. That is all we are, lookers-on. Nobody really wants us.

Now that we look at her closely . . . I find I won't be able to say nasty things about her after all. (Barrie, 1911, pp. 236, 239)

When Peter Pan himself then flies in, exults at Mrs Darling, bars the window to keep out the returning children, and finally relents, he is nothing more than the embodiment of this narrating voice gone wild.

I said at the beginning of this chapter that it is clear from the first lines of Barrie's text that the narrating voice itself occupies the place of the one child who does not grow up. In this sequence of the children's return, that voice declares itself as the onlooker who, like Peter Pan, is excluded from the scene which he watches from outside. But by the end of the chapter, this same voice has pulled itself together, and has reconstituted itself as a narrator in the conventional sense of the term, that is, as a narrator who can sagely comment on the place of the outsider as the unique and exceptional dilemma of Peter Pan: 'He had ecstasies innumerable that other children can never know; but he was looking through the window at the one joy from which he must be for ever barred' (Barrie, 1911, p. 247). This passage is one of the best known from the book, as are the lines on which it finally concludes: 'thus it will go on, so long as children are gay and innocent and heartless' (Barrie, 1911, p. 267). They give back to the reader that poise and security in language which the rest of *Peter and Wendy* so blatantly reveals as a fraud.

Put another way, we could say that Barrie's 1911 *Peter and Wendy* acts out the question of whether or not to take up a position in language, whether or not to settle down and find a place (whether or not to grow up). It is not the case, therefore, that *Peter Pan* is the sweet and innocent story of a boy who will not grow up, which then somehow cannot be written (Roger Lancelyn Green expresses bafflement at what he senses as the book's 'failure' (Green, 1954, p. 115)). Rather it is the case of the 'cannot be written or spoken' which lies behind any attempt to constitute oneself stably in speech. *Peter Pan* is the story of that impossibility, which reveals itself as unmanageable in the 1911 text.

In his book, *The Child's Concept of Story* (Applebee, 1978), Applebee gives the following anecdote about his child:

C. (appearing suddenly before me in the bathroom): How do you make things?

D. What things?

C. Babies and poems and things like that? (Applebee, 1978, p. 39)

Applebee is describing the child's acquisition of narrative form. He sees the ability to recognise and understand the concept of authorship as a crucial stage in the child's development. His anecdote makes it clear that the concept of authorship revolves around a fantasy of origins – Freud used the term 'family romance' to describe the way that the child represents to itself the enigma of birth (Freud, SE, IX (1908) 1909, PF, 7). We can take this anecdote with the emphasis on the *content* of the question and its (obvious) reply; or else we can take it with the stress on its form, on the fact that it is a *query* in which the child momentarily holds in suspense its relationship to its own beginnings and to the coming of the word. Applebee is right, of course, that recognition of parentage and of the conventions of writing effectively puts the lid on any uncertainty beneath. His anecdote confirms the close link between the child's sexual curiosity and its access to language – if the question is answered, then the child discovers at one and the same time what it is exactly that parents, and language, can *do*.

Applebee gives a number of conventions which he sees as indicating the child's developing concept of story. Most of these, such as the formal opening phrase and the consistent use of the past tense, are thrown into crisis one way or another by Barrie's 1911 text. Applebee's model is clearly the 'Once upon a time there was ...' of story-telling, in which the neutrality of the form guarantees the truth and ordering of events. This is exactly what Barrie's text fails to provide. Even the title of Barrie's work is a problem, since Barrie called his book *Peter and Wendy*, but it was subsequently published as *Peter Pan and Wendy* (Barrie, 1915 and 1921) and is now distributed as a Puffin paperback under the title of *Peter Pan* (the cultural phenomenon wins out over the written text).

One of the most striking things about *Peter Pan* is precisely the way that it undermines the very idea of authorship which Applebee looks for in the developing child. *Peter Pan* seems to be recognised and known in almost direct proportion to the extent that its authorship is problematic. Barrie himself always expressed his relationship to the text either in terms of refusal (the hesitation to write) or as a denial. The first drafts of the play were entitled 'Anon', and on the opening night in 1904, the actress who played the part of the maid – Ela Q. May – was billed as the author on the programme. When Barrie eventually published the play in 1928, he prefaced it with a dedication denying any recollection of having written it (a quotation from this Preface formed the last lines of Andrew Birkin's television trilogy, *The Lost Boys*, first screened on BBC television in October 1978).

All of this can, of course, be taken as symptomatic of no more than a writer chary of his craft and his creation. Barrie himself described his difficulty as part of his desire to hold on to the five Llewellyn Davies boys, whose loss to him was definitively sealed once he published the play. It can also be attributed to *Peter Pan*'s own ephemeral nature and to the impossibility of pinning him down: 'he is independent of print and paper' (Noyes, 1911, p. 131). This last quotation comes from a review of *Peter and Wendy* (*The Bookman*, December 1911). Its eulogistic tone cannot quite conceal the strangeness of praising Barrie's book by so totally extrapolating Peter Pan from his material form.

In fact it is virtually impossible to place Barrie in relation to his text – which makes it all the more striking that *Peter Pan* has come to be discussed in almost exclusively biographical terms. When Barrie is present as the creator of his work, he appears, as we have seen, in the form of a disturbance of intention and voice. Where he is not present, it is precisely because he has been displaced, and someone else is writing the story. This is how G. D. Drennan describes *Peter Pan* in his Preface to his own narrative version of the play which was published in 1909:

> Unto few men is it given to create a legend. It is sufficiently great to evolve the vital germ of one; to coin and set in motion that initial magnetic idea which by virtue of some mysterious quality of 'appeal' gets carried along down the centuries, ever attracting and gathering and embodying new material, like the snow-ball, until it becomes a great formless mass of priceless folklore [*sic*]. It is considered even a greater thing to take this concreted mass and mould or hew it into a legend, into 'literature'. (Drennan, 1909, p. 35)

Barrie has created 'literature' out of the 'vital germ' of legend, but he has not written a children's book. Drennan is one of the many who try to do that for him. His comment simply testifies to the vast distance which *Peter Pan* demonstrates as separating terms which seem to sit so easily together: literature, legend and writing for the child.

Applebee is not the only writer to relate literary and sexual genesis as far as children's fiction is concerned. Roger Lancelyn Green, writing on the failure of *Peter and Wendy* to become a nursery classic, states that it has 'somehow failed of its birthright' (Green, 1954, p. 115). The child understands the book when it sees it as something conceived and brought to birth; *Peter and Wendy* is born (or rather fails to be born) into the world of children's literature. Again these metaphors suggest that, in discussion of children's writing, it is the book *as* child, at least as much as the *children's* book which is at stake. But Roger Lancelyn Green's remark points up a further anomaly in *Peter Pan*'s history, which is that Barrie's text was 'born' into a world of children's literature where it was *already* meant to occupy a place. It was because of that place, predestined and claimed for it by its status as a classic of childhood ('his immortal child's play', *The Bookman*, January 1907, p. 161), that it was written as a book at all. Writing a book in order to confirm or establish a place inside children's literature is not, however, the same thing as writing a children's book. In the first case, the implied addressee is the child reader; in the second, it is children's literature itself. The difference can be compared to the difference between entering into a world, and taking it up in your hands as an object of scrutiny or play. When Barrie wrote *Peter and Wendy* in 1911, what seems to have happened is that, instead of establishing the anticipated status, the book made the relationship of *Peter Pan* to the world of children's literature both clearer and more problematic.

Peter and Wendy is a little history of children's fiction in itself. It brings together the adventure story for boys, the domestic story and the fairy tale – three forms of writing which were all central to children's literature in the half a century leading up to the time when *Peter Pan* was first produced. The lines between them cannot be rigidly drawn – fairies (or at least brownies) had often been brought into the nursery (Ewing, 1870; Mulock, 1852, 1872), and there is a long-standing connection between the fairy tale and the exploration fantasy (this has already been discussed: Barrie, like Garner after him, could be said to make this connection into a subject of his story). All these forms of children's literature were equally present in the structure of the play. But *Peter and Wendy* makes its relationship to literary tradition more explicit (it establishes its own tradition *through* that literature), by picking up the associations and commenting on them, giving them as part of the book's own reference and history: 'Jas. Hook, of whom it is said he was the only man that the Sea-Cook feared', 'the same Bill Jukes who got six dozen on the Walrus' (Barrie, 1911, pp. 80, 79). Both these references are to Robert Louis Stevenson's *Treasure Island* (Stevenson, 1883) (as Roger Lancelyn Green points out, there is no Bill Jukes on the Walrus and Hook is not part of the story – not that this diminishes the effect of quotation).

But this amalgamation of different strands of children's writing speaks a relationship and yet at the same time *too much* of a relationship, something of a pastiche with nothing that really corresponds to these types of literature at the level of their form. For, as close as *Peter and Wendy* comes to the world of children's books, at the same time it removes itself – by the very nature of its writing – from their domain. If we look back at the form of literature which Barrie most explicitly conjures up in his text, we will see not continuity, but difference. For all the similarities between Barrie, Ballantyne and Stevenson (listings of Barrie's literary sources normally come second only to biographical details in discussions of *Peter Pan*), the disparate voices of Barrie's text set him apart from the other two. The difference at this level, and the difficulties which it has produced in classifying *Peter and Wendy*, suggest that the history of children's fiction should be written, not in terms of its themes or the content of its stories, but in terms of the relationship to language which different children's writers establish for the child.[3] How, therefore, do these earlier works present their world to the child reader; what are the conditions of participation and entry which they lay down?

This is the narrator of Ballantyne's *The Coral Island* (Ballantyne, 1858) offering his document to the reader in 1857:

> I was a boy when I went through the wonderful adventures herein set down. With the memory of my boyish feelings strong upon me, I present my book especially to boys, in the earnest hope that they may derive valuable information, much pleasure, great profit, and unbounded amusement from its pages. (Ballantyne, 1858, Preface dated 1857);

and the story begins: 'Roving has always been, and still is, my ruling passion, the joy of my heart, the very sunshine of my existence. In childhood, in boyhood and in man's estate' (Ballantyne, 1858, p. 9). This is a narrator who knows, absolutely, who he is and from where he is speaking. Darton has commented that what is specific to this form of writing is a 'fusion' between father and son (Darton (1932) 1982, p. 297). I would say 'evolution', the idea of an assured progression from one stage to the next, with memories to vouch for the ease of the transition. The truth of the document – and this form is characterised above all for its insistence on literal truth – testifies first and foremost to this logical sequence leading from childhood directly to man's estate.

In *The Coral Island*, there is an explicit link made between moral order and linguistic truth. The book is a type of 'look and learn' where the children acquire knowledge of the natural world and an understanding of their moral superiority over the savages at one and the same time. Seeing with their own eyes, telling the truth and documenting without falsehood – what characterises the child's vision is its innocence in both senses of the term (moral purity and the undistorted registering of the surrounding world). The stress is constantly on empirical verification, on objects and on facts. When the hero, Ralph Rover, presents cannibalism, or the bark and foliage of a tree, the difference between them is flattened out by the way that he presents them to the reader – his repeated insistence that he does not 'exaggerate', 'mislead' or 'deceive': 'Oh reader, this is no fiction' (Ballantyne, 1858, p. 321).

In a book like *The Coral Island*, it is impossible to separate out the morality and the adventure, by calling – for example – the former colonialism and Christianity, the latter the beginnings of a progressive new literary form for the child. The morality *is* the adventure because it is a morality seen to arise naturally out of the objects of the visible world which the children discover and explore (it is something which is simply *found*). Put another way, I would say that the only morality that matters is that of the very mode of representation itself constantly vouching for its own truth.

Published a quarter of a century later, Stevenson's *Treasure Island* (Stevenson, 1883) is, in this sense, no different, although it is often seen as a major breakthrough against the earlier moral and ideological constraint. But while it may have dropped the most obvious trappings of the colonialist ethos, the form of its writing makes exactly the same claims – a story told by the child

hero[4] who is also the only real explorer (twice during the adventure
he breaks away from his crew in order to discover *more*). Jack
Hawkins, the narrator, takes up his pen in the 'year of grace 17—'
(Stevenson, 1883, p. 1), an historical allusion to the earliest days
of colonialist venture and, more importantly, to its associated
forms of writing, which should signal to the reader that the way is
not forward, but back. *Treasure Island* is written on the model of the
earliest novels in which the chief protagonist tells the story and
offers it to the reader on the basis of the truth of his experiences (cf.
Robinson Crusoe (Defoe, 1719)). Writing is discovery, document
and also apprenticeship. The child is still learning, but this
process has become so completely assimilated into the adventure
that it is almost invisible:

> I was so pleased at having given the slip to Long John, that I
> began to enjoy myself and look around me with some interest on
> the strange land that I was in.
>   I had crossed a marshy tract full of willows, bulrushes, and
> odd, outlandish, swampy trees; and I had now come out upon
> the skirts of an open piece of undulating, sandy country, about a
> mile long, dotted with a few pines, and a great number of
> contorted trees, not unlike the oak in growth, but pale in the
> foliage, like the willows. (Stevenson, 1883, p. 110)

If anything, *Treasure Island* is remarkable for the way it perfects
this form for the child reader. Praising the book for its freedom
means praising it for the way that it *conceals* the slide between
nature study and suspense. In this sense, *verisimilitude* is no more
than a way of closing the reader's eyes to the mechanisms of the
book by dissolving what is in fact a very sophisticated writing
strategy into the objects of the visible world. We have seen this
ethos of literary language before (Alan Garner and Rousseau). I
think it is important that this mode of representation, which
Barrie's writing so completely violates, is reaching its maturity in
children's literature at exactly the same time that he was writing
Peter Pan. The obvious connections – the Neverland sequence of
Peter and Wendy is packed with references to the genre – conceal the
more fundamental disparity, which has made it almost impossible
to think of *Peter and Wendy* as a children's book in the conventional
sense of the term.
  This aesthetic is not restricted to the boy's adventure story. It is

given one of its fullest nineteenth-century expositions in an anonymous article on 'Children's Literature' published in *The London Review* in 1860, which argued for the importance of fantasy and fairy tales for children. The article has an almost identical stress on concrete impressions, discovery and perception; it also has a notion of how best to affect the child reader by letting the story 'sink' imperceptibly into the child's mind. Its basic terms are very close to those of Locke – that the child's cognitive processes develop on the basis of concrete sensations: 'if [the child] grasps principles at all, it must be in the concrete; he must hold them as sentiments, as impressions, not as propositions. In the order of logic, abstract truths are antecedent to all events, and explain them; but in the order of discovery, they come last' ('Children's Literature', 1860, p. 485). For Locke, however, fantasy was mere 'chimera'; whereas for the writer of 1860, the same concepts are being put forward in the name of childhood imagination.[5] Fantasy – the argument anticipates Bruno Bettelheim – is best suited to promote the growth of that 'wonderfully organised instrument' which is the child's mind ('Children's Literature', 1860, p. 486). The link between the fairy tale and the exploration fantasy crystallises at the point where fairy tales are seen as the supreme tool in the child's discovery both of the world and of its own mind. Similarly, in 1882, Mrs Ewing argued that fairy tales were justified for children on the grounds of the knowledge which they convey 'of the world . . . of the world at large' (Ewing, 1882, Preface, p. vi).

The argument for fantasy in terms of concrete impression, and the building of adventures around an ever-expanding discovery of the real world suggests the proximity between the two forms. What the fairy tale and the adventure story have in common across the diversity of content is this insistence on the concrete reality of what they describe. Mrs Gatty takes up her position as a type of privileged traveller in her opening to *The Fairy Godmothers* (Gatty, 1851): 'There are many beautiful bays on the coast of England, and there is one especially, my dear little readers, which you and I know of . . . beautiful as this little bay is, of which I speak, and fond as we are of it, it is nothing, I do assure you, compared to the bays in Fairy Land!' (Gatty, 1851, p. 1); and we have already seen how the interest in the fairy tale in the nineteenth century depended at least partly on its status as chronicle: 'my chronicle is a consistent chronicle of its kind . . .

stoutly verified by the peasants' (Mulock, 1852, p. 12). The assurance, or consistency, is the crux of the representation. As with Ralph Rover describing the horrors of savagery in *The Coral Island*, the reliability of the narrator acts as check and balance to everything else.

Together with this, we can also notice the preoccupation with honesty – never tell a lie to a child: 'their trustfulness should be always recognised and assumed' ('Children's Literature', 1860, p. 477), 'I do not believe that wonder-tales confuse children's idea of truth' (Ewing, 1882, Preface, p. vi). Thus children's writing becomes the place where the very ethics of language are worked out. In this context, the nursery stories of the 1880s and 1890s, represented by a writer like Mrs Molesworth ('For you see children, I am telling you the history of a *real* little boy and girl' (Molesworth, 1891, p. 43)), appear less as an innovatory form of new domestic realism (realism as content), than as a domesticated-cum-sophisticated version of this preoccupation with the irrefutable honesty of the speaker. The banalisation of the content and the narrator's disclaimer ('Why Carrots should come to have his history written, I really cannot say' (Molesworth, 1891, p. 1)) so clearly work to establish the greater credibility of the writer.[6]

The claim to a new realism (real children) can be traced back to a writer like Catherine Sinclair who in 1839 had offered stories about giants and fairies to a species of natural child which she saw as threatened with extinction: 'In these pages the author has endeavoured to paint that species of noisy, frolicsome, mischievous children which is now almost extinct' (Sinclair, 1839, Preface, p. vii) (here fairy tales and a more realistic representation of childhood are being placed in deliberate association). It seems as if the basic components of *Peter Pan* – adventure, fairy and nursery story – can appear in any combination, provided that the reference is to some incontrovertible truth: a knowledge of the true nature of the child (the author of the 1860 article 'Children's Literature' talks of the science of 'paedology'), or the utter veracity of the one who is speaking.

As a mode of writing, the new 'realism' can be seen to take its most important step when the child is given his or her own story to tell – the form most popularly associated with the writings of E. Nesbit. But this form had also been presaged, by Charles Dickens in 'Holiday Romance' written in 1868:

This beginning-part is not made out of anybody's head you know. It's real. You must believe this beginning part more than what comes after, else you won't understand how what comes after came to be written. You must believe it all, but you must believe this most, please. I am the Editor. (Dickens, 1868, p. 1)

This is an infantalising of the narrative voice, but paradoxically it means that children's writing has grown up – to the point where there is as small a gap as possible between the narrator and the protagonist of the story.

There are, of course, exceptions which get through, writers who work at or deliberately represent as problematic this whole ethos of language as always reliable or true. Carroll is again the most obvious, although it is interesting in this context to notice how important it has been to identify the narrator of the story – the White Knight of *Through the Looking Glass* (Carroll, 1872) who, everyone agrees, is Carroll himself (Gardner, 1965, p. 296, n. 4; Greenacre, 1955). For this certainty takes control of the play and deformation of language which the *Alice* books ceaselessly enact by subordinating them, again, to the biography of the author. There are others, such as Thomas Hood who, in *Petsetilla's Posy* (Hood, 1870) parodies the very notion of a language holding court over its subjects: 'violations of syntax were visited with capital punishment without benefit of clergy' (Hood, 1870, p. 9). What Carroll and Hood share is an inclusion of language rules as something available for satire.[7] But, for the most part, I think we would be wrong to associate the new fun, the bold adventure, the flights of fancy (all of which are included in *Peter Pan*) with anything radically different at that level where a certain relationship to language, to objects and to knowledge is being established for both writer and child.

Peter and Wendy picks up almost everything about these forms *except* the mode of their writing. The book is therefore a dual travesty – a travesty of the basic rules of literary representation for children, and a mixing of genres which, at every other level but this one, were busily differentiating themselves from each other. In almost direct and inverse proportion to their shared claim to a realism of representation – with its associated idea of what constitutes the mind of *the* child (all children) – these same types of literature were being separated out along the lines of a sexual division. The distinction between the domestic and fairy story on the one hand, and the adventure story on the other, was also a division between literature for girls and literature for boys (Mrs Molesworth and Mrs Gatty for girls, Ballantyne and Stevenson for boys). It is a distinction which seems to have held less at the point of readership (the evidence suggests that girls, at least, read both),[8] than at that of status. *The Boys' Own Paper* and *The Girls' Own Paper*, for example, were started in 1879 and 1880 respectively. The first issue of the former ran a series by Kingston and Ascott Hope and rapidly built up a list of contributors which included Ballantyne, Verne and Reed. In the first issue of *The Girls' Own Paper* for 1880, there was not a single contribution by an established or acknowledged literary writer.[9] Boys' literature seems to have represented tradition and genre (the boys' adventure story and later the public school tale); girls' literature more of a 'miscellany'. In the distinction between the two, literature for boys appears as the marked term of the opposition which stakes out its territory against the rest.[10]

In fact the very emergence of the distinction between boys' and girls' literature tends to be associated with the development of the adventure story for boys and its creation of a wholly new literary space for 'juveniles' (father and son) as opposed to 'children and babies' (the distinction is Darton's (Darton (1932) 1982, p. 246)). The sexual differentiation of children's literature was, therefore, not so much an equal division as a breaking away of one form into a more 'adult' space. In this sense, girls' literature is best described as what got left behind (an old story).

Peter and Wendy (boy meets girl) brings together these two strands in a collision which is part war, part intercourse, between the opposite poles of a literary taboo. Barrie's book therefore shows up a polarity inside the children's literature to which it was addressed. The home–adventure–home sequence which is such a familiar pattern of children's writing (Garner, Sendak and Enid Blyton) stands out here as something more in the nature of a sexual divide. It is a divide which can be seen as determinant in the creation of both these different forms of writing, but which neither side commented on as such. *Peter and Wendy* can also be seen as telling the story of these two strands of children's writing – the story of the difficulty of their relation.

Peter Pan's position within children's literature was, therefore, f a metalanguage or commentary on that literature before it ritten as part of it. Writing the play as a children's book involved the (secondary) elaboration of something that was already there, of a place that it already had. When *Peter Pan* was written, we could almost say that children's literature appears within its discourse as parapraxis (a slip which reveals a hidden truth). *Peter and Wendy* was, as we have seen, the response to a demand, the demand for a 'classic', the definitive written text for children. Something definitive is, however, exactly what Barrie's text failed to provide – either inside the book (the sliding of the narrator) or outside the book (all the other, more simple, versions which were to follow).

In 1914, a primer called *The Progress to Literature* (Wilson, 1914(b)) was published for use in the public elementary schools. The first volume of the series is called 'Wendy's Friends' and it opens with 'Wendy's Sampler':

Who is Wendy, and what is a sampler?

Wendy was a little girl who lived with her brothers, John and Michael.

Her first name was Wendy, and her last name was Darling. She had other names in between but they do not matter.

Now the children had a nurse named Nana, and Nana was a big dog!

Do not say that this could *not* be, or you will spoil the story.

Wendy loved to play at mothers; and as mothers used to sew very much, Wendy used to sew too.

She could also darn socks very well: and after a time she made a SAMPLER. . . .

'Come, Wendy,' said Mrs. Darling 'what shall we work on your sampler?'

'Peter, of course,' said Wendy at once. So they worked Peter Pan in his boat right in the middle of the canvas.

(The story of Peter and Wendy is to be kept for another time; but perhaps you know it already).

'We must now,' said Mrs. Darling, 'work in the names of some of your friends.'

Then Wendy got up and went to the bookshelf. She took down three books and brought them to her mother.

'You will find the names on these books, mother,' she said. 'They are rather long, so I must copy them down with a pencil.'

Then she wrote:—

Dear Lewis Carroll
Dear Robert Louis Stevenson
Dear Hans Christian Andersen
They were the names that Wendy worked on her first sampler. I
wonder why she loved them so much. (Wilson, 1914(b), Part
1, pp. 7–9)

Despite the parenthesis ('The story of Peter and Wendy is to be
kept for another time . . .'), the story of Peter and Wendy is never
told in the whole series which ends with extracts from Carroll,
Kingsley, Grahame, Hood and Alcott, but not Barrie. Barrie's
1911 *Peter and Wendy* is referred to once in a footnote, but it is never
given in the form of an extract to be read by the child (it is not part
of the child's own 'progress' to literature). *Peter Pan*'s status is not,
therefore, that of a children's book, but rather that of a concept or
class – the whole category of children's literature out of which all
these other stories are produced. A convenient way of sidestep-
ping everything which constitutes the fundamental *illegibility* of
Peter Pan.

It is part of *Peter Pan*'s folklore that Wendy's 'Sampler' was the
stage curtain for the opening night of the play in 1904. But the true
facts behind this proclaimed relationship to the world of children's books only became clear when *Peter Pan* actually came to be
written. It would not be going too far to say that *Peter and Wendy*
constitutes something of an attack on, or at least an affront to, the
very concept of children's literature with which it is most often
linked. The question we have to ask now, therefore, is how this
could have happened, how, indeed, *Peter Pan* happened at all. By
which I mean, not what Barrie himself was thinking or doing at
the time, but how *Peter Pan* went into circulation and then took off.

4

Peter Pan and Commercialisation of the Child

Children are a good sell

The House Governor of the Great Ormond Street Hospital is concerned to stress that *Peter Pan* is not dead. He has good reason. Since 1929, when Barrie left the rights on *Peter Pan* to the Hospital for Sick Children, it has accounted for anything up to a third of the hospital's annual income. The exact sum remains undisclosed. Barrie himself stipulated that it should be kept secret.[1]

The association of money and childhood is not a comfortable one. Money is something impure. It circulates and passes from hand to hand (children are warned that coins are *dirty*). Money relies on traffic. The value of a piece of money depends on what it can be exchanged for (goods) and what it can be compared with (more, or less, money). As a system, money can be compared with language where each unit is part of a web of complex relations. The word 'mutton', for example, stands for something which we recognise and can buy, but its precise value in English rests on the distinction – a distinction which the French do not have – from the word 'sheep'. A unit of money, like a word in language, never stands on its own or purely for itself. It is contaminated by association and exchange. Not so childhood. In Rousseau's tract, the Emile who compares, socialises, circulates amongst men, and has intercourse with women is, by definition, no longer a child. Childhood is always a moment *before* – once it is contaminated, it is lost.

Peter Pan focuses a particular dilemma in this context. Not just because it is worth a fortune, a fact which makes, but which could also break, the myth – hence, presumably, Barrie's stricture of secrecy which prevents the money from becoming too *real*; but because of the way in which *Peter Pan*'s history constantly shows up this uneasy conjunction between money and the child. The story of *Peter Pan* can also be told as the story of money – of theatre speculation and the publishing trade, of prizes, publicity, spectacle, licences, charity and the welfare state. But this way of discussing children's fiction has gone out of favour. Writing in the *Times Literary Supplement* on the reissue of Harvey Darton's *Children's Books in England* (Darton (1932) 1982), Julia Briggs criticises it for being weighted towards the industry at the expense of the meanings of individual books for the child (Briggs, 1982). Perhaps talking about children's fiction as commerce makes it too clear that what we are dealing with is an essentially adult trade. The association of children and trade is, however, a dangerous one: 'It may come as a shock to you to learn that the fairies you are seeing on the stage these holidays are as carefully licensed and as closely watched as if they were public houses or pawnbrokers' shops. It does sound a little unromantic, doesn't it? A pixie with a licence to ply: at first it sounds like printing *Alice in Wonderland* in basic English' ('The Truth About Pantomime Fairies', *The Listener*, 10 January 1952). The idea of a child with a licence brings us smack up against the English tongue at its most 'basic' and the crudest symbols of material exchange.

Peter Pan has always been part of such exchange. The material investment in *Peter Pan* has been vast, matched only by a seemingly contradictory investment in *Peter Pan* as an ethereal substance, or disembodied child, unstained by lucre or blood. In the case of *Peter Pan*, the two conceptions – of money and innocence – appear to go hand in hand, endlessly calling each other up and cancelling each other out. It would seem that provided each one is big enough, they cease to contradict each other, turning instead into the two sides of a singular and monstrous inflation.

Peter Pan is not dead. For two years (1979–80, 1980–1), it did not run in London for its annual Christmas season, apparently brought down by the scale of its own production which was prohibitive in a time of theatrical (and general) recession (Roberts, 20 December 1979). In fact, a major new Broadway production was launched in New York in 1979 which ran for so long that it was impossible to transfer it to London as originally planned. The end of *Peter Pan* in London was, therefore, its relaunching elsewhere. At the time of writing (October 1982), a new contract had been negotiated with the Royal Shakespeare Company at the Barbican for a new production to open with a gala performance in December 1982. The venue is appropriate. The Barbican – the new cultural centre for the arts opened in 1981 – has been heralded as the new emblem of our culture (in all its vast generality). Built out of the ashes of London from the funds of the City (the project was started after the Second World War), it more appropriately symbolises the continuing wealth of investment available for such a project during a time of industrial decline and recession in Britain today.

It is, of course, the very definition of *Peter Pan* that he will always return. This seems to have made *Peter Pan* a type of emblem for the durability, or survival, of the trades to which it belongs. 'Reproduction' is another of those ambiguous terms: it can refer both to the reproducible commodity and to the newborn child. We can add to these the theatrical revival; the faithful reproduction of the original spirit of the play against which productions of *Peter Pan* tend to be measured (the cutting of the Lagoon scene in the last two London productions caused an outcry);[2] and the recollections of earlier performances by producers, actors, actresses and reviewers ('Margaret Lockwood, my first Peter in Portsmouth . . . thirty years ago' (*Guardian*, 21 December 1979)) which have become the obligatory refrain for its launching every (or almost every) year: 'like some diva making positively her last appearance for the umpteenth time' (*The Sunday Telegraph*, 23 December 1979). On Broadway in 1979, *Peter Pan* opened a season which included revivals of *Oklahoma!*, *West Side Story* and *My Fair Lady*. *Time* magazine headed their review 'Remembrance of Things Past' (17 September 1979); the *New Yorker*, less sympathetically, saw the production as a sign of the 'current backing-and-filling state of affairs on Broadway' (17 September 1979). Yet, in words which echo almost exactly those of 1907 ('The play ought to share the eternal youth of its hero' (W. T. Stead, Foreword to O'Connor, 1907, p. i)), and of 1915 ('Peter Pan is achieving his desire . . . he is no whit older or more grown up than when we first made his acquaintance' ('New Theatre *Peter Pan*', Enthoven, 1915)), another reviewer greeted *Peter Pan* as 'one of the theatre's most enduring treasures (and disarming characters) . . . seventy-five years old and as charming and timeless as ever' (*The Star-Ledger*, 7 September 1979). Thus *Peter Pan* continues to attract the two opposite meanings belonging to something which never gives up – stubborn durability and endless renewal or perennial youth.

Peter Pan has, in fact, always managed to glide over its status as a commodity by a constant reference to the second of these terms. In the commerce of children's literature, however, the link between the most material forms of calculation and the most natural, or seemingly natural, of physical processes, is by no means restricted to *Peter Pan*: '[A children's magazine] must always change without seeming to do so. Its public is perpetually undergoing, in mass, the metabolism of the human body, which renews itself every seven years . . . That period, oddly enough, is just about the duration of one generation of child readers' (Darton, Appendix to Darton (1932) 1982).[3] 'Oddly enough' perhaps – but the history of *Peter Pan* suggests that, in the case of children's fiction, this relationship between the business of the trade on the one hand, and the self-generating body of the innocent child on the other, is of an essential, rather than a contingent, nature.

'Backing-and-filling' goes back to the beginning of *Peter Pan*. *Peter Pan* has often been described as a major breakthrough in the history of theatre – as the origin of a form of children's theatre which did not exist as such before 1904 when it was first performed. The most familiar story is the one which tells of Barrie effectively blackmailing his producer, Charles Frohman, into producing *Peter Pan* by offering him another play, *Alice Sit-By-The-Fire*, as a guaranteed financial investment, with Frohman immediately enamoured of *Peter Pan* and investing his all in its realisation. The success of *Peter Pan* is then measured in terms of its novelty, daring and risk – with the anxiously awaited telegram of the opening night (*'Peter Pan* all right. Looks like a big success') as the climax. It is a narrative which follows the classical format of adventure and suspense – with Barrie and Frohman as boy heroes (the rumour was that Frohman died with Peter Pan's own words on his lips: 'To die will be an awfully big adventure'). As always, boldness produces its reward – Peter Pan as one of the theatre's 'most enduring *treasures*'. And treasure involves not just danger but also, and equally importantly, the risking of financial assets: 'it implied faith, the financial risks of the stage being infinitely heavier than those of books' (Darton (1932) 1982, p. 312), 'Faith had to be pumped into this production . . . No half measures.

Never mind the risk' (Mackail, 1941, pp. 356–7). In *Treasure Island* (Stevenson, 1883), the cost of the *Hispaniola* – whether it was bought for a trifle or horribly oversold – is discussed before there is any mention of the hiring of Long John Silver to the crew; as if the danger of the second can only be fully established on the back of the first.

This way of describing *Peter Pan* makes for a good story but it deprives it of a history, and to be without history, like being born out of thin air, is a conception which we have seen constantly returning in relation to *Peter Pan*. The innocence of *Peter Pan* is not, therefore, just the innocence of a boy child; it is also, and perhaps more centrally, the innocence of a cultural phenomenon which cannot be explained other than in terms of individual daring and/or magic. Thus *Peter Pan*'s elusiveness starts to draw into its general aura and accompanying haziness the more specific historical and cultural factors which surround and produce it: factors which exceed the individual inspiration of Barrie, just as the more troubled aspects of that inspiration are our, as much as they are his, concern. In this context, *Peter Pan*'s loss of childhood comes to mean the loss of its own past and history (with *Peter Pan* at the service of that second and more general form of disavowal). As regards money, the haziness is crucial to the essential mystique ('one can only gape and gasp at the mystery of Frohman's finances' (Mackail, 1941, p. 330)), and the child is clearly part of that mystification: 'His innumerable companies were as children to him' (Barrie on Frohman, Preface to Marcosson and Frohman, 1916, p. iv). All the words that most readily come to mind with reference to that first moment of *Peter Pan*'s production – magic, aura, inspiration and prodigy – share the implication of something which has been conjured up out of itself.

But even magic has a history. Compare, for example, the following passages, the first from Andrew Birkin's description of the preparations for the 1904 *Peter Pan*, the second from an 1880 account of the preparations for a pantomime, an account which the theatre historian, Michael Booth, takes as merely *typical* of that taste for spectacle ('existing only because of the techniques of spectacle' (Booth, 1981, p. 81)) which characterised the Victorian theatregoer between 1850 and 1910:

The 'living' fairy, now renamed Tinker Bell, was to have been achieved by means of an actress moving behind a giant ig lens, but the complications were too great; so was the agle that was meant to lift the pirate Smee from the deck of the ship by the seat of his trousers and carry him off across the auditorium on a trapeze wire. On December 21st, the night before the play was due to open, a mechanical lift collapsed taking half the scenery with it. Dion Boucicault, who had worked himself almost to death, was forced to postpone the opening until the 27th. The scenery for the final Kensington Gardens scene was still not finished, and as the stage hands refused to work over the Christmas holiday, Barrie was obliged to think again. He too was dangerously overworked, and was suffering appalling headaches as a result. Nevertheless he repaired to an empty dressing-room, axed the final twenty-two pages of the script, and spent most of Christmas Day rewriting what was by now the fifth revised ending. (Birkin, 1979, pp. 112–14)

You sit with the scenic artists in the stalls or the circles – sometimes in one, sometimes in the other – to judge of the artistic effect, and to dispose the lighting of the various sets or pictures. The fly-men (that is, the carpenters up aloft), the cellar men (those below the stage), and the stage-carpenters have never yet worked together; and it appears almost marvellous, looking at the crowded cloths and borders, wings and ground-pieces, with the complicated ropes and pulleys above, and cuts and bridges in the stage, not to mention the traps and sliders, gas-battens and ladders, how a series of fifteen or sixteen scenes, besides the elaborate transformation scene, which, perhaps, demands the united skill of fifty or sixty men to work its marvels and develop its mysterious beauties, can ever be worked with such systematic regularity and unerring correctness. A good master-carpenter is a general, and all his men depend on his head in time of action. Then there are the gas-men, who have to raise or subdue the floats or footlights, the ground-rows, the wing-ladders, the battens or border-lights, and the bunch-lights or portable suns . . . And to think that this life was led for ten weeks, without one moment's peace, without time for eating, drinking, or even sleeping. (Augustus Harris, quoted in Booth, 1981, pp. 76–8)

What distinguishes Augustus Harris's description is its confidence. But there is the same emphasis on the prodigious character of the scenic effects and their essentially demanding nature;[4] and elsewhere there is the same reference to the incomplete state of the pantomime script which was never finished and was constantly altered during rehearsal and then cut after the opening night. Pantomime *was* experiment (the two were inextricably associated) – experiment in the form of a lavishness or enterprise, where the meaning of each production was its challenge to the one that went before. The novelty and daring of that first production of *Peter Pan* does not, therefore, single it out from theatrical tradition; it decisively places it within it. The link is confirmed by the presence of Dion Boucicault, director of *Peter Pan*, and son of the producer, D. L. Boucicault, who had produced one of the most famous pantomime extravaganzas – the Covent Garden *Babil and Bijou* – thirty-two years before.

Spectacle always signifies money. In the late nineteenth-century theatre it also signified imperial display – the idea of endlessly expanding material possibilities opening up throughout the world, like the faerie transformation scene of pantomime, where gauzes lifted one after the other to reveal layer upon layer of scenic effect. Pantomime was a 'symbol of our Empire' (*The Star*, 27 December 1900, quoted Booth, 1981, p. 89). The spirit – new vistas, expanding horizons – was mirrored in that other branch of children's literature, the publishing trade, whose 'ebullient expansionist atmosphere' was a factor of 'incalculable influence' on the development of English children's books (Alderson, Appendix to Darton (1932) 1982, p. 320).[5] In the theatre, Charles Frohman was seen by the Stock Exchange as the model of this expansion – the business speculator who had only recently ousted the actor–manager from the central position in the institutions of the stage ('Theatrical Finance by a Member of the Stock Exchange', *The Green Room Book*, 1907, pp. 479–81).

Peter Pan has, however, always been carefully differentiated from the pantomime (children's theatre is *not* pantomime). But this claim for total difference starts with a contingency. The 1904 Drury Lane pantomime, *The White Cat*, introduced a drinking scene which offended contemporary notions of childhood purity and brought down the wrath of the reviewers. The *Daily Mail* entitled their review 'Not a Children's Pantomime' and commented in a separate article:

The Drury Lane pantomime is a national institution and we do not like to say hard words about such matters. But as will be seen from our comments elsewhere Drury Lane is fast falling into the category of theatres which must be looked at doubtfully before children are taken there. (The *Daily Mail* quoted in A. E. Wilson, 1934, p. 212)

The White Cat was the only pantomime of 1904 which was put on for less than 125 performances.

The symmetry of these two moments – the 'decline' of Drury Lane and the lifting off of *Peter Pan* – seems to have fostered an exaggerated generic opposition between the pantomime and *Peter Pan*; *Peter Pan* taking on the image of purity lost to Drury Lane, and this image then being set against the pantomime *per se* which is described for comparison as 'blinding', 'vulgar', 'mangled' and 'spattered', as the mere repository of theatrical extravagance and excess. By this simple act of severance, *Peter Pan* becomes a haven, or refuge, from everything that is most decadent about theatre itself:

> The typical Christmas pantomime was a version of some fine and famous story, mangled almost past recognition, spattered with the banalities and vulgarities of the Lion Comique of the music-halls, set in a blaze that half blinded and to music that half deafened the spectator, and generally lasting from four to five hours and sending everybody home more or less a wreck. In place of these inflictions, *Peter Pan* offered the nursery of Mr. and Mrs. Darling's three children. (Walbrook, 1922, p. 98)

Peter Pan is home, balm and nursemaid, replacing vulgarity with the irrefutable niceness of the nursery – saving us from an excessive display of the material facts of theatrical life.

Thus *Peter Pan* comes to be read as both innocent and not extravagant (the one as the consequence of the other), and hence as a *new* type of theatrical production, theatre *for* the child (the 'innocence' displaced from the content of the story onto the production itself). In fact it is clear from all accounts that *Peter Pan* was a vast financial concern, arriving in the provinces 'in truck after truck, and *still* kept on arriving . . . not a little pocket-folding production, but one of the biggest affairs there is' (Drennan, 1909,

p. 37), and having the corresponding status of privilege or fantasy identified with the London stage:

> I wondered as I left the theatre whether some of our wealthy men who do not know what to do with their riches could lay up for themselves treasures in heaven by taking up the theatre and packing it from floor to ceiling with the poor children of London town to whom seats in a Theatre are as unattainable as a Dukedom. (W. T. Stead, Foreword to O'Connor, 1907, p. i)

This last problem has not gone away. The price of tickets for the Los Angeles run of the Broadway production in 1981 started at thirteen dollars and went to twenty-seven dollars fifty. 'Nothing small about that', commented John Schubeck reporting for the Los Angeles Audio Video Services (11 September 1981) (the reference is, I think, to the scale of the production as well as to the price of the tickets).

Peter Pan's disengagement from the pantomime has been a central plank in its claim to uniqueness of status: 'no pantomime jokes were ever built into the script' (Angus Macloed, director of the Daniel Meyer Company, which had rights on *Peter Pan* after 1929, in a letter to *The Times*, 21 December 1971). Barrie himself had dealt a symbolic death-blow in *Pantaloon, a plea for an ancient family*, a one-act parody of/apology for pantomime which was put on at the Duke of York's theatre four days after the close of *Peter Pan*'s first run. Despite this relegation to the back drawer of family history ('an ancient family'), I see this in itself as confirmation of the links between *Peter Pan* and the pantomime,[6] a link only too clear in the first versions of the play which included a harlequinade sequence in Kensington Gardens as the ending, with all the components (columbine, harlequin, constable and clown) of those concluding the Drury Lane pantomime every year. In *The Bookman*'s Christmas Competition of 1920, a winning entry described *Peter Pan* as 'first in a long list of pantomimes' (*The Bookman*, December 1920), and the connection is there, latent to the title itself: 'Mr. Barrie's *Peter Pan*-tomime' (Enthoven, 27 December 1904). The reviewer of *The Green Room Book* for 1909 who confirmed the play's distance from the pantomime, did so only in so far as it was *not* a play for children (many of whom classify it as 'rot'), but for adults, the child 'despite the murmurs of the critics' preferring the pantomime itself (*The Green Room Book*, 1909, p. 541).

Peter Pan's lofty dissociation from this part of theatre tradition is, therefore, one in a list of repressions, or suppressions, which have characterised its history. For the connection with pantomime goes deeper, and has more important implications, than these anecdotes, contingencies and hurriedly effaced connections might suggest. Pantomime had (and still has) a strange status in English theatre – venerated as a relic of the institution (compare comedy and vaudeville), castigated for its display of artifice and machine (its essential *lowness*) and, especially in the late nineteenth century, expensive (like *Peter Pan*). Since the 1830s and 1840s the pantomime had been changing; by 1900 the harlequinade had virtually disappeared (just as it did in *Peter Pan*), and the fairy sequence, which was originally an opening piece, had been extended and had become a central part of the performance (Booth, 1981, p. 75). Although Barrie had edited out much of the fairy element of *The Little White Bird* when he moved *Peter Pan* onto the stage, it remains centrally in the form of Tinkerbell (the 'living' fairy). If we add to the technical difficulties and the expense, the harlequinade and the fairy component, then we are getting very close to the *fairy drama* which already, before *Peter Pan*, had become associated with nothing short of a theatrical cult of the child.[7] This cult had started with child-based sentimental dramas such as *Bootle's Baby* (Globe, 1888) and *The Little Squire* (Lyric, 1890), and had more recently surfaced in musical fairy plays such as *Ib and Little Christina* (Prince of Wales, 1900) and the dream play *Bluebell in Fairyland* (Vaudeville, 1901) (the connection between this play and *Peter Pan* has often been noted). Together with the pantomime, it is this cult of the child in late Victorian theatre which can give the more appropriate genealogy for *Peter Pan*.

This is the *Era* writing on the 1894 revival of *The Little Squire*:

> Bachelors and elderly cynics – 'brutes', as the ladies call them – may contemptuously declare that no such children as Adrien de Coursay and Lise de la Riviere ever existed, adding the rider that if they did exist, they ought to be slapped. But soft-hearted mothers, with tender hearts and pretty pocket handkerchiefs, will enjoy *The Little Squire* immensely . . . and if all the mothers flock – as we believe they will flock – to the matinees at the Lyric

Theatre, Mrs Greet and Mr Sedger may easily be indifferent to those who can see nothing in the juvenile business of *The Little Squire* but sentimental twaddle. (*Era*, 10 April 1894, quoted in Crozier, 1981, p. 157)

'Mothers will flock' – the image is exactly that of the Beautiful Mothers, the assorted mothers of London who rushed onto the stage to claim the Lost Boys in the scene which concluded the first performance of *Peter Pan*.

A number of these child-based plays were already classics of children's literature (*Hansel and Gretel*, Daly's, 1894; *The Water Babies*, Garrick, 1902). *Alice in Wonderland* was one – Carroll agreed to the 1886 adaptation on condition that it was free of any 'coarseness' or innuendo. But that solicitousness does not automatically lead, any more than in the case of Barrie's play, to an audience consisting of children. The 1898 revival of *Alice* was put on, not for mother-and-child matinees, but for the general public evening performances, demonstrating the extent to which 'fantasy themes associated with childhood had become acceptable to adult audiences by the turn of the century' (Crozier, 1981, p. 222). Unlike *Alice*, *Peter Pan* was not a children's classic – yet. It acquired that status only by being performed as a play (hence perhaps the need to insist that it is *the* children's play). But in 1904, when *Peter Pan* is first performed, it merely epitomises a moment of theatre which found one of its chief sources of pleasure and 'delight in watching children on stage' (*Lady's Pictorial*, 19 April 1890, quoted Crozier, 1981, p. 158).

On stage or off stage, the central focus here is on the child as spectacle. By a strange twist, half a century later, a reviewer could insist that the true spirit of pantomime lived on, and take as his image a child – watched by an adult – at a performance of *Peter Pan*. His remarks climax on the child and are worth giving in full:

According to the older generation the old Pantomime died when the curtain first rose on *Peter Pan*. The rollicking songs gave place to mawkish ballads and the evening was sicklied over with the wan cast of thought. But Barrie knew how children relish in the game of make-believe. Should you find yourself at *Peter Pan* this Christmas, the unanimous affirmative to 'Do you believe in fairies?' will show you how the children are entering into the spirit of entertainment. When the first baby laughed, said Barrie, that laugh broke into a thousand pieces, and every piece became a fairy, and 'whenever a child says "I don't believe in fairies"', a fairy falls down dead.' There in a nutshell is the essence of true Pantomime, a charming fancy, a pleasing softness, and just a tinge of sadness.

It is refreshing to recapture for an hour or so our damaged sense of wonder. Of all the comforts that nature can offer, one of the loveliest and most comforting is the unrestrained laughter of children. Unresponsive must be the souls of those who can without delight watch a little girl twisting her hands between her knees and throwing her head back in an ecstasy of laughter. There lies the true function of Christmas Pantomime. (Stanley, *Queen*, 13 November 1956)

The voyeurism of this, the weight of investment in that image, is surely unmistakable – the link between sexuality and the child reemerging here with reference to *Peter Pan* and (or rather *as*) pantomime. What *Peter Pan* gives us better than pantomime, more of than pantomime (perhaps this is the essential difference) is the right to look at the child.

On stage, Peter Pan is, of course, both child and woman. The transvestism was not new, and it goes beyond the traditional role of the principal boy.[8] Michael Booth talks of the centrality of the female image to Victorian pantomime, of the preponderance of young women in the cast (the 'mass transvestism' of the procession on stage) – of a 'sexual, pictorial, and spectacular combination of ideal purity and handsome flesh' (Booth, 1981, p. 79). We have come across all these terms before. What Barrie seems to have managed in 1904 is a skilful recombination of all these components of late Victorian theatre (fairy, purity and flesh) which *Peter Pan* gives back to the spectator in the image of the child.

Once again the sexuality in this clearly exceeds J. M. Barrie both inside and outside the theatre. For this strange focus on a child always innocent and yet sexualised by that very focusing of attention (cf. also the Victorian child photographer, pp. 29–30 above), could also be seen in late Victorian England in such an apparently different context from the stage as the campaign for the sexual protection of children, which has been seen as one of the drives leading to the Criminal Law Amendment Act of 1885. The child prostitute was seen both as a symptom and a cause of social decay (symbol of the moral degeneracy of the time and a potential source of venereal disease). The 'discovery' of the existence of child prostitution in the late nineteenth century caused an outcry (precipitated by the revelations of W. T. Stead in 1885, popular journalist and keeper of the Victorian conscience, who also wrote the foreword to the *Peter Pan Keepsake* in 1907 (see p. 95 above)). But the campaign – the scandal it revealed – can in itself be seen as an act of political displacement, in so far as the focus on morality served to close off the more difficult questions about social inequality and poverty of which prostitution was in itself the sign (Gorham, 1978; Walkowitz, 1980). The child prostitute became the emblem for a social conscience which saw in the repairing of her moral and sexual innocence a corrective to fundamental problems of social inequality which would not otherwise be amenable to such highly personalised, caring and nurturing forms of redress. This child – object of social legislation – was at once (and this is the key) totally sexualised and totally innocent. The call for attention, the felt need and anxiety, all centred on the seeming paradox of a sexuality which could *only* be seen at the very moment when it was to be blotted out.

Peter Pan is not, therefore, the only place where a highly sexualised form of attention to childhood takes onto itself the meaning, and the objective, of innocence. The link is confirmed by the fact that the audiences of the London theatre (the upper middle classes whose definitive takeover of the London stage is attributed by theatre historians to exactly this time) were the same social group who were at the centre of the other campaign (witness the presence of W. T. Stead to both). This is not to suggest that the cult of the child in the theatre was the reflection of this social malaise, with the second as the simple determinant or cause of the first (there is 'theatre' essentially in both). Rather it is to point to a circulation in which childhood, innocence and sexuality all figure in central but uneasy relation. And that the concept of innocence can carry the weight of such social and sexual contradiction is shown in another guise by the phenomenon (everything that went with it and came before it) of *Peter Pan*.

Thus it becomes increasingly difficult to see *Peter Pan* simply as a children's play without interrogating both poles of the definition. The first reviewers saw the play entirely from the adult's point of view, commenting on the skilful management of the 'child scenes' which they clearly recognised as a *genre*. And even if it has become the case that *Peter Pan* can attract an audience composed 60 per cent of children, while the ratio of child to adult at the traditional pantomime has on occasion dwindled to one in ten, the mistake is to take this fact and project it back to the beginnings of *Peter Pan* as if it were its primary intention or cause.

I think we have gone wrong by seeing *Peter Pan* solely as the creation of its author, a dramatist whose more obvious affinities lie with the new playwrights such as Ibsen and Shaw. In this context, and in the context of Barrie's earlier work, *Peter Pan* looks like a major break and hence as a radical and innovatory moment in the history of theatre itself. It was in fact more of a moving sideways on the part of its author into another equally popular, less esteemed, but no less financially viable section of the London stage.

For what is most striking finally about *Peter Pan* in the theatre is not the similarity of content with other contemporary plays, nor the links of spectacle and pleasure, but the *status* of the dramatic forms to which *Peter Pan* owes its strongest allegiance. In 1905 two new theatres were opened in London – the Aldwych with a second edition of *Bluebell in Fairyland* and the Waldorf with a light operatic season by the San Carlo company, the types of drama which were seen as the safest objects of financial investment in a period which was generally characterised as one of artistic 'decline'. This paradox of 'high' investment and 'low' drama reaches perhaps its peak in the late Victorian pantomime, but it has a longer history than this. Raymond Williams has suggested that it resulted from the pressures of middle-class development on an art form whose roots belonged to preindustrial Britain, the failure of the new class to appropriate the drama producing a split between theatrical expansion (the theatre as business enterprise) and a decline in the drama represented by a series of hybrid theatrical forms: 'farce, pantomime, burlesque, spectacular shows, and then, from the beginning of the nineteenth century, melodrama' (Williams, 1961, p. 263).

Despite the emergence of the new drama (the 'bourgeois' drama of Ibsen and the works of Shaw), the vestigial elements of the paradox that Williams describes can still be identified in the theatre in 1904 when *Peter Pan* was first produced: in the 'machine-made' dramas of Hall Caine (*The Green Room Book*, 1907, p. 390), the musical comedies of Seymour Hicks, and a 'growing taste' for light opera and opera comique (*The Green Room Book*,

1907, p. 392). *Peter Pan* only became renowned as a musical with the American production of 1954, but its affinity to these forms of drama goes back to the beginnings of its history. Its appearance alongside *Oklahoma!* and *West Side Story* in 1979 signifies, therefore, not just the nostalgia of Broadway but this other, earlier, proximity of form (*Peter Pan* not as play, but as light entertainment or show).

In the early part of the century, the criticism of the prevalent dramatic forms was constant. It was directed both against the genre ('light, humorous, superficial comedy' (*The Green Room Book*, 1909, p. 535)) and against the class content of the drama ('the prejudices and conventions of the English upper-middle class' (*The Theatre Magazine*, 1 (5), 1907, p. 22; see also Wilson, 1951, p. 2)). Children's theatre first has its place in this context – the first matinee, which was classified as a 'juvenile performance', was staged at Drury Lane in 1853 and repeated by 'desire of numerous families of the nobility and gentry' (quoted in Armstrong, 1959, p. 56).

The theatre therefore seems to have been characterised by an upper-middle-class content within a series of hybrid dramatic forms – opera comique, pantomime and musical comedy. Children's theatre was the product of these elements of the declining adult drama (residue as opposed to autonomous new form). Legally the child had been covered as theatrical employee since 1879, but it was not legally recognised and protected as spectator until the Children's Act of 1908. In the list of plays published in the first edition of *The Green Room Book* in 1907, there is only one play explicitly classified as a children's play, and it is not *Peter Pan* – *The Two Naughty Boys*, 'a musical fairy play for children' (Gaiety). The list does, however, include three fairy plays (one of these is *Peter Pan*), one fairy comedietta, a new stage adaptation of *Alice*, the revival of *Bluebell in Fairyland* and three pantomimes.

Thus *Peter Pan* emerges at a vacuum point in the drama somewhere between the musical comedy and the pantomime, both of which were considered to be representative of the low condition of the English drama. It was produced at a time when there was, if anything, a plethora of fairies and children on the stage, and also when closer links between the drama and the novel (the 'dramatist novelist' such as Hall Caine, W. J. Locke and J. M. Barrie)[9] were bringing a number of children's classics onto the stage (Kingsley's *The Water Babies* and Dickens's *The Cricket on the*

Hearth, both at the Gaiety in 1903). Any consideration of the success of *Peter Pan* must be seen first in this context, and not as the autonomous creation of a new children's theatre based on the success of a single play:

> There was also, from *Peter Pan*, a further effect, so far as children were concerned . . . it was perceived that plays meant specially for children were a necessity – in fact, there eventually appeared a theatre specially for children. *Pinkie and the Fairies, Where the Rainbow Ends, Alice* adaptations, Treasure Island on stage may all be called in some sort the offspring of *Peter Pan*. (Darton (1932) 1982, p. 312)

Peter Pan's tenacity has therefore retrospectively invested it with a false status as the origin of children's theatre (*Alice* and *Bluebell* both preceded *Peter Pan*). Thus repetition imperceptibly translates itself into infinity (in the beginning there was *Peter Pan* . . .).

To the extent that *Peter Pan* can be seen to represent that moment when light domestic drama, fairy and childhood were on the point of being offered to a child spectator, then it merely takes up a place in a long history of children's literature where a degraded literary form is handed down to the nursery (we could compare this with the fairy tale in seventeenth-century France). *Peter Pan* did not found a new type of drama so much as revivify a number of old ones. Thus the novelty and freshness of children's theatre neatly suppresses the decadence, both institutionally and sexually, of what went before.

Children are not the cause of this literature. They are not the group for whom it is created (the presence of the child image within it proves nothing on this score). In relation to *Peter Pan*, children are more the fillers-in ('backing-and-filling') for a dying fantasy of theatrical life: 'A show that should be seen with children for maximum enjoyment', 'If you don't have kids, rent them' (William Cottens, *Philadelphia Enquirer*, 8 September 1979; Dennis Cunningham, *CBS TV*, 1979).

*   *   *

There is one question asked by children which is almost as hard to answer as where babies come from and that is how money is *made*.

How can you explain to a child how you make something which always comes from somewhere or somebody else? Perhaps it is because of this difficulty, and not just because of the seeming insatiability of children's demands, that we so often resort to insisting that 'money doesn't grow on trees'. We could try saying simply that money doesn't *grow* at all. But it does. It accumulates according to processes that are often as invisible to us as to children. Making money, like sex, is another one of those always mystified processes which then gets converted into a childhood taboo – which might be another reason why it is so difficult to trace its movements, other than symptomatically, in the history of literature for the child.

Peter Pan, as has already been mentioned, accumulated vast sums of money. But whereas we could see that money (its quantity) as helping us to define the value of *Peter Pan* (just what is it worth?), instead it only makes it more obscure. One look at the extent of the commercialisation of *Peter Pan* is enough to establish that we do not really know what we are talking about when we refer to *Peter Pan*. In its history to date, *Peter Pan* has stood for, or been converted into, almost every conceivable (and some inconceivable) material forms: toys, crackers, posters, a Golf Club, Ladies League, stained glass window in St James's Church, Paddington, and a 5000-ton Hamburg–Scandinavia car ferry. As if only too aware of the infinite convertibility of their gift, the Great Ormond Street Hospital asks in its contracts (Legitimate stage Rights, Musical in Arena Production Rights, Animated Cartoon Rights, Live Motion Picture Rights, Puppet Rights and Television Rights) for a percentage on merchandise which is double that on producer's profits.

Peter Pan is, therefore, more than *one* – it is repeated, reproduced, revived and converted in a seemingly endless spiralling chain. But it is seen to represent *oneness*. And that oneness conceals the multiplicity of commodities, the accumulation of money, and the non-identity of the child audience and reader to whom it so awkwardly relates. In the case of the play, we have seen the easy confusion, or conflation, of child-spectacle, child-performer and child-audience – the idea of the third allowing us to gloss over the more insistent and difficult reality of the first two. In the book trade, we are dealing not with the relative homogeneity of an upper-middle-class audience which finds the most perfect image for its own self-identity in the child, but with different markets and

different readers. And these differences make all the more
apparent the mystification which we perpetuate whenever we
take as a simple point of reference the idea of *a* book for *the* child.
We can start with the crudest level of value – the price of the book,
that is, its own declaration of what it is worth.

In *The Bookseller* for August 1981, a new edition of J. M. Barrie's
Peter Pan and Wendy is advertised for £7.95. It appears in the
advertisement section for the over-fives along with gift books
which include Kay Nielsen's illustrated edition of *The Fairy Tales
of Hans Christian Andersen*. This last book is priced at £6.95, the
same price as the other collection of Hans Christian Andersen
fairy tales which is advertised. The fact is worth noting only
because these books (with *Peter Pan and Wendy* at the fore) are
conspicuously the most expensive books on the page. In 1979, an
advertisement in the *Peter Pan* programme of His Majesty's
Theatre, Aberdeen, offered Eleanor Graham's retelling of *Peter
and Wendy* at £3.95, and a facsimile of the 1921 edition at £7.95: 'to
mark the centenary of the birth of Mabel Lucie Attwell and the
75th anniversary of *Peter Pan*'s first appearance a special gift
edition containing Sir James Barrie's full length story together
with Mabel Lucie Attwell's original illustrations has just been
produced'. As is the case in the theatre, when *Peter Pan* appears, it
carries with it the weight (and the price) of its history. *Peter Pan*
can be retold (£3.95), or else it can be issued as a prized relic of
publishing history (£7.95), and relics are worth their weight in
gold.

Peter Pan was in this sense a relic before it started. First
published as *Peter Pan in Kensington Gardens* in 1906 in an 'Edition
de luxe', it belonged to the category of collector's items, first
editions and important works, which already included a number
of books problematically identified with a child audience, such as
Andrew Lang's *Green Fairy Book* of 1893 and Arthur Rackham's
first big illustrated, *Rip Van Winkle*, which had been published in
1905. These books represented the 'best' of publishing – they were
the 'leading items' of artistic production (*The Bookman*, January,
1906, p. 150). Barrie's book was oversubscribed, and reviewed in
the Fine Art and Archaeology sections of *The Athenaeum*
(December 1906) and *The Book Monthly* (December 1906). This is
where *Peter Pan* first appears as a book – a children's book only to
the extent that these venerated archeological treasures were
classics which had already been (although not originally), or else

were on the point of being, associated with, and then given to, the child.

A gift can be an aggressive act. Marcel Mauss, the anthropologist, has described communities which exchange gifts of gradually ascending value in order to drive their opposite number into economic collapse (Mauss (1925) 1954). Children's gift books are better seen as belonging somewhere between a bribe and a demand – a bribe of the purchasing adult and a demand on the receiving child. John Newbery's first book for children was advertised in 1744 as a guarantee of strength, health, virtue, wisdom and happiness in the receiving child (a tall order) (Newbery, 1744). One of the chief ways of ensuring the circulation of children's books has been their use as prizes, with the book as a reward for a correctness which it is intended to encourage. In my school, prizes had to be selected from a fixed list of books (presumably in case we went wild). According to the historians of children's fiction, it was the late Victorians who turned the use of children's books as prizes into a 'standard trade' (Alderson, Appendix to Darton (1932) 1982, p. 322).

The period when *Peter Pan* was first produced as a book shares with the last three decades of this century its expansiveness in the field of children's books. In the first half of the nineteenth century, booksellers redefined themselves as 'publishers', establishing themselves as what could be recognised as the British book trade by the second half of the century. In the last three decades of the twentieth century, children's books have once again become (after a comparative lull) a 'major field of publishing and international exchange' (Lewis, Preface to Kirkpatrick, 1978, p. vii). The value of these glossy books of the late nineteenth century, of which Barrie's text was one, can therefore be seen as the celebration of an expanding industry, the spectacle-on-paper of a growing financial concern. Books, no less than theatre, were part of a visual display in which children offered up some of the richest potential for the trade. The late nineteenth-century child was 'grist to the mill' of the miscellaneous bookseller (*The Bookman*, December 1891, p. 105). In 1896, *The Bookman* added a special section on children's books to its Christmas Supplement on illustrated books which, together with popular magazines and fairy tales, were the most commercially viable products of the market. The fairy tale was, therefore, good business first; the idea of children's books came second. The confused association between children and fairies reproduces itself in the commercial history of children's books, and continues to this day. Writing on the recent expansion in output of children's books, Naomi Lewis talks of the popularity of 'books about children or fairies; or both' (Lewis, Preface to Kirkpatrick, 1978, p. vii).

In his Appendix to the 1982 edition of Darton's *Children's Books in England* (Alderson, Appendix to Darton (1932) 1982, pp. 316–31), Brian Alderson lists as the main factors in the late nineteenth-century publication of children's books: the private consumption of books in the home, the establishment of the prize, the beginnings of children's book criticism, and the expressiveness of a writer like Beatrix Potter, 'the uncompromising story teller, knowing that *her* way is the way that the story needs to go and that the children will follow her' (Alderson, Appendix to Darton (1932) 1982, p. 328). Alderson lists these features in order to demonstrate that the new freedom in children's writing started in the late nineteenth century, as a corrective to Darton's belief that the main breakthrough came later (with the appearance of *Peter Pan*). There is an irony in this (the perverseness, as Alderson puts it, of associating freedom in children's literature with the moment when it becomes an object of investigation by adults). For what this list offers is children's literature as an uncompromising, newly self-conscious, self-promoting and self-commenting material concern ('children *will* follow'). The freedom of children's literature seems to lie somewhere between the freedom of a market economy and *Peter Pan*.

In this context, the heavy commercial promotion of *Peter Pan* becomes more than an incidental factor of its history. It reveals both how marketable the child was for the book trade, and the gap which could in fact hold between this reality and something which might finally reach its destination as literature for children. Hodder and Stoughton, who published *Peter Pan*, were not children's publishers, but Barrie was one of their most successful and heavily promoted writers, and they had their own publicity journal, *The Bookman*, which was started in 1891 (this was exactly the time when the publicity journal was castigated by booksellers for its commercialisation of the trade). The advanced promotion for *The Little White Bird* included a half-page advertisement in *The Publisher's Circular* (1 November 1902) which announced that it was to be 'the great success of the season' (15 November 1902, p. 539). Between 1903 and 1911, *The Bookman* produced no less than seven portfolios and supplements on *Peter Pan*. The 1905 Christmas number, for example, with a Barrie photograph on the cover and a supplement of photographs from the play, had reached a 200 per cent premium on its original price by November 1906 (*Peter Pan* already a 'collector's item'). It was on the back of this that *Peter Pan in Kensington Gardens* was issued in the following year.

The publication of *Peter Pan in Kensington Gardens* therefore had very little to do with a child reader. Rather it illustrates just how far the child had become one of the chief fantasies – object of desire and investment – of the turn of the century publishing trade. Thus its publication has been taken to show that children were now considered 'worthy of loveliness, not to say aesthetic luxury' (Darton (1932) 1982, p. 311) – as if they could assimilate into themselves, and render innocent (again), the more glaring commercial realities of the trade.

Luxury is never a neutral concept. In the world of children's books, it signals both class and excess ('the well-to-do classes almost forced their offspring into a surfeit' (Darton (1932) 1982, p. 311)) – not so much an achievement, or consummation, as the beginnings of a divide. If *Peter Pan in Kensington Gardens* was indeed eloquent of 'child glorification', then that eloquence and its associated value had its reverse image in contemporary complaints about the debasement of literary value and the cheapening of literary taste. The advent of the cheap (seven pence) reprint was seen by its critics as leading to the overproduction and general devaluation of fiction: 'Fiction, like every other article should have a fixed value' (*The Bookman,* June 1909, p. 636). This already shows the volatile and contradictory nature of ideas of literary value at this time. But, in relation to children's fiction, the importance of the cheap reprint lies in the fact that it was associated by its critics with the development of a new child reader – not the receiver of the Christmas gift, but the child who was emerging from the recently compulsory elementary schools. The overproduction of fiction meant, by implication, an overproduction of the educated child:

Quantity not quality – is that what is now demanded in a reprint? Every year thousands of new readers are being sent forth by the Board Schools, and naturally they are first attracted to books by what may be called the 'story interest' of these. But by-and-by the same readers evolve a minority who

take a deeper critical interest in what they read. That then is the
road which leads to a scholarly reprint, and so, ultimately, its
fortunes are secure. (*The Book Monthly*, February 1906, p. 292)[10]

Only a minority (the argument anticipates F. R. Leavis) (Leavis,
1930) can ultimately ensure the value (and the price) of books.

The idea that there was a sudden expansion of literary output to
encounter the new literacy is now thought to be mistaken. The
point here, however, is that *commercially* the child did not form a
homogeneous market. When *Peter Pan* was written, that market
was divided between the child *recipient* of the Christmas gift and
the child *reader*, the former the object of a new and increasing
commercial attention (aesthetic luxury and value), the latter the
displaced focus of anxieties about the commercial and literary
effects on the book trade of the changing educational policy of the
state (overproduction, devaluation).

Thus the question of what children were reading carried the
weight of anxiety about literary degeneration and cultural decay.
'Blood and thunder' stories were a 'menace to juvenile civilisation' (Darton, Appendix to Darton (1932) 1982, p. 341); they were
rubbish ('What Boys Do Read – the Need for Stemming a River of
Yellow Rubbish', *The Book Monthly*, September 1910, pp. 883–5),
and were leading to a decay of the infantile mind: 'when our books
are bought as rubbish, sold as rubbish, and received as rubbish, it
is perhaps natural for anyone to suppose that they are read and
written in the same spirit' (*Guardian*, 2 May 1900). The objection
was as much to the form in which these books appeared (papers
rather than bound books) as it was to the content of the stories.

In the attacks on the quality of this literature, it was compared
with the contemporary music hall, with the complaint that the
better books by Verne, Henty, Reed and Kingston normally
associated with boys' literary culture were now only bought by
parents and their friends. The distinction between the two
different types of child reader was, therefore, a distinction
between a classic children's literary culture still largely dominated by the adult market (literary tradition) and the emergence
of an autonomous children's literature which was being nega-
tively identified with aspects of working-class culture. The
'cheapness' ascribed to the latter clearly went beyond the
question of price, since the same journals which criticised the
development of cheap boys' fiction were simultaneously praising

the new technology of the three-colour process which made it possible to produce colour illustrated books for children at a lower price than before. This new gift book was not *cheap*, it was *natural* ('The New Gift-Book, the Arrival of Naturalness and the Three-Colour Picture', *The Book Monthly*, January 1907, pp. 223–38) – as 'natural', that is, as the comfort of the nursery which this new gift book mirrored back to itself: 'Now the nursery is getting what it most likes, a mirror of itself' ('The New Gift-Book', p. 224).

The Peter Pan Picture Book (O'Connor and Woodward, 1907), published at five shillings by Bell in 1907, probably falls into this category of the cheaper colour illustrated book for children. Unlike *Peter Pan in Kensington Gardens*, it was listed as a children's book by *The Book Monthly* when it was published in 1907, and again in a new edition at three shillings and six pence in 1911, to the exclusion of J. M. Barrie's *Peter and Wendy* which was published that year.

In this context, the circulation of *Peter Pan* (it has by now been published in every conceivable price range), and its value, take on a new meaning – that of a wholly generalised concept of culture which cannot see the divisions on which it rests. The aestheticisation, the glorification, the valuing of the child – to which its first publication so eloquently bears witness – act as a kind of cover for these differences, of reader and address, differences which manifest themselves in the very physical substance of the book. If we look at the children's book market, its identity falls apart, exposing the gaps between producer (writer), distributor (bookseller or publisher), purchaser (parents, friends and/or children) and the consumer (ideally, but only ideally, the child). These spaces, missed meeting points, places of imposition, exploitation (or even glorification of the child) are not entirely different in kind from those which characterise other aspects of the literary life of our culture. They are not exclusive to the world of children's books. But there is something about the totality, the oneness, of *Peter Pan*'s status as a myth which makes them appear as an affront – the affront, for example, of claiming, as I would, that J. M. Barrie never wrote a version of *Peter Pan* (on stage or on paper) for children.

I would say that the responses of children to *Peter Pan* (for responses there have undoubtedly been) can in no sense be deduced from its material success (great as this, equally undoubtedly, has been); but that this success, and the corresponding status of *Peter Pan*, say something about the fantasies which our culture continues to perpetuate – about its own worth, its future and its traditions – through the child. That the child serves above all as a fantasy in all of this is given perhaps most clearly in the image of the little girl with twisted knees and head thrown back in ecstasy, an image off which we read that a fragment of our cultural history still survives; or else in the image of the beautiful book, the imprint or insignia of a value which, at the beginning of the century at least, we could still see as infinitely expanding throughout the world.

One of the strongest weights which *Peter Pan* carries is something which I would call the aesthetic mode – a system of values attaching to language and literature which we tend to take for granted, and whose very universality serves to close off the divisions in culture of the type which I have described in this chapter in relation to children's literature. A week after Barrie died in 1937, the *Times Literary Supplement* published a long article in which the question of *Peter Pan*'s survival drew onto itself the whole question, not just of Barrie's survival as a dramatist, but of what – in general – *can* survive, of what *is* endurance, perpetuity and eternal worth. This worth, defined by the article as true literature or literature as truth, finally dispenses with the present, with what might be the responsibility now. Because if *Peter Pan* survives, we all survive, and the problem of the present, and its difficulty, no longer has to be asked:

> No dramatist has ever been more perilous to criticism than Barrie within a week of his death . . . when everything has been said of the technical adroitness, the darting humour, the narrative skill of his other plays, the problem of Barrie's survival remains the problem of *Peter Pan*; and this not by any means because he is to be recognised as a 'one-play' dramatist but because what will cause his other plays to endure, if anything does, is that element of fantasy, or, as some would have it, of the seer, in them which in *Peter Pan* has its most concentrated expression. . . . If *Peter Pan* is fashionable senti-mentality . . . then the whole of Barrie's theatre is refused its major claim. But if *Peter Pan* is in the succession to *Cinderella*, if it is not a Christmas pantomime but one of those stories that embody and perpetuate the intuitive wisdom of childlike

humanity, then Barrie's work will be in flower when all the 'intellectual and social forces' of our time, Ibsen, Strindberg or Shaw, have vanished even from the encyclopedias. *Peter Pan* is, in this sense, the greatest of all critical gambles . . . The problem may be grappled a little more closely if we are prepared to grant that the test of validity in any work of art is its realism *on its own plane*. Whether it makes a contribution to contemporary thought is not relevant; whether it represents superficial experience, past or present – whether or not it is 'like' something that its audience recognises – is not relevant; whether it is moral, immoral, or non-moral is not relevant. The test is that an artist has not polluted his own imagining, whether naturalistic, fantastic or mystical, with stuff borrowed from others or from a different self, and that, having thus preserved the purity of his idea, he has struck fearlessly for the whole truth – that is the essence of it.

It is upon this ground – that it blinks its own truth – that those who condemn *Peter Pan* must justify their criticism . . . It is possible to point to the continuing vitality of the play during a quarter of a century, to remember what delight many – but not all – children have in it, and to say:— 'This is work which, in fact, confounds your analysis. You may prove a thousand flaws in it, but still it goes on. It goes on because its audiences are unaware, as Barrie himself was unaware, that it is spiritual autobiography.

'To them the confusions, the contradictions, the avoidances that you complain of resemble the inconsequence of their own dreams, and the thing before their eyes has the quality of a legend that they are making up for themselves.' If this be true, it means that Barrie had the power which is much greater than that of story-telling of compelling successive generations to invent his story afresh, to tell it to themselves and in their own terms – that is to say, he was able not merely to instruct or entertain but to impregnate the collective mind of his audience. And if he did, indeed, possess this power, which is precisely the power of the great fairy-tales, criticism may as well throw its pen away, for then he is immortal by election and there is no more to be said about it. (*Times Literary Supplement*, 26 June 1937, pp. 469–70 (front page feature))

If, therefore, *Peter Pan* survives, it is because there is a realm of literature which stares unblinkingly at the truth, which strides over flaws and inconsistencies, over the intellectual and social forces of our time, straight into the collective mind of its audience. 'Intuition', 'wisdom', 'truth' and the 'childlike humanity' of the collective – these are all terms which have appeared together before. What is different here is the way that they are assimilated to a concept of the *literary* as truth (the whole truth) – staring unblinkingly and, I would say, blinded by the feat. In this context, that *Peter Pan* should end up at the Barbican is fitting in another sense. For it fulfils the wish which I have often seen expressed that *Peter Pan* should at last be freed from the wrong connotations of infancy (mere childishness) and into the upper reaches of our cultural life ('the intuitive wisdom of childlike humanity'), by being interpreted by a director such as Peter Brooke (Michael Billington in the *Guardian*, 23 December 1977) or performed at the National Theatre (Eric Shorter in the *Daily Telegraph*, 6 December 1979) as a wholly serious play.[11] (See the Note on the 1982 production at the end of this chapter.)

It is the very generality of this recognition which for me perpetuates the fundamental blindness – to the contradictions and difficulties which more urgently need to be addressed in relation to how our culture constitutes and reproduces its image of the child, contradictions which can be seen in the production, promotion, language and reception of *Peter Pan*. I want to end this book, therefore, by going back to the child reader who was emerging at the time when *Peter Pan* was written, because it is not strictly true to say that *Peter Pan* completely by-passed this reader or had nothing to do with him or her at all. It did once – when *Peter Pan* was accepted by the state educational machinery for use in the schools. Looking at this moment, we will see that even here, the idea of a child reader is not simple, but is divided over again on itself. It seems appropriate to end this book by examining that moment when one of the most general of our cultural myths about childhood, and the most public of childhood institutions, actually came face to face.

A NOTE ON THE 1982 ROYAL SHAKESPEARE
COMPANY PRODUCTION AT THE BARBICAN
THEATRE, LONDON

The 1982 production of *Peter Pan* by the Royal Shakespeare
Company at the Barbican Cultural Centre for the Arts was
heralded, and mainly received, as a new beginning for *Peter Pan*
which restored the original intention of the author and gave back
to the play its tragic and fully adult dimension. The production
reintroduced scenes and lines cut from earlier productions (the
seduction between Tiger-Lily and Peter), a version of the
once-performed 1908 ending ('An Afterthought') and the narrator of the 1911 novel. All residual links with the pantomime
were severed and the part of Peter Pan was played by a man.

For the directors – John Caird and Trevor Nunn – the changes
were justified, or even demanded, by the status of the Royal
Shakespeare Company as a subsidised theatre whose proper task
is to 'take such works, clean and dust them, and restore an original
intention' (*Omnibus* interview with Richard Baker, BBC Television, 16 January 1983). Thus *Peter Pan* becomes a major
masterpiece of our culture (as opposed to a pantomime or merely
a children's play): 'the RSC have seized the advantage of taking
the work out of mothballs and elevating it from the ghetto of
children's theatre into a national masterpiece' (Irving Wardle,
The Times, 18 December 1982). 'However you take it, this makes
the play a tragedy' (Michael Billington, *Guardian*, 17 December
1982).

This renovation of *Peter Pan*, which reintroduces many of the
elements carefully excluded when its status as myth relied more
closely on its presumed appeal to children, then throws into
question its relationship to the child audience: the predominantly
adult audience of the Barbican theatre, the restricted number of
matinees, and the fact that the box office advised on booking not
to bring any child under the age of eight to the performance.

Despite these changes, however, there is a sense in which
nothing seems to have altered. One reviewer acknowledged the
link with Freud ('it seems to anticipate Freud or to be an example
of simultaneous discovery', James Fenton, *Sunday Times*, 19
December 1982), but for the director John Caird the play
illustrates a fundamental truth: that children are capable of

intense but wholly asexual feelings for one another ('prepubescent' and therefore 'nothing to do with sex', *Omnibus* interview, 16 January 1983). The programme and accompanying commentaries recognise the centrality of death as a motif in the play but invariably divest it of its psychic meaning for children by reducing it to a fact of Barrie's personal biography. And the narrator becomes Barrie himself, a sage and untroubled Edwardian commentator: the famous opening line of the 1911 novel 'All children, except one, grow up' is divided into two halves in the production's opening sequence with 'All children grow up' spoken by the narrator and 'Except one' as the first line and challenge to him by Peter Pan himself, which neatly disposes of the idea that one person could speak from the two places at once. (Even this diluted presence of the narrator was too much for someone in the audience who complained that he 'rather breaks the magic'.)

Finally, sponsored by Nederlander Associates Inc., linked to the first 1904 production by its extravaganza and risky effects (the critics were unanimous about its *spectacular* quality), this production speaks money, like the Spielberg film, *ET* ('Spielbergian ecstasy', Billington, *Guardian*, 17 December 1982), which also tells the story of an alien who can only be seen and understood by children and who represents the eternal childhood of man: 'Generations grow up and get boring but Peter Pan might just be there at your window' (*Omnibus* interview, 16 January 1983); 'If you think it is your house, you're probably right, because it wanders around London looking for anyone who needs it' (the narrator, Act I, 1982 production); 'Peter Pan goes straight to your centre ... to something about which you are defenceless' (*Omnibus* interview, 16 January 1983).

Thus, this final extravagantly financed and fully reciprocal love affair between *Peter Pan* and *ET* (*ET* includes sections from *Peter Pan* which the mother reads to the child), between the Barbican and Hollywood, reinscribes the eternal myth of childhood – childhood *as* eternal myth – over and above anything else.

5

Peter Pan, Language and the State
Captain Hook goes to Eton

In 1925, Barrie wrote a short story called 'Jas Hook at Eton, or The Solitary' for inclusion in an anthology of short stories for children, *The Flying Carpet* (Barrie, 1926(b)). Instead of being published in that anthology, the story was delivered as a speech to the First Hundred at Eton on 7 July 1927, and published in *The Times*. It was replaced in the anthology by a sequel to 'The Blot on Peter Pan' (see pp. 39–41 above), a short story called 'Neil and Tintinnabulum' which describes how the male narrator loses his godson when he is absorbed into the life of a public school – the title reflects the loss as the little boy's name is changed at school from Neil to Tintinnabulum, from English to Latin. Latin is the element which connects the two stories. The autograph manuscript version of Barrie's 1927 story is accompanied by a leaf of manuscript in an unidentified hand which gives the following Latin inscription for James Hook: 'Gratissimus Almae Matris filius magistro inform. et alumnis omnibus avete hoc ivto Iunii die MDCCC? ex Moluccis Iacobus Hook Floreat Etona' (Beinecke, 1927).[1] The sequence from the earlier story 'The Blot on Peter Pan', which turns on the child's use of language as picture puzzle, to 'Neil and Tintinnabulum', therefore, describes the passage from the most elementary of child's play in language to the most elevated of linguistic/cultural norms.

The story 'Jas Hook at Eton' is presented by Barrie as evidence for the Latinate and public school credentials which are given in Hook's dying words – 'Floreat Etona' – which he utters as he jumps off the edge of the ship in the last sequence of the play. The reference goes back to *The Little White Bird* which ends when the public school master, Pilkington, steals (that is how it is expressed) the boy David and his friend Oliver from the narrator of that story and carts them off to school. In the 1911 *Peter and Wendy*, Barrie spells the association out in the form of a revelation or scandal – as the ultimate and most carefully guarded secret of his story:

> Hook was not his true name. To reveal who he really was would even at this date set the country in a blaze; but as those who read between the lines must have guessed, he had been at a famous public school. (Barrie, 1911, p. 203)

By writing a story (or giving a speech) to Eton about Hook at Eton, Barrie is going over the traces of his story, elaborating (confessing, exposing) its cultural code, bringing out into the open something which, prior to this, had operated purely at the level of allusion or aside. Making Hook's cultural allegiance explicit is, therefore, a little like drawing back the veil on a mystery, or else breaking into a sanctuary, with the implication that neither the hitherto protected scenario nor the onlooker will survive the revelation. The story Barrie tells of Hook's relationship to Eton describes just such a violation – it is not the story of his schooldays, but the story of how he broke into the school one night after 'Lock Up time' to destroy all record of his ever having been there. This cleverly disposes of two problems at once – the fact that the infamous Captain Hook would threaten the good name of the school had he indeed once been its pupil, and the fact that (as the records will show) the whole idea is a fantasy, or lie.

The idea of breaking and entering also has a history which goes back to the first Peter Pan story in *The Little White Bird* when Maimie Mannering broke the rules and stayed in Kensington Gardens overnight, where she (and we as readers) meet Peter Pan for the very first time. Thus there is a second circuit which overlays the passage from language as play to language as privilege with the notions of exclusion, barriers and taboo. At the simplest level the overlapping of these two moments suggests that the desire to get back to the beginning and make everything perfect takes the form of the familiar desire for better opportunities, and a fantasy of public school life. That the secret Latin reference is as much a risk to the purity of *Peter Pan* as the partly spoken fantasies about origins and birth is confirmed, however, by the fact that in 1915, when the London County Council's Books and Apparatus Sub-Committee accepted Barrie's *Peter and*

Wendy as a reader for use in the schools, every vestige of this reference was systematically cut.[2] In 1915, the public elementary school child, object of compulsory education since 1880 and recently redifferentiated from the middle-class child by the second Education Act of 1902,[3] did not speak Latin but English, and an English which was carefully distinguished from literary language by its reference to experience, to the 'sights and sounds, the thoughts and feelings of everyday life' (Government Circular, 1912 (BOE, 1912, p. 27)). Against this language was set not only Latin, but literary language in general or, more specifically, the language of the literary trope. Matthew Arnold, HM Inspector of Schools from 1852–86 offered the following two extracts in 1867 to illustrate the gulf which then separated the privately educated middle-class child from children in the elementary schools:

> My dear parents, – The anticipation of our Christmas vacation abounds in peculiar delights. Not only that its 'festivities', its social gatherings, and its lively amusements crown the old year with happiness and mirth, but that I come a guest commended to your hospitable love by the performance of all you bade me remember when I left you in the glad season of sun and flowers.

> Dear Fanny, – I am afraid I shall not pass in my examination. Miss C says she thinks I shall. I shall be glad when the Serpentine is frozen over, for we shall have such fun; I wish you did not live so far away, then you could come and share in the game. (Arnold, 1899, pp. 131–2)

The pseudo-classicism which Arnold is commenting on in the language of the privately educated middle-class child is picked up by Barrie in his 1927 story about Captain Hook: 'But even so, what ardour to excel, how indomitable is the particle man' (Beinecke, 1927, p. 3). It also appears at various points in *Peter and Wendy*: 'O man unfathomable' (Barrie, 1911, p. 202); 'the elegance of his diction, even when he was swearing, no less than the distinction of his demeanour, showed him one of a different caste from his crew' (Barrie, 1911, pp. 80–1). Along with all mention of Hook's educational history, this language is edited out of *Peter and Wendy* when it is accepted by the schools. Thus the censorship does not only apply to the explicit references to the

institutions of schooling. Equally, and more crucially, it takes out
any signs of their associated forms of linguistic style.

For *Peter Pan* to become a *reader*, the overconscious signs of its
status as *literature* must be erased. The distinction is one which was
written into state educational policy on language in the first
decades of the century, when the state faced a potential contradiction between an increasingly generalised policy of state aid to
schools (the 1902 Education Act provided state aid for the first
time to the previously private domain of secondary education),[4]
and the need to secure a differentiation between classes of
child.

The language of the child – the language which it speaks, the
language it reads, and the relationship between the two – was one
of the central arenas within which this contradiction was played
out. Here, the question of language becomes the question of
literacy, and the question of literature hands over to that of *literary
language* (how and what to speak, what to read and to what end?).
By this almost imperceptible shift, both language and literature
are released as objects of *policy* – policy by means of which the
child's relationship to its culture can be defined. Language is not
simply there to be spoken, any more than literature waits to be
read, like matter almost to be imbibed by the child ('When you
give your child a bath, bathe him in language' – the exhortation of
the 1974 Bullock Report on literacy, *A Language for Life* (Bullock,
1974, p. 58)). Both the language and the literature available to the
child fall inside institutions which constitute them differentially
and with different values and meanings at different times. The
point of examining *Peter Pan*'s encounter with the schools is not,
therefore, so much to demonstrate an outrage – the repressive
educational machinery clamps down on the book for the child – as
to show how both language and literature are constituted by just
such 'machinery' in the first place. In this context, natural
language or the idea of language as naturally expressive – a
concept which we have seen to be so central to writing on
children's literature – appears not as something outside the range
of these determinations, but as one pole of a fully structural
opposition between natural and cultured language in the
schools.[5]

This is how the Board of Education Circular of 1912 on the
teaching of English in the public elementary school concludes its
final section on English teaching for its senior classes:

in teaching children, failure to use a direct, simple, unaffected style is doubly harmful: it makes the teaching more difficult for the child to understand and remember, and it corrupts his natural taste ... To preserve and develop naturally the unsophisticated virtues of children's language is worthy of an effort and will indeed require an effort on the part of a grown-up teacher. He need not revert to 'childish' language, but if he can recover some of the directness and simplicity of thought and expression which education too often impairs, he will find that his effort has been of as great advantage to himself as to the children. (BOE, 1912, pp. 31–2)

This from the opening section of the 1910 Board of Education Circular on English teaching in the secondary schools:

It would only be wasting words to refute the view that knowledge of English in any real sense of the term will be 'picked up' naturally, or that though systematic instruction is necessary in such subjects as mathematics or foreign languages, the mother-tongue may safely be left to the occasional direction and influence of home, or to the rare chance of spontaneous liking for its study. The instruction in English in a Secondary School aims at training the mind to appreciate English literature, and at cultivating the power of using the English language in speech and writing. These objects are equally important, and each implies the other. Without training in the use of language, literature cannot be fully understood or properly appreciated. Without the study of literature there can be no mastery over language. (BOE, 1910, p. 3)

We should remember that the relationship between these two types of school was not one of a sequence – a journey through the educational system of an individual child (elementary *then* secondary). The age groups of the two schools partly overlapped (10 to 14 for the senior classes of the elementary school and 12 to 16 for the secondary school). The elementary school stopped at 14 because this was considered the appropriate educational span for the working-class child; and the secondary school made it clear that its methods should also be used for the elementary training of its pupils ('the whole spirit of the Circular must be regarded as applying equally to pupils of this more elementary stage' (BOE,

1910, p. 3)). The differences between these recommendations on language – an unsophisticated language on the verge of 'childishness' versus literature as the precondition for mastery over language itself – cannot therefore be resolved into the stages of a continuous development or growth. They remain, precisely, a difference.

The language of the elementary school child was to be natural – which meant a vocabulary based on concrete objects, and written composition constructed on the basis of speech ('No attempt should be made to impose a difference in style in written and oral composition'; 'Written composition should be subordinate to oral' (BOE, 1912, pp. 16, 14)). It meant literature based on physical actions, and on facts which could be added to the child's stock of information. The child should read literature for its story, poetry for its matter rather than its form. If literary taste was to be developed, it too should 'grow naturally by feeding on the best' (BOE, 1912, p. 25) – although the child will not be fully cognisant of the process ('they will rarely be able to show reasons for their preference' (BOE, 1912, p. 25)). In the secondary school, the priorities are almost exactly reversed. Since literary language predominates, so the child's speech is encouraged towards cadence and quality, its composition towards structure and style. Books of fiction are the one form of writing to be excluded from its reading. In the final stages, the study of literature leads to the analysis, appreciation and mastery of the classicism of Milton's style. Literature is to be selected for its 'specially fine passages' (BOE, 1910, p. 6) which the child commits to memory by learning them by heart ('not so much a method as the presupposition of all methods' (BOE, 1910, p. 6)). Literary language therefore becomes the fully internalised model of the child's own mental processes which reflect not everyday concrete experience, but 'remembrances', 'unconscious associations' and a 'widening experience of life' (BOE, 1910, p. 6). The image is that of a subjecthood which 'ripens' (BOE, 1910, p. 6) in accordance with the truly organic nature of a literate culture ('nature' appearing with opposite connotations on either side of the educational divide).

Thus the secondary school remained, even after it had been taken partly under state control, the repository of a notion of literacy, whose objective was the classicism which Arnold's quotation (p. 117 above) shows us so slavishly imitated by the middle-class child. Meanwhile, the public schoolboy was himself learning English for the first time (a 'new subject' in 1906 according to the Assistant Master of Harrow School), but English as 'pure literature' (*The Public Schools from Within*, 1906, pp. 49, 48), with composition taught on the earlier models of Latin prose.[6] In this context, therefore, Barrie's Latin reference places *Peter and Wendy* in the midst of a struggle about the appropriate ownership, patronage and reproduction of linguistic and cultural privilege in the schools. Even for Matthew Arnold, who pleaded for a 'humanising' (Arnold, 1899, p. 87) influence to be exerted on the raw, uncultivated information of elementary education, Latin literature represented the one cut-off point of his cultural *largesse*: 'we do not want to carry our elementary schools into Virgil or Cicero' (Arnold, 1899, p. 166).

Elementary language is, however, no more natural than this classical prose. When *Peter Pan* was written, elementary language, with its emphasis on natural expression, can clearly be seen as something in the process of being *constructed* as one half of an opposition whose other term it necessarily evokes. As if symptomatically, the 1912 Board of Education Circular recommends *Tom Brown's Schooldays* (Hughes, 1857) along with the more predictable *Robinson Crusoe* (Defoe, 1719) and *Masterman Ready* (Marryat (1841–2) 1878) as reading for the elementary schools. The first (which was first in a long line of books for children written in the second half of the nineteenth century about public school life)[7] demonstrates the uneasy but always present relationship between the different sectors of the educational system (their constant reference to each other); the second two are the wholly appropriate representatives of an old empiricism of language and a colonialism of adventure whose long association with childhood was now to receive the sanction of the linguistic-educational policy of the state.

This can be seen most clearly in a new synthetic method for teaching English which was devised in 1914 in direct response to the 1912 Government Circular by R. Wilson, whose *Progress to Literature* (see pp. 85–6 above) had already revealed something of *Peter Pan*'s problematic relationship to the world of children's books. Its objective – which it defined against the previous analytic method of teaching English by grammar, spelling and dictation – was to teach the child language by means of the visual image, in such a way that language should be seen to arise directly, and without interference, out of the objects of the visible world:

1 To name in turn various objects represented by the artist, eg.: I see a horse.
2 To close book and name objects from memory, eg. I saw a horse, or, I have just seen a horse.
3 To say what he will see when he opens the book, or, what his companions will see, eg. I shall see a horse, etc. He will see a horse, etc.
4 To name 'actions' or 'states' represented by the artist, eg. Grazes in the field . . . (Wilson, 1914(a), Teacher's Lesson Book 1, pp. 12–13)

The method was appropriate for a child whose future was most likely to involve the physical manipulation of objects in manual work. (This has in turn produced a new crisis of literacy since this form of language is now considered unsuitable for a workforce no longer employed predominately in manufacture, agriculture and mines (Bullock, 1974, p. 4)). But the stress on the visible and manipulable aspects of physical experience, on concrete impression and on language as the direct extension of the visual sign, can also be seen as the linguistic prototype for a late nineteenth-century imperialism (increasing control of an empirically knowable world) which was simultaneously bringing subjects like geography, religion and comparative ethnography for the first time into the elementary schools. The paradox was that the social group which actually serviced the Empire (the public school élite)[8] was prevented by the counterweight of their own classical-linguistic privilege from allowing, other than with the greatest difficulty and reluctance, either the newly celebrated mother-tongue[9] or the subjects appropriate to the ideology of imperialism into their schools.[10]

There is, as I argued in the second chapter of this book, a long colonial history which lines up under one banner childhood, the beginnings of language and the origins of the race – with *Robinson Crusoe* often serving as the link between the three (it was the one book recommended by Rousseau for children). *Robinson Crusoe* is appropriate not just for its fantasy of a primary and natural state of man, but also because it presents language as a record which directly captures experience much as physical labour puts man in immediate contact with the land. Accordingly, the Government Circular of 1912 takes this text as its image for the most proper, that is, physical and concrete, relationship between literature and the elementary school child:

> a child should not be expected to write a single composition upon a whole book or story, eg on *Robinson Crusoe*; it will be found far more profitable to call for a description of some particular scene or incident which is specifically interesting, or even to frame two or three pointed questions on some portion of the book; eg., what were the difficulties which Crusoe found in building his boat, and by what means did he overcome them. (BOE, 1912, p. 26)

We can compare this with the use of literature in the secondary school, where the child's consciousness is directed at the language of the author (whose words 'express the meaning better than any other words can do' (BOE, 1910, p. 8)); the aim being to produce an attention to language itself rather than to by-pass it in the name of the concrete event which it records.

This moment of educational history is, therefore, particularly helpful in allowing us to bring into sharper focus what it is we mean when we talk about language for the child. Children's language is not a concept which comes as readily and easily to mind as that of children's literature, although it is clear from the encounter between *Peter and Wendy* and the schools that they are inseparable, in so far as what is allowable to the child as fiction – its literature – is in part an effect of what it is permissible at any one moment for the child to speak. 'Children's language' tends to be a differential term, meaning 'not adult' and associated with babbling, rhythm, puzzle or play. But the one moment when this language of puzzle or play surfaces in the history of *Peter Pan* ('The Blot on Peter Pan' (Barrie, 1926(a))) has conspicuously been discarded by the myth. For the elementary schools in 1912, there is no doubt that any trouble which children's literature might pose at this level of impossibility and/or nonsense is to be subsumed under the correctness of the child's mother-tongue:

Lesson XXIV 'Who'
Write down two sentences.

Alice was a little girl. She had many adventures in Wonder-
land.
　　Now join them by substituting *who* for she. Note that *who*
comes near to the noun for which it stands.
　　Now offer the following for similar treatment.
　　Red Riding Hood was a little girl. She met a wolf in the wood.
　　Tom was a boy sweep. He was turned into a water baby.
　　Peter Pan was a little boy. He did not wish to grow up.
(Wilson, 1914(a), Teacher's Lesson Book 3, p. 43)

There is an obvious repressiveness involved in turning all these
unlikely or miraculous characters (metamorphosed – Tom, in
danger – Red Riding Hood, or desiring the impossible – Peter
Pan) into familiar people 'who . . .'. But this deflation of the
content conceals the more important transformation, which is the
fundamental *ordering* of the language through which it takes place.
　　It would, therefore, be misleading to describe the relationship
between elementary and cultured language as an ideal sequence
from linguistic underdevelopment into literate civilisation – a
sequence which, at the turn of the century, was only available to
one class of child. First, because the same child did not attend the
elementary and secondary schools, and secondly because to
conceive of the differences between them as a sequence can give
the impression that the more simple language is uncorrupted and
true, or else simply deprived – with the idea of the elementary as
something lacking, or left out, as far as these educational
determinants are concerned. The 1912 circular ends, indeed, by
recommending the teacher to put back the clock on her language
and to start speaking almost like a child. But the fact that this
statement comes at the end of a document designed to lay down
the principles of natural language, plus the fact that it has to
sidestep so carefully the more incoherent of children's speech,
suggests that the idea that there could ever be a natural language
is a myth. Rather there are two ideologies *of* language – one based
on the visible, knowable and controllable of the physical world,
the other based on the more numenous reaches of our higher
cultural life. The most rudimentary laws of how to organise
narrative fall under the rubric of each: for the elementary child,
actions and their immediate consequences ('What happened and
what happened next' (Wilson, 1914(a), Teacher's Lesson Book 6,
p. 3)); for the secondary school, the circular motion of a fully

integrated teleology of prose ('the end would be in view from the beginning . . . the whole piece of composition shall be an organic whole in which each portion is related to all the rest' (BOE, 1910, p. 12)).

Barrie's *Peter and Wendy* belongs on both sides of this cultural division. The confusion of tongues between adult and child on the part of the narrator, which was analysed in Chapter 3, carries with it an oscillation between these extremes of language, between elementary English and the periodic cadences of a more Latinate prose:

> Wendy came first, then John, then Michael.
>
> It was just at this moment that Mr and Mrs Darling hurried with Nana out of 27.
>
> He was a little boy and she was grown up.
>
> Fell from their eyes then the film through which they had looked at victory.
>
> the elegance of his diction, even when he was swearing, no less than the distinction of his demeanour, showed him one of a different caste from his crew.
>
> That passionate breast no longer asked for life. (Barrie, 1911, pp. 3, 56, 262, 174, 80–1, 228)

The Latin style is conspicuous; the elementary English fades into the invisibility of an apparently natural and universally comprehensible linguistic form. But, as educational policy at the turn of the century makes clear, the most natural of languages only has a meaning in relation to that other stylistic quality against which it is set. There is no natural language (least of all *for* children); there is elementary English and cultured prose, evoking each other, confronting each other, or else coming together as here, only to be carefully orchestrated apart.

When *Peter and Wendy* comes up against the schools, it therefore reveals, almost accidentally, that it is speaking to two different children at once, and that its language is not cohered but divided down the middle. But, at a time when the state was particularly concerned to secure a differentiation in the language of its subjects-to-be, such a conflation was impossible to accept and every sign of it therefore had to be edited out.

The effect of that editing is to take with it almost all the other forms of disturbance which have been described so far in relation to Barrie's text of 1911. The authorised school version removes:

all syntax (periodisation, inversion) or tropes (metonymy, synecdoche) which are resonant of a classical literary style;

all specific cultural and material references (not just to Hook's educational history, but also the more middle-class associations of the nursery: Mr Darling's stocks and shares, and Mrs Fulsome's kindergarten for the children);

all signs of play or parody of its own language, especially those which comment on language as institution or practice (' "I, George Darling, did it. *Mea culpa. Mea culpa.*" He had had a classical education' (Barrie, 1911, p. 19). 'Feeling that Peter was on his way back, the Never Land woke into life. We ought to use the pluperfect and say wakened, but woke is better and was always used by Peter' (Barrie, 1911, p. 75)); the implication here seems to be that language must not be seen to comment on itself;

all those moments when the sexuality of the text becomes explicit (in the Lagoon sequence, when Hook is being taunted by an invisible Peter, 'He felt his ego slipping from him . . . In the dark nature there was a touch of the feminine, as in all the great pirates', p. 135 – Hook then resorts to a guessing game with Peter; the text drops the 'ego' and the 'feminine' but keeps the game, which was the one 'judicious form of play' recommended by the 1912 circular (BOE, 1912, p. 6));

all episodes which disturb the logical narrative sequence of the story (*Peter and Wendy* describes the children's escape retrospectively, that is, it gives the outcome and then leads up to it; the school version picks out the story of what happened but drops the frame which gave it the status of a memory).

Above all, the school version cuts out virtually all signs of the presence of an identifiable narrator – that narrator who so uncomfortably forces on the reader's attention the question of who is telling the story (with all the instability in language that this implies). The school version is told almost entirely by an anonymous third person narrator who never appears explicitly in the text to trouble its linguistic norms or its utterly sustained cohesion of address. Thus, after dropping the first ten pages of Barrie's text completely, it opens 'The children were in bed' (Barrie, 1915, p. 5), a sentence which it lifts clean out of this one from the original: 'On the night we speak of all *the children were* once more *in bed*' (Barrie, 1915, p. 14) (my italics).

Barrie's text is not the only version of *Peter Pan* accepted after alterations for use in the schools. Three years before *Peter and Wendy* was approved, D. O'Connor's *Keepsake* had been admitted as a reader (O'Connor, 1912). The complexity of the operation carried out on this text is less because its challenge is less. It was, after all, a summary version of the play which went into circulation largely because of the difficulties of Barrie's own relationship to his text (in which context it is significant that O'Connor's text should be accepted before Barrie's own, which had appeared the year before). The *Keepsake* is not so much dramatically cut as corrected and its vocabulary simplified where this is too ponderous or literary: 'voracious saurian' to 'greedy crocodile', 'wierd apparation' to 'strange figure', 'become inaudible' to 'died away'. Above all its syntax is simplified, which means that for a sentence like this one 'he was the best father who never forgot to be a little boy' (O'Connor, 1907, p. 19), which grammatically can be read in at least three different ways ('of those fathers who never forgot to be a little boy, he was the best', 'he was the best father because he never forgot', 'he was the best father and never forgot') the easiest and most banal is the meaning which is retained: 'He was the best of fathers; and he never forgot to be a little boy' (O'Connor, 1912, p. 49) (the separation of the two clauses breaks the otherwise total and perhaps uncomfortable identity between fathers and little boys).

Barrie's text is never *rewritten* in this way. It is *abridged*, which means that the form of language desired by the schools can be extracted out of the most recalcitrant of Barrie's prose. Unlike O'Connor, whose faulty grammar is corrected on a number of occasions, Barrie never makes a mistake. It is his precision in relation to both forms of language, which he so skilfully meshes together, that is the scandal.

In educational terms, Barrie's personal history can suggest why he might have been particularly well placed to produce something which appears in *Peter and Wendy* as a type of condensation of these forms of speech, which for the schools were rapidly coming to be seen, and were increasingly being defined, as incompatible. In relation to linguistic policy at the turn of the century, Barrie's text was full of interference or noise. In relation to Barrie, however, this can be seen as the logical outcome of a fairly remarkable educational history which stretched from the learning situation of a small domestic economy in Scotland, through the Dumfries Academy (Barrie's elder brother was, like Arnold, an HM Inspector of Schools, and the Independent Scottish Academies were renowned for their cultural standards), to Edinburgh University and then London.[11] The public school education which Barrie provided for the Llewellyn Davies boys, whom he finally adopted, is well known (Eton of course). But it only makes sense in relation to *Peter Pan*, when seen as the termination point, or fantasy, of a linguistic trajectory which runs right across the spectrum of educational institutions and practices at that time. Barrie spoke almost all their forms of language – and desired perhaps above all the one that he did not speak. But the biographical reference is important here only because it shows up the complex institutional determinants – at the level of language and education as they bear most directly on the child (Barrie included) – of a work which has given to childhood the transcendant and ahistorical status of a myth.

The alterations carried out on *Peter and Wendy* suggest that it is not just the stylistic features of literary language which clash with the linguistic demands of the elementary school. The cutting out of the narrator's comment on Mr Darling ('He had had a classical education'), and of the more infantile voice which rebels against correct grammar in the name of Peter Pan ('we ought to use the pluperfect and say wakened, but woke is better and was always used by Peter'), removes from the text any linguistic self-consciousness, any drawing attention to language as something whose origins are never safely anonymous (a third person narrator who just *speaks*), nor single, but stem from what might be a multiple and contradictory source. One of the main achievements of many works which are successfully classified as literary (amongst which *Peter and Wendy* cannot really be included) might, therefore, be the extent to which they smooth over these differences, and integrate our own divisions in language into a coherent form. The demand for stability in language (which has, I have argued, been central to one strand of children's literature since the eighteenth century and which appears in so much criticism of children's books) would, therefore, carry a double burden: the securing of our identity as subjects in the world, and a suppression of those aspects of our linguistic-educational history which, because of its cultural divisiveness, give that myth of identity in language so thoroughly the lie. The problem – like so many others – is shown up by Barrie's *Peter and Wendy*, but it is by no means restricted to that book. A more recent children's classic, Richard Adams's *Watership Down* (Adams, 1972), for example, can serve to show a different way of resolving those tensions which, at at least one point in *Peter Pan*'s history, caused it to fall so totally apart.

Watership Down follows the classical adventure format of a pursuit and a struggle for survival, carried out by rabbits who are given by the narrator something of the status of a lost tribe battling against the horrors of advancing civilisation. At the climax of the story, a final chapter suddenly brings to the reader's attention the issue of language and literacy, when a young girl, Lucy, is introduced into the book as a 'Dea ex machina' (the title of the chapter) to save the rabbit, Hazel, from destruction by the farmyard cat.

The moment stands out conspicuously from the rest of the book – because, up to this point, the humans have been villains of the story (it is their development of the land which precipitates the rabbits on their journey); because of the Latin which announces it; and because it is the first time, in a book in which rabbits speak the most finely tuned and cultured English prose (verging on the Biblical in the mythical stories they tell), that dialect comes into the story: ' "Tab!" called Lucy sharply. "Tab! Wha! you got?" . . . "Git out, Tab!" said Lucy. "Crool thing! Let'n alone!" ' (Adams, 1972, pp. 396–7). Lucy's dialect is, however, in transition. She is marked out as self-educated – the only person in the book with knowledge of rabbit life, that knowledge which the narrator provides for the reader and whose source in the work of Mr Lockley's *The Private Life of the Rabbit* is acknowledged before the book starts and at several points in the narration. And she is on her way to the grammar school: 'her father was proud of the way Lucy got on with Doctor. She was proper bright kid – very likely goin' to grammar school an' all, so they told him' (Adams, 1972, p. 398).

The moment is almost an aside, but it fleetingly allows to be

spoken the whole question of the child's relationship to knowledge, culture, language and the schools. Simply brought into
focus here, it is a relationship which forms the prehistory of the
book (the sources of the language in which the author writes) and
the precondition of its reception (the child reader). But it figures,
as it did in *Peter and Wendy*, throughout *Watership Down* – in the
range of its language, which moves from Mr Lockley's nature
study, to the mythical stories of 'El-ahrairah', through a whole
history of literature, which is celebrated in the opening quotations
to every chapter of the book (from Aeschylus and Xenophon to
Malory, Shakespeare, Dr Johnson, Tennyson and Hardy with the
occasional reference to popular literature and one children's book
(*Alice*)). In *Watership Down*, practical down-to-earth knowledge is
what matters (Lucy saves the rabbits), but literate culture is the
framework and final objective of the story (Lucy goes to grammar
school). Writing over fifty years after Barrie, Adams manages to
balance out and coordinate these disparate voices in such a way
that his version of *Watership Down* (as opposed to the film,
book-of-the-film, calendar, long-playing record and ceramic
rabbits) remains the version which is still most widely acclaimed.

What appears so sharply thrown into relief by Barrie's *Peter and
Wendy* reappears here in another form. *Peter and Wendy*'s encounter
with the schools merely reveals a history which lies, necessarily,
behind any children's book (behind any book), occasionally
commented on, but mostly suppressed, or else ordered into the
coherence of what we recognise as successful literary writing.
Children's writers may well have a special relationship to that
history – it may, quite simply, be one of the things to which they
are endlessly returning, something they are writing *about*. Adams,
for example, shares with other children's writers (Garner,
Tolkien) a working over of the origins of culture (more than once
in *Watership Down* the rabbits are described as 'primitives'), which
in his case brings with it a reprobing of the institutional
beginnings of speech (Garner has also commented on the
importance for him as a children's writer of an abrupt transition
from dialect to the Latin of the grammar school).[12] Like the
pleasure which Lucy's father takes in the fact that she is going to
grammar school, Barrie's revelation of the hidden educational
history of Captain Hook is the wholly appropriate finale for *Peter
Pan*.

The issue of literacy in relation to childhood continues to be an area of public policy and concern. In 1972, when *Watership Down* was published, the government commissioned a new report on literacy. We can see it as the official response to a set of dilemmas which were given one possible solution at the time of *Peter Pan* (a response also to some of the effects of that earlier solution). Looking forward from *Peter Pan*, therefore, I want to end this final chapter by taking the Bullock Report as the most recent officially sanctioned statement of how language and literature are in the process of being reconceptualised for the child.

The report was published in 1974 under the title *A Language for Life* – a title whose generality (*a* language for *life*) already signals the broadness of the concept of literacy and culture which it is to offer. Like *Watership Down*, the report opens a number of its chapters with quotations from, or about, literature – Dickens, Hardy, I. A. Richards, J. D. Salinger – plus one from Georges Gusdorf which begins the section on language and learning: 'Man interposes a network of words between the world and himself and thereby becomes master of the world' (Bullock, 1974, p. 47). The purpose of the report – and the effect of *Watership Down* – could therefore be defined as the integration of that more general proposition about mastery of language (and of the world through language) with literature itself.

Unlike the 1910 and 1912 government circulars, the Bullock Report does not wish to differentiate between classes of child. Rather its desire is to redress a balance, to halt a felt decline in standards of literacy (a decline which it traces to the children of the unskilled and semi-skilled workers), and to give back to children as a whole a culture whose carefully constituted divisions of half a century previously are now felt as an obstruction to the possibility of general social advance. The report explains that as a society becomes more complex, so it requires greater 'awareness' and 'understanding' on the part of its members, and its criterion of literacy will rise (Bullock, 1974, p. 11) (the implication is that standards have not necessarily declined but are now felt to be deficient in relation to social needs). For a society whose workforce is now predominantly employed, not in manual labour, but in the service sectors of industry, literacy is the *general* prerequisite for full participation in working life. Accordingly the stress is on a general language policy – language *across* the curriculum, *continuity* between schools (primary and secondary), *cross-age* tutoring and *mixed-ability* teaching (these are just some of the terms used). The idea that the problem can be resolved by these forms of continuity, and by improved teaching methods inside the schools, blinds the report almost completely to what might be some of the divisive institutional origins of the problem it addresses (such as language policy just sixty years before), and the institutional conditions of their perpetuation (the different types of schools in England today). Instead language is seen as something which can cut across and harmoniously reconcile social differences in and of itself, as if language could magically wipe out divisions of which it necessarily forms a part. The report does not address this notion of origins as institution, but sees the source of the difficulty in more privatised terms: 'There is an indisputable gap between the language experience that some families provide and the linguistic demands of school education' (Bullock, 1974, p. 54) (hence the already noted exhortation to mothers: 'When you give your child a bath, bathe him in language' (Bullock, 1974, p. 58)).

It is, I think, precisely this way of conceiving of language (fount of all things) which allows the report to give to literature a similarly universal status: 'It would have been impossible for me to have told anyone what I derived from these novels, for it was nothing less than a sense of life itself' (Richard Wright, *Black Boy*, quoted in Bullock, 1974, p. 124).[13] Quoting F. R. Leavis on the value of literary studies, on the vital *range* of their implication ('literary studies lead constantly outside themselves' (Bullock, 1974, p. 5)), it argues that literature should be allowed to *flow* where the child's interests take it. Thus the earlier distinction between natural and literary language in the schools, described in the first half of this chapter, is replaced with a conception of literature as something fully integral to the child's mind.

It follows from this that language belongs to the 'general context of childcare' (Bullock, 1974, p. 58) and 'child growth' (courses on parenthood which 'direct the emphasis away from mothercraft to child growth as an aspect of human development' (Bullock, 1974, p. 55)), an emphasis which links directly back to the time which saw the emergence of *Peter Pan*. For the word 'mothercraft' which is being moved out here in favour of 'child growth' was itself only introduced into the English language in 1907. Dr John Sykes, medical officer of health for St Pancras, London, and founder of the St Pancras school for mothers, coined the word at a time when concern about infant mortality, precipitated by low recruitment figures for the Boer War, and anxiety about the effects of this on imperialism, produced a renewed concentration on the role of the mother as 'bearer of the Imperial race' ('a matter of Imperial importance', A. Newsholme, 'Infant Mortality', *The Practitioner*, October 1905, p. 494, in Davin, 1978). This moment, taken by historians (Davin, 1978) to show the historical determinations of the seemingly natural values which attach to the status of motherhood, is only one of a number of occasions when social anxiety about one form of policy (in this case imperialism) gravitates for its solution down to the felt source of all subjectivity and social life – that is, the primary relationship between the mother and child. Once again, that which is most 'natural' – mother, child, human development and growth (the unitary condition and eternal sameness invested in the image of each) – serves to syphon off the more urgently needed recognition of the social divisions and conflicts through which their always changing meanings are constituted at any one time.

There is, therefore, no question of denying here that some of the individual recommendations of the Bullock Report may, indeed, represent an advance – better literature for all, one could say, than literature for some (that is, some literature for some children). Rather the point is to draw attention to what I would call the fundamental desire, or even fantasy, which underlines that call. A language for life and a literature for ever – it is the very innocence of the appeal which, like all the other innocents I have tried to examine in this book, requires the scrutiny. For what could be a language for life and a literature for ever, other than the eternal return of the same (the same child and the same literature) which has been one of the drives behind the very persistence of a work like *Peter Pan*?

As you look at Wendy you may see her hair becoming white, and her figure little again, for all this happened long ago. Jane is now a common grown-up with a daughter called Margaret; and every spring cleaning time, except when he forgets, Peter comes for Margaret and takes her to the Neverland, where she tells him stories about himself, to which he listens eagerly. When Margaret grows up she will have a daughter, who is to be Peter's mother in turn; and thus it will go on, so long as children are gay and innocent and heartless. (Barrie, 1911, p. 267)

I started this book by suggesting that there is a way of reading Freud's psychoanalytic writings which offers a decisive challenge to this very *sameness*, which has been given one of its most salient representatives in the shape of *Peter Pan*; that Freud's theory of the unconscious is a challenge above all to just this sameness in that it undermines the idea that psychic life is continuous, that language can give us mastery, or that past and future can be cohered into a straightforward sequence, and controlled. Above all it throws into question the idea that the child can be placed at the beginnings of this process (origins of culture, before sexuality and the word), or, indeed, at the end (the guarantee of a continuity for ourselves and our culture over time). This is not the only reading of Freud, nor is it the one which has received the greatest currency in writing on children's books. It is not, for example, that of Bruno Bettelheim, the psychoanalyst whose writing on children's literature is most widely known.

Psychoanalysis may seem to be remote from the questions of language and literacy which have been the concern of this chapter. But, as if completing the circuit, a recent book by Bettelheim – *On Learning to Read* – brings psychoanalysis into the schools (Bettelheim and Zelan, 1981). The book is important for its insertion of psychoanalysis (the child's subjectivity) into the pedagogic arena – its emphasis on the complexity of the child's access to the processes of 'reading' and 'meaning'. *On Learning to Read* links up the areas which I see as surrounding, producing and perpetuating *Peter Pan*, by demonstrating the proximity between our conceptions of psychic life, of literacy and of writing for the child. It also illustrates what I take as problematic in one way of conceiving their relation.

On Learning to Read belongs firmly in that tradition which wishes to redress a felt degradation of cultural life through the child. In response to a generally acknowledged decline of literacy in America, it makes two main recommendations: an improvement in the literary quality of primary school books, and a fundamental respect for the child's inability to read which, it suggests, is often the child's unconscious response to their essentially degrading lowness. Lowness refers both to a lack of meaning and to an impoverishment of culture as a whole. The new citizenship is being deprived since, faced with the demand to read the present books on offer, some children defeat their teachers by not learning to read at all: 'a Pyrrhic victory that robs the child of his chance to become fully educated, and with it deprives society of a well-educated citizen' (Bettelheim and Zelan, 1981, pp. 138–9). It is a definition of education, literature and culture which carries with it, quite explicitly, a notion of origins ('the first literature probably consisted of myths' (Bettelheim and Zelan, 1981, p. 306)), which is not, I think, unrelated to the emphasis on the living speech of the child (oral culture as the primary truth and the written word as its contamination). The other true speech and supreme embodiment of culture is the Bible: 'in the beginning was the word, and the word was with God, and the word was God' (quoted Bettelheim and Zelan, 1981, p. 53).

What is most striking is the concept of reading and of psychic life which goes with this definition of culture. Reading is magic (if it has never been experienced by the child as magic then the child will be unable to read); it is also an experience which allows the child to master the vagaries of living, to strengthen and fortify the ego, and to integrate the personality – a process ideally to be elicited by the aesthetic coherence of the book. A good book (the Bible, fairy tales and a New England Primer of 1727) is an experience 'in which the total personality is fully involved in the messages conveyed by the text' (Bettelheim and Zelan, 1981, p. 47). Thus the possibility or preservation of culture, the strength of the child's ego, and the integrity and coherence of literary writing are placed in a mutually dependent relation.

There are, however, a number of problems here which are acknowledged by Bettelheim. We can compare, for example, the statements 'I am' and 'we are here', the first words of a Swiss primer which he commends for their assertion of selfhood, with his earlier examination of the nonsense represented by the expression 'I made a simple mistake' (since a contradictory and erring 'I', like the mistake it makes, is never simple) (Bettelheim and Zelan, 1981, pp. 200–1). And we can ask what it means to say that the insights of psychoanalysis, which allow conflict and division to be spoken, could, or should, in any direct way contribute to the educability of the child (this problem is also discussed). More important, what questions about the contents of culture does that very project require us to leave on one side?

For the Bullock Report also recommended fairy tales for the 'strength and simplicity of their origins' (having quoted Tolkien on the accidental and arbitrary nature of their association with childhood (Bullock, 1974, p. 129)); and it also states that 'books compensate for the difficulties of growing up' (Bullock, 1974, p. 125), and that although the names of the most widely read authors vary from one decade to the next, 'the characteristic feature of their books remain much the same' (Bullock, 1974, p. 125) (this after having recommended the introduction of more new modern fiction in the schools). In their emphasis on meaning (a unity), on culture (under threat), and on the integrity of the child's self-expression and growth (the means of ensuring the identity and preservation of the first two), *A Language for Life* and *On Learning to Read* are quite remarkably resonant of each other. With this difference, that, for Bettelheim, it is the very unconscious of the child which, in its resistance to the low quality of con-temporary writing, speaks the truth of a dying culture which goes back to the beginnings of the word.

Once again, this is not to enter into the question of the value of the recommendations made by either piece of writing – the value, for example of the work being done by Bettelheim and Zelan in the schools (the value of that intervention) – but to underline a repetition of terms. It is also to show how the question of writing for children is something which leads off to, or invokes, both psychoanalysis and literacy in the schools (seen here in one historically specific form of relation). Children's fiction does, indeed, 'lead out' of itself – to language, as it is being constituted and culturally defined, to psychic life and subjectivity, as they are being examined, elaborated or repressed. *Peter Pan* is not excep-tional for belonging in the middle of all this. Nor is it, finally, exceptional for the way in which it has managed, or been used, to conceal so much of it from view.

Conclusion

Instead of asking what children want, or need, from literature, this book has asked what it is that adults, through literature, want or demand of the child. By putting the question in this form, I have tried to foreground some (although by no means all) of the complex meanings concealed inside an expression like 'literature for children' whose very clarity and self-evidence (the idea of a service rendered or a gift) seems to work like a decoy or a foil. There is a famous story by Edgar Allan Poe, called 'The Purloined Letter', which has been amply commented on by psychoanalysts and others,[1] in which a detective hired to recover a stolen letter finds it when he abandons the obvious procedure of turning the suspect's apartment upside down and starts looking, not for what is hidden, but for what is *offered* – an opened envelope in the letter rack which is there for all to see. The story can serve as an analogue for the starting-point for this investigation, without the implication, however, that what carries on in the name of children's literature is the perpetration of a crime.

Peter Pan has been at the centre of this enquiry, not because it is the most important, popular or even representative of children's literature (none of these statements is finally tenable), but because it shares with the term 'children's literature' a similar clarity or purity, which has been at the very heart of its mystique. *Peter Pan* has always been assigned the status of a truth (lost childhood, nostalgia or innocence). But if something is too often presented as true, then it starts to look false (like the word 'mystique' itself with its dual connotation of transcendance and of downright mystification). There has always been criticism of *Peter Pan* (normally dismissed in exactly these terms – 'there will always be critics of *Peter Pan*'), and more recently the suggestion

137

that it is dated (Lewis in Kirkpatrick, 1978). But my point has not been to criticise *Peter Pan* or to accuse it of limitation with reference to a world of children's writing which, by removing *Peter Pan* at the appropriate moment, will itself remain intact. The importance of *Peter Pan*, finally, is not whether or not it belongs to the world of children's literature (with the suggestion that if it does not then it has failed). Rather it lies in what *Peter Pan* demonstrates about a fantasy of childhood, with children's literature as just one of the arenas in which this fantasy is played out. Nor is the fantasy which I have described here restricted to the domain of childhood itself. Thus George Boas, describing the myth of the Noble Savage and its remarkable tenacity in the face of the empirical facts (the discovery of primitive man), lists the Child, Woman, the Folk, the Irrational and Neurotic and the Collective Unconscious, as the various places to which this myth has migrated. They are connected by a fantasy of origins – the belief that each one represents an ultimate beginning where everything is perfect or can at least be made good.

The concept 'children's literature' has not – any more than *Peter Pan* itself – been allowed to go unquestioned. Attention has been drawn to the fact that there is no easy way of establishing a relationship between its two terms ('children' and 'literature' (Meek, review of Heins (Meek, 1978(a)), Hunt, 1979). My aim has been to contribute to that discussion by suggesting one of the essential ways in which they might be linked. I see this link as language – not as a simple tool of communication which ensures the passage between the two terms, but language and its vicissitudes, that is, the ordering and structure of language, together with the constant movement, play and instability which underlines its most basic of rules.[2] All writing can be seen as a return to, or reworking of, language; in the case of children's literature this idea of a return is given added meaning by the text's own stated drive towards the child. Children's literature brings together two concepts of origin – that of language and that of childhood – whose relationship it explores. This book has tried to describe some of the restrictions (injunctions, defences) which have historically prescribed the limits of that exploration. For me children's literature cannot be understood as the passive reflection of changing values and conceptions of the child (images *of* childhood); instead I see it as one of the central means through which we regulate our relationship to language and images as such. So often has it seemed to be the case that what is at stake in an image of the child is not the child first and then the image, but the child as the most fitting representative for the gratifying plenitude of the image itself.

The account of children's fiction which I have given here does not claim to be a general history. Its analysis is offered as symptomatic and typical, but not exhaustive. Around children's fiction since the eighteenth century I see a set of barriers constructed which assign the limits to how far children's literature is allowed to go in upsetting a specific register of representation – one which may well be the most coherent, but which is historically delimited and formally constrained. Children's fiction seems to be circumscribed by a moralism which goes way beyond the more transparent didacticism and pedagogy of its earliest modes and into the heart of writing. I would call it an *ethos* of representation, characterised by its basic demand for identity in language, that is, for language as a means to identity and self-recognition. This identity is the prerequisite for the internalisation of rules, precepts and laws which individual books may or may not then require of the child reader, but this form of subjection is, I would argue, secondary and, finally, marginal to the first.

There is a whole domain surrounding children's fiction which is normally placed in opposition to the canons of narrative fiction in the name of rhythm and play. This is the order of folklore, nursery rhyme and nonsense which I have barely touched on in this book. It is, however, the separating out of these two modes of representation which is worthy of note. For as long as the first (rhythm and play) is seen as melody or archaic lore which stretches back in time, and the second (narrative fiction) as the forward progression of advancing literary form, then the challenge of the one to the other, the idea that one might actually erupt inside the other, forcing open the issue of what constitutes continuity in speech, is effectively denied. They remain worlds apart, the distance between them working to transmute and becalm what might otherwise be felt as too present and insistent a difference. Classifying 'otherness' in language as infantile or child-like reduces it to a stage which we have outgrown, even if that stage is imbued with the value of something cherished as well as lost. In the end, the very association of linguistic rhythm and play with childhood becomes a way of setting the limit to what we are allowed to conceive of as a language which does not conform to the normal protocols of representation and speech.

Recently there has been an increasing focus on the shifting registers of language in relation to children's books. This can be seen, for example, in a deliberate foregrounding of narrative conventions (Aidan Chambers, who is in fact classified as a writer for 'new adults', is perhaps the obvious example (Chambers, 1978)), or in the new stress on the narrative activity of the children's writer who thereby becomes a 'fabulator', spinning stories out of words and calling on children to appreciate and actively participate in his task (Margaret Meek on William Mayne (Meek, 1982)). .

All of this relates to, but is finally distinct from, the point which I have wished to make here. I am not asking for a form of writing which, by calling attention to its own fabrication, can claim to be language at its most true, nor for an awareness of language which gives to children's writing the physicality and intimacy of the lost story-telling of long ago. It is the constant association of language in all its forms with a register of truth which is for me the problem (it is no criticism of these writers, therefore, that whenever the possibility of a different language for children is mooted it slides back into the return of the same). My questioning does not bring with it some ideal form of writing which I am wishing to promote for the child. It is a questioning of language itself as the means through which subjective identity, at the level of psychic and sexual life, is constituted and then imposed and reimposed over time. In this context another separation is worth noting in commentaries on children's books which seems to divide up and redistribute the different components of this emphasis, between a new attention to language (the 'poetics' of children's writing) which does not speak of psychic and sexual conflict, and an attention to psychic and sexual conflict in, for example, the fairy tale (Bettelheim) which does not speak of the divisions of language itself.[3]

Children's writing seems to operate according to a régime of attraction which draws the child straight into the path of identification – with the intimacy of the story-telling itself,[4] or with the characters in whom the child recognises himself or herself on the page. I would not call this the 'oppression' of children (the French writer on children's fiction, Marc Soriano, uses this term in a recent interview (*Guardian*, 24 January 1982)). I understood as an activity hideously carried out by the child (no crime). What I am referring to is the very co___ the adult as a subject, a process which the adult then *repeats* through the book which he or she gives to the child. 'Repetition' is more appropriate than 'oppression' because of what it implies by way of something uncertain which therefore has to be constantly reenacted. But I will take from Marc Soriano the idea of restrictive 'determiners' to convey the sense of another scene which lies behind this process, and which continues in force while mostly remaining unspoken.

What is touched on by this issue of the limits of writing is, therefore, the extreme edge of subjectivity, of what is permissible in language before communication and identity start to crumble and break down. All subjects – adults and children – have finally to take up a position of identity in language; they have to recognise themselves in the first-person pronoun and cohere themselves to the accepted register of words and signs. But it is the shift of that 'have to' from a necessity, which is shared by both adult and child, to something more like a command, which passes from one to the other, that seems to find one of its favourite territories in and around the writing of children's books.

The difficulty of this process is partly spoken by *Peter Pan* (it can only ever be spoken in part), but *Peter Pan* has also stood for its denial. The hesitancies of both language and sexuality which have appeared throughout its history cannot be separated from the very force of its image as purity itself, embodied by the eternal child. *Peter Pan* seems to have operated constantly on this edge, as if liable at any one moment to offer its disturbance to view but choosing instead to turn the other face of innocence. Borrowing (and distorting) for a moment one of the most ecstatic moments of *Peter Pan*, we can perhaps compare its success to the success of the high-flier who is greeted with rapturous applause as he or she comes back down to earth. So beautifully does their escapade express the worst fears of one's imagining, and yet also sets these fears to rest by bringing it all back safely to ground. *The Little White Bird*, *Peter and Wendy*, 'The Blot on Peter Pan' all suggest in their different ways that *Peter Pan*'s most dangerous flight has been its passage through the hazards of language. It is perhaps not strange that a work which so totally represents the myth of the eternal child should also show, in some of these lesser-known texts, how adults and children – the language they share and the stories they tell – are bound up in this problematic.

The relative exclusion of modernist experimentation from children's books could possibly be investigated in similar terms. Modernism has been assimilated into popular consciousness very unevenly in relation to the different art forms. I would place children's fiction, together perhaps with experimental film, at the bottom of the list as far as this acceptability is concerned.[5] The resistance to modernism in children's writing, however, requires an explanation which goes beyond questions of facility of reading and ease (the idea that modernist writing is too difficult or disturbing for children who *need* the regulation of narrative form). The investment in a specific theory of literature which is often carried by such a concept of 'need' (literature as a bastion against cultural decay) has been discussed in this book. But it is perhaps also worth pointing to the highly selective way that childhood or children can appear inside this argument. To take the simplest and best-known instance – the early resistance to Picasso's drawings which was couched in the form of a complaint that 'any child could do it' (to which his reputed reply – 'if an adult can still draw like a child at forty he is a genius' – may also be apposite here).[6] For what does this complaint indicate if not that childhood and modernism have some *necessary* relation which in this instance is being critically juxtaposed to the true domain of 'high' or mature art? Which is not to say that the observation about Picasso is right, or that the almost forced separation of children from modernism in literary writing is wrong. It is simply to underline the availability of 'the child' as a concept to buttress different arguments and positions in the establishment of our relationship to changing cultural forms.

Children's writing belongs unequivocally in this wider domain. One of the most important things which *Peter Pan* demonstrates is the way in which children's literature leads off to the multiple centres of our culture where we rediscover the child being constituted by other institutions and practices in their various forms (education, theatrical history, legislative and social reform). Children's literature is not a reflection of these institutions and practices (there is no straightforward relationship of determination between them and children's literature, nor can they be understood as providing the 'context' or 'background' to children's books). Children's literature is one such institution in itself with its own force and its own history (its own regulations and laws), equally active and determinant in its way. Its status as a social entity does not have to be guaranteed with reference to values which are constructed somewhere else – in the space of what is seen as a somehow more social reality. But the fact that children's fiction has its own impetus and its own laws does not mean that it exists as an isolate. One of the risks, as I see it, in establishing a 'poetics' of children's writing, which could undoubtedly develop our understanding of the internal features of children's books, is that it will reinforce the idea of children's literature as something self-contained which can be examined exclusively with reference to itself or to other forms of writing. *Peter Pan* has repeatedly broken the bounds of such a definition, setting a challenge to the integrity of the literary object itself. In doing so it has thrown up a more general problem of history and childhood, which goes beyond the now established historical contingency of our modern conception of the child (Ariès, 1960; Middleton, 1970). For *Peter Pan* has appeared not just as a part *of* history, but equally it has served as a response *to* history, that is, as a response to some of the most divisive and contradictory aspects of one particular historical moment whose difficulties it has been used to disavow. No divisions of culture and literacy (the cry of a literature asserting its freedom from the world), no impingement on the family by the state (the reaction of the state to the mishaps of its earlier policies), no differences finally between children (the same the world over – no class barriers here). Instead the eternal child. The story of *Peter Pan* cannot be fitted into a framework which sees the child as a historical entity which literature reflects. It shows history as a divided entity which is given a false unity in the image of the child.

* * *

In 1987, the Great Ormond Street Hospital's rights on *Peter Pan* will expire. For the past fifty years, by means of the careful selection and negotiation of contracts, the hospital has been able to regulate the interpretation of *Peter Pan*. It has been able to keep *Peter Pan* within certain limits which can be seen as true to the original spirit of the play. Thus the Great Ormond Street Hospital has been the guardian of *Peter Pan*, the bearer of a tradition entrusted to its keeping.

By means of this gift, Barrie gave to *Peter Pan* the meaning of a charity for children, a fact in itself that will be seen by many as more than amply compensating for any ambiguity of readership and address towards the child which might exist in the work itself. Charity is, however, only ever a supplement to deficiency. Even in this link to the hospital for sick children, *Peter Pan* can now tell another story.

In 1948, eleven years after Barrie's death, the National Health Service was founded in England as part of the welfare state with the ideal of sufficient funding which would end the dependency of the health sector on the private benefactions of charity. The 1970s and 1980s have for many been the period which has seen the definitive collapse of this ideal, as public spending has been cut and the existence of the National Health Service has been thrown into question. With advances in medical technology outstripping public funding and nursing budgets overspent, for the Great Ormond Street Hospital the importance of the *Peter Pan* gift has increased in proportion.[7] A bizarre confrontation in which this most precious gift for children, and the state's provision for children, meet and register a fundamental disparity of interest.

The possible loss of *Peter Pan* by the hospital in 1987 consequently has two meanings – the dispersal of *Peter Pan* into the world of free and potentially wild interpretation, and the increasing confrontation of the hospital for children with the limits of its own means. If there is to be an end to *Peter Pan* as we know it, it will therefore be a crisis of meaning (just how far can you go with *Peter Pan?*) and of money (funds for the survival of children as a problem of the state). Thus the dissolution of *Peter Pan*, cultural emblem of our time, will simply release back into the public domain the most pressing and dramatic questions of its history.

Notes

INTRODUCTION

1 Andrew Birkin's book *J. M. Barrie and the Lost Boys* (Birkin, 1979) was dramatised as a three-part television serial for BBC television in October 1978.

CHAPTER 1: PETER PAN AND FREUD

1 References to Freud, by volume number, year of writing (in parenthesis) and first publication of work and page number, are to *The Standard Edition of the Complete Psychological Works of Sigmund Freud*, 24 vols (London: Hogarth, 1953–74), and to the Pelican Freud where available.
2 'the first time he is founded in a *Lye*, it should rather be wondered at as a monstrous Thing in him, than reproved as an ordinary Fault' (Locke, 1693, pp. 153–4).
3 There is no room here to discuss in detail Bettelheim's work on the fairy tale, but it should be noted that, while he interprets Little Red Riding Hood, for example, predominantly in terms of the girl's mastery of Oedipal conflict, he does stress throughout the book the partial nature of his reading and the multifarious and contradictory meanings which fairy tales carry in themselves, and which they may represent for different children at different moments of their psychic life. In fact, I see a tension between Bettelheim's stress on this complexity and his fundamental aesthetic – his belief in the artistic coherence of the fairy tale, the facility of the child's identification with its characters and meaning, and the assumption of its final and necessary resolution of psychic and sexual conflict. For the proximity of this concept of aesthetic form to realist forms of representation, see Chapter 2, pp. 60–5 below.
4 For more explicitly psychoanalytic discussions of *Peter Pan*, see John Skinner, 'James M. Barrie or The Boy Who Wouldn't Grow Up' (Skinner, 1957), Martin Grotjahn, 'The Defenses Against Creative Anxiety in the Life and Work of James Barrie' (a commentary on John Skinner's article) (Grotjahn, 1957), and G. H. Pollock, 'On Siblings, Childhood Sibling Loss and Creativity' (Pollock, 1978).
5 See however Frederick Meisel, 'The Myth of Peter Pan' (Meisel, 1977) – one of the few articles I have found which attempts a reading of *The Little White Bird* and *Peter Pan*, not through Barrie's personal history, but in terms of the

unconscious scenario of narcissistic anxiety and defence which the stories might symbolise for the child.

6 'At lunch, the children asked about "the beginning of the world." Dan (six years one month) insists, whatever may be suggested as "the beginning", there must always have been something before that' (Matthews, 1980, p. 22).

7 References to Beinecke and date refer to the J. M. Barrie collection at the Beinecke Rare Book and Manuscript Library, Yale University; full details are given in the bibliography.

8 For a fuller discussion of this question of stage space in relation to classical and Shakespearian tragedy see André Green, *Un Oeil en trop, le complexe d'Oedipe dans la tragédie* (Green, 1969, trs. 1979), pp. 11–29.

9 The adventure in Sendak's book can be read as a dream. On the first night of *Peter Pan* in 1904, one critic objected that the adventure in *Peter Pan* could not, but his concern was for the adult rather than the child: 'Having regard to the mother's feelings, it is customary in such cases to invoke the aid of the dream. We cannot imagine why Mr. Barrie has not done so.' 'Mr. Barrie's *Peter Pan*-tomime' (*Enthoven*, dated 27 December 1904).

10 Both John Skinner (Skinner, 1957) and Martin Grotjahn (Grotjahn, 1957) (see note 4 above) comment on the failure of the Oedipal resolution in *Peter Pan* (Grotjahn criticises Skinner for not making this explicit enough), but make this the basis of an aesthetic (and moral) condemnation of Barrie himself.

11 On the reinstatement of the *Afterthought* and other aspects of the play mentioned here (e.g. the episode with Tiger Lily) see Note on the 1982 Royal Shakespeare Company production at the Barbican pp. 113–14.

12 See for example Paul Schilder, 'Psychoanalytic Remarks on *Alice in Wonderland* and Lewis Carroll' (Schilder, 1938) which describes nonsense as the effect of incomplete object relations and analyses the *Alice* books in terms of anal regression (a long note to this effect was cut out from this article when it was reprinted in *Aspects of Alice* (Phillips, 1972)); Martin Grotjahn, 'About the Symbolisation of Alice's Adventures in Wonderland' (Grotjahn, 1947), replying to Schilder, rejects the moral judgement which declares the *Alice* books unsuitable for children but also defines them in terms of psychic and artistic regression; John Skinner, 'Lewis Carroll's Adventure's in Wonderland' (Skinner, 1947) does take account of the child's pleasure in illogicality, but again concentrates mainly on Carroll's biography; an exception is Alwyn Baum, 'Carroll's *Alices*: The Semiotics of Paradox' (Baum, 1977) which discusses the *Alice* books in terms of the operations which they carry out on language. There is an interesting intellectual parallel between the psychoanalytic readings of the works of Carroll and Barrie, both analysed psychobiographically in terms of artistic and psychic regression, both receiving attention more recently in terms of the internal structure of the fantasies which their books represent and how these fantasies are symbolised for the child (Baum, 1977; Meisel, 1977). Baum has this to say on the limits of psychobiography in dealing with children's fiction: 'If we accuse Carroll of aberrance in his fantasies, we would similarly have to charge human society, as collective author of the world's traditional literature, with neurosis' (Baum, 1977, p. 87).

CHAPTER 2: ROUSSEAU AND ALAN GARNER

1 'When Rousseau revolutionised the whole frame of children's existence, another era came in, with his notions of teaching in play, and of preserving *uncontaminated* the minds of children by arranging for them an *arbitrary* world' (my italics). 'Literature of Childhood', 1840, p. 143.

2 *Red Shift* (Garner, 1973) is more complex than Garner's other books in terms both of linguistic structure and sexuality; it is now advertised as a book for 'older readers' (Frontispiece to *The Stone Book*, Garner, 1976).

3 Compare for example '[children's] speaking voice has no accent; they cry out, but their words are not accented; and as there is very little energy in their speech, there is little emphasis in their voice' (Rousseau (1762) 1763, I, p. 202). Rousseau is here commenting on the child's inability to combine the three voices of man ('the speaking or articulate, the singing or melodious, and the accented or pathetic', Rousseau (1762) 1763, I, p. 202).

4 See also Hugh Crago, 'Cultural Categories and the Criticism of Children's Literature' (Crago, 1979).

5 For further discussion of Rousseau's philosophy of childhood in relation to colonialism, and the challenge to that conception represented by Marx and Freud, see Richard Appignanesi, 'Some Thoughts on Freud's Discovery of Childhood' (Appignanesi, 1979).

6 The origins of children's publishing are usually identified with the publishing houses of Newbery (Newbery, 1744, 1756) and Boreham (1740–3; see also Muir, 1954); Thomas Day's book was not the first extended narrative for children; a similar use of child actors as the link between collections of stories was used by Sarah Fielding in *The Governess or The Little Female Academy* (Fielding, 1749) which tells the story of Mrs Teachum's [*sic*] boarding establishment for girls.

7 Compare 'Children and the poor understand eloquence, for eloquence speaks to the feelings, which the most unsophisticated have ever the most open to impressions.' 'Literature of Childhood', 1840, p. 158.

8 There were numerous unofficial and pirated editions of the *Peter Parley* books. Goodrich himself licensed the stories to the English publisher, Thomas Tegg, who, although he did not stick to the terms of their agreement, was largely responsible for distributing the tales in England. The tales were also issued by the London publisher John Parker in 1837; for fuller bibliographical detail, see Darton (1932) 1982, pp. 223–6 and Goodrich (1827) 1977, pp. xxi–xlv.

9 'Whether all this Americanism is desirable for our children we doubt, were it only that, for them if possible, we would keep the "pure wells of English undefiled," and cannot at all admire the improvements which it pleases that "go-a-head" nation to claim a right of making in our common tongue.' 'Literature of Childhood', 1840, p. 149; 'the whole fill-page family of the Peter Parleys, with their skin-deep gloss of colloquial familiarity – their "well's," and "you know's," and "what do you think's,".' 'Children's Books', 1844, p. 12.

10 Much controversy surrounds the provenance, authorship and audience of Charles Perrault's fairy tales; these questions, together with the issue of their relationship to oral and literate culture in the seventeenth century, are

examined in Marc Soriano, *Le dossier Charles Perrault* (Soriano, 1972) and in the introduction to Perrault's *Contes* (Perrault, 1967).
11 See Francis Mulhern, *The Moment of Scrutiny* (Mulhern, 1979).
12 In *On Learning to Read*, Bettelheim himself uses Piaget's concepts of assimilation and accommodation to describe changes in the child's response to external stimuli (Bettelheim and Zelan, 1981, pp. 41–2).
13 See especially Rosemary Stones, 'To the Salt Mines' (Stones, 1980) and Jill Paton Walsh, 'The Devil and the Deep Blue Sea' (Paton Walsh, 1980).

CHAPTER 3: PETER PAN AND LITERATURE FOR THE CHILD

1 'A task to be taken up at odd moments, rather than carried through under any kind of pressure. Yet why, one may perhaps wonder, did he tackle it at all? Certainly not to make money. Possibly to please Hodder and Stoughton, or Charles Scribner who were always hoping for a word of new manuscript, but had had none since 1902. Perhaps for the interest of keeping his novelist's hand in. Or perhaps with a wish to fix the story – which was already being re-told by others – in an official and tangible form' (Mackail, 1941, p. 400).
2 The title of this chapter is taken from a famous article by the Hungarian psychoanalyst Sándor Ferenczi, 'Confusion of Tongues between Adults and the Child' (Ferenczi (1933) 1955).
3 Responses to modern writers of children's fiction confirm this interdependency between the classification of children's books and narrative technique; see David Rees, 'Beyond Childhood' (review of Aidan Chambers *Dance on my Grave*) (Rees, 1982) and Josephine Karavasil, 'A Psychological Friend' (review of Helen Cresswell's *Dear Shrink*) (Karavasil, 1982): 'Although said to be for "younger teenagers", the target market for *Dear Shrink* is in fact difficult to determine because [of] the shifting identity of the first-person narrator' (p. 794). Aidan Chambers also suggests that William Mayne places himself outside the range of the child reader by his use of distancing narrative techniques (Chambers, 1977, esp. pp. 73–4) (see also note 4 below).
4 The narration of *Treasure Island* shifts to the Doctor in the centre of the book, but this in no sense upsets the fundamental cohesion of its narrative voice (the Doctor *covers* the story for Jack while he is away), but Stevenson does make use of a more distanced narrator in *Kidnapped* (Stevenson, 1886). Kathleen Tillotson's response to this book (which she compares, along with books including *David Copperfield* and *Great Expectations*, to Charlotte Bronte's *Jane Eyre*) gives an interesting illustration of the importance of a centrally cohered narrator, not just to children's writing, but to aesthetic appraisal of the nineteenth-century novel as a whole (its importance for children's writing embedded in this nineteenth-century aesthetic): 'These are master-pieces of first-person narrative, but they all sacrifice something which *Jane Eyre* retains: the ironic hovering [in *Kidnapped*] sets the reader at a further distance from the central character – invited to understand it better than it does itself, he admires it, and identifies himself with it a shade the less' (Tillotson, 1954, p. 295). Compare Chambers: 'There is an ambivalence about Mayne's work that disturbs his relationship with his child reader. And this is made more unnerving by a fracture between a narrative point of view that seems to want

to ally the book with children, while yet containing a use of narrative techniques that require the reader to dissociate from the story – to retreat and examine it dispassionately' (Chambers, 1977, pp. 73–4).

5 'Children should use and trust their senses for themselves at first hand . . . It is from direct sense stimulus that imagination is born.' (Lucy Boston quoted in Chambers, 1977, p. 86) – Locke's conception of the child's unmediated relationship to the world of sensation so diffused now that it can pass without comment.

6 In *This and That* (Molesworth, 1899), Mrs Molesworth attempts to replicate the child's speech in the form of its incomprehensibility to the adult: 'Sandford was six and Cecilia was five, and though they talked plainly and distinctly on the whole, they had words and ways of their own of speaking, which required explaining to a stranger . . . .' ' "No, That. This doesn't like a 'ouse builded in that way . . . This likes it all along ways, low down" ' (Molesworth, 1899, pp. 1 and 4); but the experiment is finally subordinated to the religious/allegorical motif of the story (the little girl grows up to understand the true moral significance of the story of Faithful which is told to her at the end of the book by her aunt).

7 For other contemporary parodies of literary convention, see Andrew Lang, *Prince Prigio* (Lang, 1889) and Alice Corkran, *The Adventures of Mrs. Wishing-to-be* (Corkran, 1883); Norton Juster's *The Phantom Tollbooth* (Juster, 1962) is often described as a contemporary *Alice*, but I see it more as a sophisticated moral fable (parody of the world and its dis-logic, but also a celebration of the virtues of endeavour and fortitude – Dischord and Dynne banished, Rhyme and Reason restored – which at many points brings it closer to Bunyan than to Carroll).

8 E. Salmon in *Juvenile Literature as it is* (Salmon, 1888), quoting from a questionnaire of 2000 boys and girls, lists Dickens, Kingston, Scott, Verne and Marryat as the five most popular writers for boys, Dickens, Scott, Kingsley, Charlotte Yonge and Shakespeare for girls; also *The Boys' Own Paper* is cited as the second favourite magazine for girls after *The Girls' Own Paper*; see also Amy Cruse, *The Victorians and their Books* (Cruse, 1935, Chapter 14: 'A Young Victorian's Library') and Eleanor Farjeon, *A Nursery in the Nineties* (Farjeon, 1935).

9 The first two serialised stories in vol. I of *The Girls' Own Paper* (1880) ('Zara' and 'Three Years of a Girl's Life') are anonymous; Dinah Mulock is listed as a contributor to the second volume; other writers such as Alice Corkran also became contributors to the magazine. The first serialised story of *The Boys' Own Paper* (1879) ('From Powder Monkey to Admiral, or, the Stirring Days of the British Navy') was by W. H. G. Kingston. Darton describes *The Boys' Own Paper* as an 'institution', *The Girls' Own Paper* as 'useful' rather than 'inspired' (Darton (1932) 1982, p. 304).

10 Charlotte Yonge in *What Books to Lend and What to Give* (Yonge, 1887) includes a separate chapter on books for boys, but not for girls: 'Boys are here treated as a separate subject. The mild tales that girls will read simply to pass away the time are ineffective with them. Many will not read at all' (Yonge, 1887, p. 29). The statement is all the more remarkable in that Charlotte Yonge was herself one of the most popular writers for girls (see note 8 above). However her comment can be misleading. The construction of girls' books as a

'miscellany' – the absence of the adventure story and the lack of an equivalent institution for girls to the boys' public school which was to become the basis of a whole literary genre (see Chapter 5, note 6 below) – can easily give the impression that books for girls are somehow undetermined or without history. In fact the book for girls can be traced right back to the beginnings of children's fiction in the eighteenth century (Sarah Fielding, *The Governess or The Little Female Academy*, 1749); in Mrs Sherwood's *The Fairchild Family* (Sherwood, 1818) the pedagogic format is picked up and domesticated (Mrs Fairchild educates her children at home); the domesticated/moral stories associated with girls' writers of the nineteenth century could be seen, therefore, as giving continuity to this earlier literary history.

CHAPTER 4: PETER PAN AND COMMERCIALISATION OF THE CHILD

1 Some figures have, however, slipped through. The Broadway production of 1954 made £27 500 ('*Peter Pan* earns Hospital £27,500', *Daily Mail*, 26 February 1955); in 1962, Berkeley Films paid £35 714 for the film rights which led to a legal dispute between Berkeley and Disney followed by a new agreement in 1967 that £5000 was to be paid for a twelve-month option on the film and £45 000 on exercise of option ('Appeal in *Peter Pan* Film Case', *The Times*, 25 January 1967); Universal Pictures had an option on the film which expired on 4 April 1975; the film is now contracted to Paramount. By 1964, the royalties on *Peter Pan* were reported as totalling £500 000 used to build a new wing, X-ray department and 26-bed ward ('Before Tomorrow's Diamond Jubilee: The Story Behind the Story of *Peter Pan*', *Daily Mail*, 17 December 1964).

2 Milton Shulman in the *Evening Standard* ('Barrie's Heroes Win Through', 21 December 1979) and Irving Wardle in *The Times* ('*Peter Pan*', 21 December 1979); also: 'Part of the attraction of *Peter Pan* is that the production never changes' (Jane Ellison, 'Tinkerbell Lives', *Evening Standard*, 21 December 1978) and 'The fantasy, nearly three-quarters of a century old now, can still keep one listening and watching; however this speech or the other seems ripe for cutting, it is clear that the strange old piece is uncuttable' (*The Lady*, 18 January 1979).

3 F. J. H. Darton, 'The Youth of a Children's Magazine', *Cornhill*, May 1932, reprinted as Appendix 4 to Darton, *Children's Books in England*, 1982 edition, edited by Brian Alderson (pp. 339–48).

4 See also G. R. Sims, *Without the Limelight* (Sims, 1900, Chapter 1 'The Christmas Fairy', pp. 1–18); Sims starts his account of theatrical life with a description of the dress rehearsal of Dick Whittington at the Theatre Royal, Northerton.

5 Brian Alderson, 'Some Additional Notes on Victorian and Edwardian Times', Appendix 1 to Darton, *Children's Books in England*, 1982 edition, edited by Brian Alderson (pp. 316–31).

6 Writing in 1954, Roger Lancelyn Green describes the pantomime as 'a dying tradition fifty years ago' and yet singles it out from among the changes that

Barrie carried out on his earlier versions of the play as an element which 'fought harder for expression' (Green, 1954, p. 65).

7 I am indebted in this section to Brian Crozier's unpublished PhD thesis, 'Notions of Childhood in London Theatre 1880–1905' (Cambridge, 1981).

8 The Lost Boys were played by girls up to 1928 (Green, 1954, p. 80).

9 See J. T. Grein, 'The Drama in London in 1907' (*The Green Room Book*, 1908) (references to John Valentine, *The Stronger Sex*, W. S. Maugham, *Lady Frederick*, W. J. Locke, *The Morals of Marcus*); Sidney Dark, 'The Theatrical Season of 1908, a Retrospect and Review' (*The Green Room Book*, 1909) (references to Charles Dickens, *The Mystery of Edwin Drood* and W. J. Locke, *The Beloved Vagabond*); J. M. Barrie's *The Little Minister* (1891) was produced in a stage version in Washington and London in 1897; the link – from book to play – also worked the other way round, with booksellers commenting on the popularity of books connected with the stage or based on contemporary plays ('Wholesale Report of the Bookselling Trade', *The Bookman*, 22 (127), April 1902).

10 Frederick Farrar, author of *Eric, or, Little by Little* (Farrar, 1858), makes a similar point in relationship to the reading of his youth: 'the blight of cheap literature had not yet descended upon the land . . . the schoolboy of those days was at least saved, in spite of himself, from becoming the debauchee of shoddy fiction' (quoted in Darton (1932) 1982, p. 288).

11 Also Francis King in the *Sunday Telegraph*, 24 December 1978: 'I long to see some director like Jonathan Miller or John Dexter take a totally new look at one of the few indisputable masterpieces of the twentieth-century English theatre, with Peter played either by a boy – as Barrie originally intended – or by some male adult with the boyish physique and choreographic and theatrical gifts of a Wayne Sleep.' In the 1982 Barbican production Peter Pan was played for the first time by a boy (severance of the last link with pantomime and passage into maturity).

CHAPTER 5: PETER PAN, LANGUAGE AND THE STATE

1 'A most grateful son of our Dear Mother to the headmaster and to all her pupils. Greeting! this 4th day of June 18—, from the Moluccas, James Hook, Eton for ever.'

2 'Report of the Books and Apparatus Sub-Committee, July 19, 1915', Greater London Record Office and Library, London County Council Education Minutes, 1915, 2, 28 July 1915, p. 164. Originally set up in 1872 under the School Boards to give instructions to local school managers (and then teachers from 1899) on the selection of books for use in schools, the policies of this Committee were adopted by the County Council in 1904.

3 The 1870 Education Act legislated for the state provision of elementary education by locally elected agencies, the School Boards, to supplement, where necessary, schooling provided by religious denominations; the Act is related by historians to shifts in the workforce in the second half of the nineteenth century which released the working-class child as an object of education (the development of a casual labour force) (see Simon, 1960, pp. 337–67 and Middleton, 1970); attendance became compulsory in 1880. The

1902 Education Act was directed primarily at secondary education; it was introduced partly as a check to the increasing infiltration by the School Boards, via High Grade Technical and Evening Classes, into the domain of a predominantly private secondary education. The Act provided for state aid to the voluntary schools (thus secured to the state) and for denominational instruction in the state schools (a victory for the Anglican High Church Party in collaboration with the Liberal-Unionists). It was resisted by the Nonconformists and by the School Boards which were effectively liquidated when the whole of educational policy became assimilated to the County Councils (see Halévy, 1926 and Rogers, 1959).

4 The Taunton Commission of 1864–8, investigating 'middle' (that is non-public) schools, had recommended a class-based tripartite division of the educational system (upper and professional, mercantile and higher commercial, upper working class). Despite the inclusion of secondary education in general state policy after 1902, it is clear that the three types of school – public, secondary and elementary – correspond to and reinforce such a division. Sir Francis Sandford makes the distinction between elementary and secondary education the basis of his introduction to Matthew Arnold's *Reports on the Elementary Schools 1852–82* (Arnold, 1899): 'Education should be based upon three principles – the mean, the possible, the becoming, these three. The term "mean", used here in the ordinary Aristotelean sense, seems, as applied to elementary education, to be equivalent to what Mr. Forster called "a *reasonable* amount of instruction"; not confined to the three R's on the one hand, not trenching on the domain of secondary education on the other' (Sandford, Introduction to Arnold, 1899, p. viii).

5 For further discussion of this issue and of the general argument on which this chapter is based, see René Balibar's examination of national educational policy on language in post revolutionary France (Balibar, 1974).

6 In 1864, the Clarendon Commission, investigating the nine leading public schools, recommended the retention of classical languages and literature as the central part of the curriculum, together with the introduction of arithmetic or mathematics, one modern language, one branch of science, either drawing or music, ancient or modern history, and a command of 'pure grammatical English' (quoted in Darwin, 1929, p. 110); for the public school response to the Commission and their resistance to the introduction of new subjects, see *The Public Schools From Within*, 1906, esp. Introduction, p. xii, and T. E. Page (Assistant Master of Charterhouse School), 'Classics' (pp. 3–11); also Darwin, 1929, Chapter 8: 'The Curriculum and the Upheaval of the Royal Commission' (pp. 100–11) and Mack, 1941, Chapter 1: 'The Public School Commission' (pp. 3–49).

7 Thomas Hughes, *Tom Brown's Schooldays, Rugby, by an old boy* (Hughes, 1857), Frederick W. Farrar, *Eric, or, Little by Little, a tale of Rosslyn School* (Farrar, 1858), Francis Anstey, *Vice Versa, or, A Lesson to Fathers* (Anstey, 1882), Talbot Baines Reed, *The Fifth Form at St. Dominic's, a school story* (Reed, 1887). Thomas Hughes' book was by no means the first school story (see Fielding, 1749), but his book can none the less be seen as a decisive moment in the establishment of the boys' school story as a *genre*.

8 Classics were still the basis of the civil service entry examinations; on the close links between the public schools and the civil service, see Mack, 1941, esp. Chapter 7: 'Imperialism' (pp. 209–64); Guttsman, 1954; Woodruff, 1954

and Wilkinson, 1964; also Pitcairn (ed.), *Unwritten Laws and Ideals of Active Careers* (Pitcairn, 1899), esp. Rev. J. E. C. Welldon (late schoolmaster of Harrow), 'Schoolmasters' (pp. 269–85) and *The Public Schools from Within* (1906), esp. Rev. T. L. Papillon, 'The Public Schools and Citizenship': 'Thus equipped he goes out into the world, and bears a man's part in subduing the earth, ruling its wild folk, and building up the Empire' (p. 283).

9 See Henry Wyld, *The Place of the Mother Tongue in the National Education* (Wyld, 1906) and Brian Hollingsworth, 'The Mother Tongue and Public Schools in the 1860s' (Hollingsworth, 1974); also Richard Wilson, *Macmillan's Sentence Building*: 'Remember also that your mother-tongue is a precious gift to you from many generations of patriotic Englishmen' (Wilson, 1914(a), Pupil's Companion, 7, p. 3).

10 This whole question has to be seen in the context of resistance to new utilitarian concepts of education on the part of the public school. Gladstone had written to the Clarendon Commission criticising the 'low utilitarian argument in matter of education' (quoted in Darwin, 1929, p. 110); Rev. T. L. Papillon specifically criticises the public school for the low level of teaching relevant to the Empire (geography, English history and literature, ethnology and religions) as part of his general exhortation 'learn to think Imperially' (*The Public Schools from Within*, 1906, p. 284).

11 Barrie's educational history was even more complex than this. It includes a Free Church School, a number of private schools, a seminary, the Glasgow and Forfar Academies as well as the Dumfries Academy which he attended before going on to Edinburgh University in 1878. Many of these changes were determined by his elder brother's career (he was classics master at Glasgow Academy from 1867 to 1871) (see Mackail, 1941, pp. 18–73).

12 'I realised that I had been taught (if only by default) to suppress, and even deride, my primary native North-West Mercian tongue.' 'All my writing has been fuelled by the instinctive drive to speak with a true and Northern voice integrated with the language of literary fluency.' Alan Garner, 'The Fine Anger' in Fox and Hammond (eds), *Responses to Children's Literature*, 1978, pp. 1–12 (p. 5 and p. 10).

13 The Bullock Report starts its section on literature by acknowledging criticism of the definition of literature contained in the idea that 'all pupils, including those of very limited attainment, need the civilising experience of contact with great literature and can respond to its universality'; however, it returns to this same definition: 'In Britain the tradition of literature teaching is one which aims at personal and moral growth, and in the last two decades this emphasis has grown. It is a soundly based tradition' (Bullock, 1974, pp. 124, 125) – the concept of personal and moral growth is given the same generalising validity as the earlier stress on civilising experience. All Leavis's work testifies to the proximity of these two definitions of literature and its values.

CONCLUSION

1 See Marie Bonaparte, 1958, vol. 2, pp. 580–3, and Jacques Lacan (1957) 1972.

2 For a different emphasis on the question of language in relation to children's books in terms of reader response, based on the psychology of the reading

process and theories of literary communication, see Fox and Hammond (eds), *Responses to Children's Literature*, 1978, and Aidan Chambers, 'The Reader in the Book' (Chambers, 1977).

3 A vivid demonstration of the gap between these two concerns is given in *Signal*, 28, January 1979: an article by Robert Westall ('How Real Do You Want Your Realism?' (Westall, 1979)) which points out the limits – in terms of sexuality and death – of what is allowed to be spoken in children's books (despite the common assumption of an ever increasing 'realism' of children's writing today); and Peter Hunt's analysis of William Mayne ('The Mayne Game: An Experiment in Response' (Hunt, 1979)) in terms of the aesthetic assumptions about language which underpin his acceptance and/or rejection as a children's writer. Although I agree with many of the points made in this article, I would none the less want to distinguish myself from Hunt's overall project which seems to be, along with that of a number of children's book critics, to establish the literary 'value' and credentials of children's writers and children's book criticism (the ultimate fantasy, perhaps, of children's book criticism that it should come of age and do what the adults (that is adult critics) have been doing all along) (see also Hunt, 1976).

4 In a rarely mentioned article, Lilli Peller discusses the story-telling situation in terms of the child's sexual curiosity about the adult's activities ('Daydreams and Children's Favourite Books', Peller, 1956).

5 A related and similar point seems to be made by Margaret Meek in a review article of Paul Heins *Crosscurrents of Criticism* in 1978: 'Underneath the very weight of it all, I shift uneasily, feeling that the collection of these pieces has produced a view of children's literature which is the survival of a nineteenth-century category without a real picture of a twentieth-century child' (Meek, 1978(a), p. 381); see also Hunt, 'The Mayne Game' (Hunt, 1979) and note 3 above; and Hugh Crago's excellent article, 'Cultural Categories and the Criticism of Children's Literature' (Crago, 1979) which challenges the assumptions on which the resistance to modernism in relation to children's writing seems to rest: 'If books can "injure" their readers through their emotional content, then so too (it seems) can children be done intellectual harm by "premature" exposure to unregulated vocabulary, complex ideas, ambiguous plot resolutions or (in the case of picture books) sophisticated or non-representational art styles' (Crago, 1979, pp. 147–8).

6 See George Melly and J. R. Glaves-Smith, *A Child of Six Could Do It!* (Melly and Glaves-Smith, 1973) esp. cartoon 64, p. 62 and cartoon 66, p. 64.

7 The possibility of abolishing the National Health Service in favour of privatised medicine has been discussed by the present Conservative Cabinet; government spending on the health sector is estimated to have increased nationally by approximately one and a half per cent under the Conservative administration of 1979–83, but this has not been adequate to meet increasing costs. In November 1982, under the pressure of an expected deficit for the coming year of £1m, the Great Ormond Street Hospital voted to close down Tadworth Court Hospital, its medical centre for the care of chronically ill children. See 'Children's hospital beds saved by grant', *The Times*, 30 October 1982, 'Whisper who cares', *Sunday Times*, 31 October 1982, and 'Must the caring stop? The Tadworth Affair, sick children at risk', *Sunday Times*, 21 November 1982. Tadworth has now been given a temporary reprieve by a government grant.

Bibliography

PETER PAN in chronological order

1. *Publications*

Barrie, J. M. *The Little White Bird* (London: Hodder and Stoughton, 1902)

Barrie, J. M. *Peter Pan in Kensington Gardens*, with drawings by Arthur Rackham (London: Hodder and Stoughton, 1906)

O'Connor, D. S. (ed). *Peter Pan Keepsake*, the story of *Peter Pan* retold from Mr Barrie's fantasy, foreword by W. T. Stead (London: Chatto and Windus, 1907)

O'Connor, D. S. and Alice B. Woodward. *The Peter Pan Picture Book* (London: Bell, 1907)

Herford, O. *The Peter Pan Alphabet* (London: Hodder and Stoughton, 1907)

Drennan, G. D. *Peter Pan, His Book, His Pictures, His Career, His Friends*, retold in story form from J. M. Barrie's dramatic fantasy (London: Mills and Boon, 1909)

Barrie, J. M. *Peter and Wendy*, illustrated by F. D. Bedford (London: Hodder and Stoughton, 1911)

O'Connor, D. S. *The Story of Peter Pan*, a reading book for use in schools, with illustrations by Alice B. Woodward (London: Bell, 1912)

E.E.L. 'Peter Pan and Wendy' a poem on the play in *English Poetry 1870–1912* (London: Stationers' Hall, 1912)

Chase, Pauline. *Peter Pan in The Real Never Never Land* (London: Horace Cox, 1913)

Edmonston, Maysie. *The Duke of Christmas Daisies and other fairy plays* adapted from *The Little White Bird* of Sir J. M. Barrie (London: Wells, Gardner, Darton, 1914)

Barrie, J. M. *Peter Pan and Wendy*, the story of *Peter Pan* extracted from *Peter and Wendy*, illustrated by F. D. Bedford, authorised school edition (London: Henry Frowde, Hodder and Stoughton, 1915)

Hassall, J. *The Peter Pan Painting Book* (London: Lawrence and Jellicoe, 1915)

O'Connor, D. S. *The Story of Peter Pan For Little People*, simplified from Daniel O'Connor's story of Sir J. M. Barrie's fairy play, illustrated by Alice B. Woodward (London: Bell, 1919)

155

Barrie, J. M. *Peter Pan and Wendy*, illustrated by Mabel Lucie Áttwell (London: Hodder and Stoughton, 1921)

Byron, May. *The Little Ones' Peter Pan and Wendy*, retold for the nursery, Mabel Lucie Attwell (London: Hodder and Stoughton, 1925(a))

Byron, May. *J. M. Barrie's Peter Pan and Wendy* retold for boys and girls, pictures by Mabel Lucie Attwell (London: Hodder and Stoughton, 1925(b))

Barrie, J. M. 'The Blot on Peter Pan', in *The Treasure Ship*, edited by Cynthia Asquith (London: Partridge, 1926(a))

Barrie, J. M. 'Neil and Tintinnabulum', in *The Flying Carpet* edited by Cynthia Asquith (London: Partridge, 1926(b))

Barrie, J. M. *Peter Pan* in *The Plays of J. M. Barrie* (London: Hodder and Stoughton, 1928)

Milford, H. *Peter Pan's Play Book* (London: Oxford University Press, 1929)

Byron, May. *The Littlest Ones, Peter Pan and Wendy*, retold for the nursery, illustrated by Kathleen Atkins (London: Hodder and Stoughton, 1930)

Byron, May. *J. M. Barrie's Peter Pan and Wendy*, retold for boys and girls, pictures by Mabel Lucie Attwell (London: Hodder and Stoughton, Colour Books, 1938)

Byron, May. *The Nursery Peter Pan and Wendy*, illustrated by Kathleen Atkins (London: Hodder and Stoughton, Nursery Books, 1938)

Barrie, J. M. The Blampied edition of *Peter Pan*, original text of *Peter and Wendy*, newly illustrated by Edmund Blampied (London: Hodder and Stoughton, 1939)

Barrie, J. M. *Peter Pan*, play edition, illustrations by John Morton-Sale, 'Peter Pan Books' (from 9 years) (London: Hodder and Stoughton, 1942)

Barrie, J. M. *Peter Pan*, illustrations by Nora S. Unwin, 'Peter Pan Books' (from 9 years) (London: Hodder and Stoughton, 1951)

Byron, May. *Peter Pan*, retold for the nursery, illustrated by Mabel Lucie Attwell, 'Peter Pan Books' (for 3 to 6 year olds) (Leicester: Brockhampton Press, 1952)

Disney, W. E. *Walt Disney's Peter Pan*, based on the play by Sir J. M. Barrie (USA: Walt Disney Productions, 1952)

Barrie, J. M. *Peter Pan in Kensington Gardens*, illustrated by Arthur Rackham, 'Peter Pan Books' (from 9 years) (London: Hodder and Stoughton, 1953)

Bedford, Annie N. *Disney's Peter Pan and Wendy*, 'Peter Pan Books' (London: Hodder and Stoughton, 1953)

Byron, May. *Peter Pan in Kensington Gardens*, illustrated by Arthur Rackham, 'Peter Pan Books' (for 6 to 8 year olds) (London: Hodder and Stoughton, 1953)

Byron, May. *The Walt Disney Illustrated Peter Pan and Wendy*, 'Peter Pan Books' (for 8 to 9 year olds) (Leicester: Brockhampton Press, 1953)

Pearl, Irene. *Walt Disney's Peter Pan*, retold from the original story by J. M. Barrie, 'Peter Pan Books' (for 3 to 6 year olds) (Leicester: Brockhampton Press, 1953)

Winn, Alison. *Walt Disney's Peter Pan*, retold from the original story by J. M. Barrie 'Peter Pan Books' (for 6 to 8 year olds) (Leicester: Brockhampton Press, 1953)

Barrie, J. M. *J. M. Barrie's Peter Pan and Wendy* (London: Hodder and Stoughton, Juvenile Productions, 1955)

Groom, A. *Peter Pan and Wendy*, with five pop-up pictures (London: Birn, by arrangement with Hodder and Stoughton, 1955)

Barrie, J. M. *When Wendy Grew Up*, foreword by Sidney Blow (Edinburgh: Nelson, 1957)

Derwent, Lavinia. *The Story of Peter Pan*, illustrated by Carla Ruffinelli (Glasgow: Collins, Silver Torch Series, 1957)

Jones, O. *Nursery Peter Pan*, specially edited for very young children, colour plates by Mabel Lucie Attwell, drawings by J. S. Goodall (Leicester: Brockhampton Press, 1961)

Graham, Eleanor and E. Ardizzone. *J. M. Barrie's Peter Pan*, the story of the play (Leicester: Brockhampton Press, 1962)

Barrie, J. M. *Peter Pan*, a fantasy in five acts, acting edition (London: Hodder and Stoughton, 1964)

Derwent, Lavinia. *The Story of Peter Pan*, illustrated by Carla Ruffinelli (London and Glasgow: Collins, Re-told Classics No. 4, 1964)

Owen, R. (ed). *The Golden Book of Peter Pan* (London: Newnes, 1965)

Barrie, J. M. *Peter Pan* (Harmondsworth: Puffin Books, 1967)

2. Manuscripts

The Walter Beinecke Jnr Collection at the Beinecke Rare Book and Manuscript Library, Yale University, contains the main collection of *Peter Pan* manuscripts. Details of the first draft of *Peter Pan* (*Anon*, 1904) and the Lord Chamberlain's Copy (*Peter Pan*, 1904) are given in Roger Lancelyn Green, *Fifty Years of Peter Pan* (Green, 1954). The following is a list of the Beinecke manuscripts which have been most relevant to this book.

Llewellyn Davies, P. *The Boy Castaways of Black Lake Island* (London: published by J. M. Barrie in the Gloucester Road, 1901) (Beinecke B276, 1901)

Barrie, J. M. *Anon*, two typescripts, with autograph manuscript revisions, of Act III of the three-act version of the play, 1904; varies from other texts of Act III in the Barrie Collection and from the text published in *The Plays of J. M. Barrie* (Barrie, 1928) (Beinecke P45, 1904)

Barrie, J. M. *Anon*, typescript of the three-act version of the play (with manuscript revisions in an unidentified hand and interleaved with lighting-plots, stage business and prompt cues in several unidentified hands) used in the 1904 production (Act III is incomplete); accompanied by one leaf labelled Scene v of a version of Act III. Produced in London 27 Dec. 1904 at the Duke of York's Theatre; varies from the text published in *The Plays of J. M. Barrie* (Barrie, 1928) (Beinecke P45, 1904–5B)

Barrie, J. M. *Peter Pan*, autograph manuscript of Scenes ii and iv from Act III, 1904–5; Scene ii is similar to the text of the same scene, P45 1904–5B; most of the text of Scene iv is published in Roger Lancelyn Green, *Fifty Years of Peter Pan* (Green, 1954) (Beinecke P45, 1904–5)

Barrie, J. M. *Peter Pan, or, the Boy Who Wouldn't Grow Up*, a play in five acts, typescript of Act I; second preliminary leaf 'A Note. On the Acting of a Fairy Play', 1905; varies from other copies of Act I in the Barrie Collection and from the text published in *The Plays of J. M. Barrie* (London: Hodder and Stoughton, 1928); 'A note. On the Acting of a Fairy Play' is published in Roger Lancelyn Green, *Fifty Years of Peter Pan* (Green, 1954) (Beinecke P45, 1905)

Barrie, J. M. *Peter Pan*, two typescripts (variants) of Acts II–V of the five-act version of the play, with autograph manuscript revisions, prepared for the first American production, 1905; produced in Washington November 1905; varies from other copies of Acts II–V in the Barrie Collection and from the text published in *The Plays of J. M. Barrie* (Barrie, 1928) (Beinecke P45, 1905B)

Barrie, J. M. *Peter Pan*, typescript of Act III of the five-act version of the play, 1905; varies from other copies of Act III in the Barrie Collection and from the text published in *The Plays of J. M. Barrie* (Barrie, 1928) (Beinecke P45, 1905C)

Barrie, J. M. *Peter Pan*, typescript of Act III of the five-act version of the play with autograph manuscript revisions, 1905; varies from other copies of Act III in the Barrie Collection and from the text published in *The Plays of J. M. Barrie* (Barrie, 1928) (Beinecke P45, 1905E)

Barrie, J. M. *Peter Pan*, typescript of Act V of the five-act version of the play, dated 13 June 1905; varies from the text published in *The Plays of J. M. Barrie* (Barrie, 1928) (Beinecke P45, 1905F)

Barrie, J. M. *An Afterthought*, autograph manuscript, with revisions, of an epilogue to the play *Peter Pan*, with a signed note dated March 1908 ('To Hilda Trevelyan, My incomparable Wendy'); produced in London, 22 February 1908 at the Duke of York's Theatre; published in *When Wendy Grew Up* (Barrie, 1957) accompanied by a signed manuscript in the hand of Hilda Trevelyan explaining how the play came to be written and produced and how the manuscript came to be given to her (Beinecke P45, 1908B)

Barrie, J. M. *An Afterthought*, typescript of an epilogue to the play *Peter Pan*, with autograph manuscript revisions and manuscript revisions in Hilda Trevelyan's hand, 1908; produced in London, 22 February 1908 at the Duke of York's Theatre; published in *When Wendy Grew Up* (Barrie, 1957) accompanied by a TLS from the Assistant Comptroller in the Lord Chamberlain's Office to Sidney Blow, concerning *An Afterthought*, 22 May 1956 (Beinecke P45, 1908C)

Barrie, J. M. *An Afterthought*, typescript of an epilogue to the play *Peter Pan*, 1908 at the Duke of York's Theatre: published in *When Wendy Grew Up* (Barrie, 1957) (Beinecke P45, 1908D)

Barrie, J. M. *Jas Hook at Eton, or, The Solitary*, autograph manuscript short story dated Jan. 1925; originally written for publication in *The Flying Carpet*, ed. Cynthia Asquith (Barrie 1926(b)), replaced by 'Neil and Tintinnabulum' (Beinecke P45, 1925, cf. also P45, 1927)

Barrie, J. M. *The Blot on Peter Pan*, autograph manuscript of a short story signed and dated 9 April 1926; varies from the text published in *The Treasure Ship*, ed. Cynthia Asquith (Barrie, 1926(a)), accompanied by page 5 of another version of the story (Beinecke P45, 1926)

Barrie, J. M. *The Blot on Peter Pan*, typescript short story with autograph manuscript revisions, dated 9 April 1926; varies from the text published in *The Treasure Ship*, ed. Cynthia Asquith (Barrie, 1926(a)) (Beinecke P45, 1926B)

Barrie, J. M. *The Truth about Peter Pan*, autograph manuscript with corrections in Barrie's hand, 1926; a revised version of this story entitled 'The Blot on Peter Pan' was published in *The Treasure Ship*, ed. Cynthia Asquith (New York: Scribner's Sons, 1926) (Beinecke P45, 1926C)

Barrie, J. M. *Capt Hook at Eton*, autograph manuscript signed of a speech delivered to the First Hundred at Eton College, 7 July 1927; published in the

London *Times*, 8 July 1927; accompanied by a typescript of the speech with autograph manuscript revisions (Beinecke P45, 1927)

Barrie, J. M. 'To the Five', autograph manuscript dedication of the play *Peter Pan*, accompanied by 5 leaves of another manuscript version of the dedication and by 1 leaf of notes (Beinecke P45, 1928)

Barrie, J. M. *Peter Pan, or, the Boy Who Would Not Grow Up*, autograph manuscript of the five-act version of the play prepared for publication, signed and dated 18 July 1928; varies from other copies of the play in the Barrie Collection and from the text published in *The Plays of J. M. Barrie* (London: Hodder and Stoughton, 1928) presentation inscription on fly-leaf ('M.S. Of Peter Pan. The only one in existence so far as I know, to Cynthia Asquith from her affectionate J. M. Barrie', December 1928); presentation inscription on verso of free front end of paper ('for Simon Asquith from his mother Cynthia Asquith') (Beinecke P45, 1928B)

Barrie, J. M. *Peter Pan or the Boy who would not Grow Up*, typescripts of Acts I–IV of the five-act version of the play with autograph manuscript revisions; similar to the text published in *The Plays of J. M. Barrie* (Barrie, 1928) (Beinecke P45, 1928C)

3. *Articles on, references to, programmes, performances based on, etc.*

Quiller-Couch, A. T. 'Mr. J. M. Barrie's New Novel *The Little White Bird*', *The Bookman*, 23 (134), November 1902

'The Little White Bird', *Times Literary Supplement*, 14 November 1902

'Mr. Barrie's New Book *The Little White Bird*', *The Publisher's Circular*, 15 November 1902

Peter Pan, programme of 1904 production, London, the Duke of York's Theatre, (*Enthoven*, dated 27 December 1904)

'Mr. Barrie's *Peter Pan*-tomime', review article, n.l. (*Enthoven*, dated 27 December 1904)

'Duke of York's Theatre', review article, n.l. (*Enthoven*, dated 27 December 1904)

'*Peter Pan*, The New Play by J. M. Barrie at the Duke of York's Theatre', *The Sketch*, 4 January 1905

'*Peter Pan*, at the Duke of York's', *Illustrated London News*, 7 January 1905

'*Peter Pan* at the Duke of York's', *The Sketch*, 18 January 1905

'Mr. Barrie's Fantasy at the Duke of York's', *The Sketch*, 15 February 1905

' "The Child Barrie's" Fantasy at the Duke of York's', *The Sketch*, 15 February 1905

'Pantomime in the Present', *The Tatler*, 6 December 1905

'*Peter Pan* at the Duke of York's', *Illustrated London News*, 30 December 1905

Noyes, A. 'The Boy Who Wouldn't Grow Up', *The Bookman*, 29, 171 (December 1905)

Peter Pan, programme of 1905 production, London, the Duke of York's Theatre, 26 January 1906

Peter Pan, programme of 1906 production, London, the Duke of York's Theatre, (*Enthoven*, dated 31 December 1906)

'News Notes', *The Bookman*, 31, 184 (January 1907)

'The Ever-Lovable *Peter Pan*', *The Tatler*, 2 January 1907

Granville Barker, H. 'J. M. Barrie as Dramatist', *The Bookman*, 39, 229 (October 1910)

Moffat, J. 'J. M. Barrie and his Books', *The Bookman*, 39, 229 (October 1910)

Noyes, A. 'Peter and Wendy', *The Bookman*, 41, 243 (December 1911)

'New Theatre, *Peter Pan*', review article, (*Enthoven*, dated 1915)

Marcosson, I. F. and Frohman, D. *Charles Frohman: Manager and Man*, with an appreciation by J. M. Barrie (London: Bodley Head, 1916)

Flower, W. N. *The Boy Who Did Grow Up* (London: Cassell, 1919)

'What the Audience Thinks. "Mary Rose" and "Peter Pan" Competitions Results', *The Bookman*, 59, 351 (December 1920)

Smith, Sheila K. 'J. M. Barrie, The Tragedian', *The Bookman*, 59, 351 (December 1920)

Sutro, A. 'J. M. Barrie and The Stage', *The Bookman*, 59, 351 (December 1920)

Walbrook, H. M. *J. M. Barrie and the Theatre* (London: F. V. White, 1922)

Darton, H. J. *M. Barrie* (London: Nisbet, 1929)

The 78th Annual Report of the Board of Management (London: Great Ormond Street Hospital for Sick Children, 1929)

Kennedy, J. *Thrums and the Barrie Country* (London: Heath Cranton, 1930)

'Barrie as Dramatist, A Divided Mind', *Times Literary Supplement*, 26 June 1937

Mackail, D. *The Story of J.M.B.* (London: Peter Davies, 1941)

Trewin, J. C. 'Creator of *Peter Pan*', *Everybody's*, 1 September 1951

'The Truth about Pantomime Fairies', *The Listener*, 10 January 1952

Lucas, C. 'Broadway Hails Mary Martin', *Daily Mail*, 2 October 1954

Green, R. L. *Fifty Years of Peter Pan* (London: Peter Davies, 1954)

'Everybody's Show Business', *Everybody's*, 1 January 1955

'Now *Peter Pan* goes Touring on Ice', *Daily Express*, 26 February 1955

'*Peter Pan* earns Hospital £27 500', *Daily Mail*, 26 February 1955

Stanley, L. T. 'The Spirit of Pantomime', *Queen*, 13 November 1956

'*When Wendy Grew Up*, an Afterthought on *Peter Pan* by Sir James Barrie', *John Bull*, 1957 (*Enthoven*)

'*Peter Pan* Film, Great Ormond Street Sells Rights', *New York Daily Telegraph*, 14 February 1962

'Before Tomorrow's Diamond Jubilee: The Story Behind the Story of *Peter Pan*', *Daily Mail*, 17 December 1964

'Appeal in *Peter Pan* Film Case', *The Times*, 25 January 1967

Dunbar, Janet. *J. M. Barrie, the Man behind the Image* (London: Collins, 1970)

Macleod, A. '*Peter Pan*', *The Times*, 21 December 1971

'*Peter Pan* as Film Musical', *The Times*, 18 January 1972

'Film of *Peter Pan*', *The Times*, 12 August 1972

'This Most Generous Gift – J. M. Barrie, *Peter Pan* and The Hospital for Sick Children', *The Great Ormond Street Gazette*, March 1973

Peter Pan 1904–1974, The Seventy Glorious Years, souvenir booklet issued with the 1974 Duke of York's production (Reading: Creative Press, 1974)

Plowman, J. *The Peter Pan Man*, an entertainment based on the life and work of J. M. Barrie (typescript), London, the King's Head Theatre, January 1975

Fraser, M. *The Death of Narcissus* (London: Secker and Warburg, 1976)

Billington, M. 'Peter Pan', *Guardian*, 23 December 1977

Lewis, Naomi. 'J. M. Barrie' in D. Kirkpatrick (ed). *Twentieth-century Children's Writers* (London: Macmillan, 1978)

Du Maurier, Daphne. 'Sylvia's Boys', *Radio Times*, 7–13 October 1978

Blow, S. 'The Secret Life of Peter Pan', *Guardian*, 7 October 1978
Morley, S. 'Last Survivor of Barrie's Favourite Five', *The Times*, 11 October 1978
Birkin, A. *The Lost Boys*, a trilogy, BBC2 *Play of the Week*, 11, 18, 25 October 1978
Bourne, R. 'Save Mole and Co!', *Evening Standard*, 13 November 1978
Ellison, Jane. 'Tinkerbell Lives', *Evening Standard*, 21 December 1978
King, F. 'Allegory in Disguise', *Sunday Telegraph*, 24 December 1978
Birkin, A. *J. M. Barrie and the Lost Boys* (London: Constable, 1979)
Lewis, Naomi. 'Peter Pan's Progeny', *Observer*, 27 May 1979
Raidy, W. A. 'Duncan Soars in Revival of *Peter Pan*', *The Star-Ledger*, 7 September 1979
Cottens, W. B. 'Peter Pan Opens Spritely', *Philadelphia Enquirer*, 8 September 1979
Clarke, G. 'Rememberance of Things Past', *Time*, 17 September 1979
Gill, B. 'The Theatre Tiny-Tot Time', *New Yorker*, 17 September 1979
'Peter Pan', *Sunday Telegraph*, 23 September 1979
Shorter, E. 'Peter Pan', *Daily Telegraph*, 6 December 1979
Roberts, Glenys. 'The Personification of Peter Pan', *The Times*, 20 December 1979
Shulman, M. 'Barrie's Heroes Win Through', *Evening Standard*, 21 December 1979
Wardle, I. '*Peter Pan*', *The Times*, 21 December 1979
Sutcliffe, T. 'Peter Pan', *Guardian*, 21 December 1979.
'Children's Hospital Beds saved by Grant', *The Times*, 30 October 1982
'Whisper who Cares . . .', *Sunday Times*, 31 October 1982
'Must the Caring Stop? The Tadworth Affair, Sick Children at Risk', *Sunday Times*, 21 November 1982
Peter Pan, programme of 1982 production, London, Barbican Theatre, 10 December 1982
Billington, M. 'Midwinter's night dream', *Guardian*, 17 December 1982
Wardle, I. 'Neverland 20 years on', *The Times*, 18 December 1982
Cushman, R. 'Renovated', *Observer*, 19 December 1982
Fenton, J. 'Flight of a great imagination', *Sunday Times*, 19 December 1982

4. *Bibliographical Information*

Beinecke, W. (Jnr). 'Barrie in the Parrish Collection', *Princeton University Library Chronicle*, 17, 2 (Winter 1956)
Cutler, B. D. *Sir James Barrie, a Bibliography* (New York: Greenburg, 1931)
Mott, H. S. 'The Walter Beinecke Jr., J. M. Barrie Collection', *Yale University Library Gazette*, 39 (1965) pp. 163–7

CHILDREN'S LITERATURE

1. *Texts*

The following list includes only those books directly referred to or having direct relevance to the argument.

Adams, R. *Watership Down* (London: Collings, 1972)

Alcott, Louisa May. *Little Women* (Boston: Roberts, 1868) (4th edn, London: Sampson Low, 1871)

Anstey, F. (Thomas Anstey Guthrie) *Vice Versa, or, A Lesson to Fathers* (London: Smith and Elder, 1882)

Ballantyne, R. M. *The Coral Island* (London: Nelson, 1858)

Blyton, Enid. *Five Fall into an Adventure* (London: Hodder and Stoughton, 1950)

Blyton, Enid. *Five Run Away Together* (London: Hodder and Stoughton, 1944)

Boreham, T. *The Gigantick Histories of Thomas Boreman* (1740–3), ed. Wilbur Stone (Maine: Southworth Press, 1933)

The Boy's Own Paper, ed. James Macauly (London: Leisure House, 1879–   )

Carroll, L. (Charles Lutwidge Dodgson) *Alice's Adventure in Wonderland* (London: Macmillan, 1865)

Carroll, L. (Charles Lutwidge Dodgson) *Through the Looking Glass* (London: Macmillan, 1872)

Chambers, A. *Breaktime* (London: Bodley Head, 1978)

Churne, W. (Francis Edward Paget) *The Hope of the Katzekopfs* (London: Burns, The Juvenile Englishman's Library, 2, 1844)

Cooper, J. Fenimore. *The Last of the Mohicans*, Bell's Literature Readers (London: Bell, 1909)

Corkran, Alice. *The Adventures of Mrs. Wishing-to-be, and other stories* (London: Blackie, 1883)

Dasent, G. *A Selection from the Norse Tales for the Use of Children* (Edinburgh: Edmonston and Douglas, 1862)

Day, T. *The History of Sandford and Merton* (London: Stockdale, 1783–9)

Dickens, C. *The Cricket on the Hearth* (London: Bradbury and Evans, 1846)

Dickens, C. 'Holiday Romance', *Our Young Folks*, IV (i–v) (January–May 1868)

Ewing, Juliana Horatia and H. K. F. Gatty. *Aunt Judy's Christmas Volume for 1874* (London: Bell, 1874)

Ewing, Juliana Horatia. *The Brownies and Other Tales* (London: Bell and Daldy, 1870)

Ewing, Juliana Horatia. *Jackanapes* (London: Society for Promoting Christian Knowledge, 1884)

Ewing, Juliana Horatia. *Old Fashioned Fairy Tales* (London: Society for Promoting Christian Knowledge, 1882)

Farrar, F. W. *Eric, or, Little by Little* (Edinburgh: Adam and Charles Black, 1858)

Fielding, Sarah. *The Governess or The Little Female Academy* (London: Millar, 1749)

Garner, A. *Elidor* (London: Collins, 1965)

Garner, A. *The Moon of Gomrath* (London: Collins, 1963)

Garner, A. *The Owl Service* (London: Collins, 1967)

Garner, A. *Red Shift* (London: Collins, 1973)

Garner, A. *The Stone Quartet* (London; Collins, 1976–8): 1. *The Stone Book* (1976); 2. *Tom Fobble's Day* (1977); 3. *Granny Reardun* (1977); 4. *The Aimer Gate* (1978)

Garner, A. *The Weirdstone of Brisingamen* (London: Collins, 1960)

Gatty, Margaret. *The Fairy Godmothers and Other Tales* (London: Bell, 1851)

The Girl's Own Paper, ed. James Macauly (London: Leisure-Hour, 1880–1908) continued as *The Girl's Own Paper and Woman's Magazine*, 1908–27

Henty, G. A. *Out on the Pampas, or The Young Settlers, a tale for Boys* (London: Griffith and Farran, 1871)

Hicks, S. *Bluebell in Fairyland* (1901) (London: Samuel French, Copyright 1927)

Hoffman, H. *The English Struwwelpeter, or Pretty Stories and Funny Pictures for little Children*, after the fourth edition (Leipsic: Friedrich Volckmar 1848)

Hood, T. *Petsetilla's Posy* (1870) (London: Routledge, 1871)

Hughes, T. *Tom Brown's Schooldays* (London: Bell and Daldy, 1857)

Ingelow, Jean. *Mopsa the Fairy* (London: Longmans and Green, 1869)

Jacobs, J. *English Fairy Tales* and *More English Fairy Tales* (1890, 1894), published as *English Fairy Tales* (London: Bodley Head, 1968)

Juster, N. *The Phantom Tollbooth* (London: Collins, 1962)

Keary, Annie. *The Heroes of Asgard and the Giants of Jötunheim, or, The Week and its Story* (London: Bogue, 1857)

Kingsley, C. *The Water Babies* (London and Cambridge: Macmillan, 1863)

Kingston, W. H. G. *The Three Midshipmen* (London: Griffin and Farran, 1871)

Kipling, R. *Stalkey and Co.* (London: Macmillan, 1899)

Lang, A. *The Blue Fairy Book* (London: Longmans and Green, 1899)

Lang, A. *Prince Prigio* (London: Simpkin and Marshall, 1889)

Lear, E. *A Book of Nonsense* (London: McLean, 1846)

Lear, E. *Laughable Lyrics, a fourth Book of nonsense poems, Songs, Botany, Music, etc.* (London: Bush, 1877)

Lear, E. *More Nonsense Pictures, Rhymes, Botany, etc.* (London: Bush, 1872)

Lear, E. *Nonsense Songs, Stories, Botany and Alphabets* (London: Bush, 1871)

Lemon, M. *The Enchanted Doll* (London: Bradbury and Evans, 1849)

Marryat, F. (Captain). *Masterman Ready or The Wreck of the Pacific* (1841–2) (London: Bell, 1878)

Mayne, W. *All the King's Men* (London: Jonathan Cape, 1982)

Molesworth, Mary Louisa. *'Carrots' Just a Little Boy* (London: Macmillan, 1891)

Molesworth, Mary Louisa. *This and That. A Tale of Two Tinies* (London: Macmillan, 1899)

Mulock, Dinah. *The Adventures of a Brownie* (London: Sampson Low, 1872)

Mulock, Dinah. *Alice Learmont* (London: Chapman and Hall, 1852)

Mulock, Dinah. *The Fairy Book* (London and Cambridge: Macmillan, 1863)

Mulock, Dinah. *John Halifax, Gentleman* (London: Hurst and Blacket, 1856)

Nesbit, E. *The Story of the Treasure Seekers* (London: Fisher Unwin, 1899)

Newbery, J. *A Little Lottery Book for Children* (London: Newbery, 1756)

Newbery, J. *A Little Pretty Pocket Book* (1744) facsimile edition M. F. Thwaite (London: Oxford University Press, 1966)

[Parley, Peter] Martin W. (ed). *Peter Parley's Annual for 1864* (London: Kent, 1864)

[Parley, Peter] Goodrich S. G. *Peter Parley's Book of the United States* (Boston: Charles Hendee (1827), 1837)

[Parley, Peter] Goodrich S. G. *The Tales of Peter Parley About America* (1827) preface by M. L. Cohen (New York and London: Garland, 1977)

Peter Parley's Universal History on the Basis of Geography (London: Parker, 1837; 6th–12th editions, London: William Tegg, 1854–67)

Reed, T. B. *The Fifth Form at St. Dominic's* (London: The Religious Tract Society, 1887) (originally published in the *Boy's Own Paper*, IV (142–180) (2 October 1881–24 June 1882)

Reid, T. Mayne. *The Fatal Cord* (London: Ward, Lock and Tyler, 1870)

Reid, T. Mayne. *The Headless Horseman* (London: Richard Bentley, 1866)

Ryland, Clara. *Snow White and Rose Red and Other Plays for Children* (London: Dent, 1896)

Sendak, M. *Where The Wild Things Are* (London: Bodley Head, 1967)

Sherwood, Mrs (Mary Martha Butt). *The Fairchild Family* (London: Hatchard, 1818)

Sinclair, Catherine. *Holiday House* (Edinburgh: Whyte, 1839)

Stevenson, R. L. *Kidnapped* (London: Henderson, 1886)

Stevenson, R. L. *Treasure Island* (London: Cassel, 1883)

Summerly, Felix (Sir Henry Cole). *The Home Treasury*, 11 vols (London: Joseph Cundall, 1843–5): 1. *Traditional Nursery Songs of England* (1843); 5. *Sir Hornbook, or, Childe Launcelot's Expedition, a Grammaticio-allegorical ballad* (1843); 6. *The Chronicle of the Valiant Feats, Wonderful Victories and Bold Adventures of Jack the Giant Killer* (1845); 7. *Beauty and the Beast*, an entirely new edition (1843); 8. *Puck's Reports to Oberon* (1844); 10. *The Pleasant History of Reynard the Fox*, told by the pictures of Albert Van Everdingen (1843); 11. *Little Red Riding Hood*, an entirely new edition (1843)

Syrett, Netta. *Six Fairy Plays for Children* (London: Bodley Head, 1903)

Watts, I. *The Improvement of the Mind* (1741) (London: Buckland and Longman, 1782)

Wyss, J. D. *The Swiss Family Robinson*, translated from the German (London: Godwin, 1818)

2. Histories, Commentaries, etc.

Applebee, A. N. *The Child's Concept of Story* (University of Chicago Press, 1978)

Avery, Gillian. *Nineteenth-century Children, Heroes and Heroines in English Children's Stories 1780–1900* (London: Hodder and Stoughton, 1965)

Briggs, Julia. 'The Childhood of History', *Times Literary Supplement*, 26 March 1982

Buchan, J. 'The Novel and the Fairy Tale' (1931) in Virginia Haviland (ed), *Children and Literature, Views and Reviews* (London: Bodley Head, 1973)

Chambers, A. 'The Reader in the Book: Notes from Work in Progress', *Signal*, 23 (May 1977) pp. 64–87

Cook, Elizabeth. *The Ordinary and the Fabulous, an Introduction to Myths, Legends and Fairy Tales for Teachers and Story-tellers* (Cambridge University Press, 1969)

Crago, H. 'Cultural Categories and the Criticism of Children's Literature', *Signal*, 30 (September 1979) pp. 140–50

Crouch, M. *The Nesbit Tradition, the Children's Novel in England 1945–70* (London: Benn, 1972)

Darton, F. J. H. *Children's Books in England, Five Centuries of Social Life* (Cambridge University Press, 1932) (third edition revised by Brian Alderson, Cambridge University Press, 1982)

Dixon, B. *Catching Them Young*: 1. *Sex, Race and Class in Children's Fiction*, 2. *Political Ideas in Children's Fiction* (London: Pluto Press, 1977)

Egoff, Sheila A. and G. T. and L. F. Ashley (eds). *Only Connect: Readings on Children's Literature* (Toronto and New York: Oxford University Press, 1969)

Eyre, F. *British Children's Books in the Twentieth Century* (London: Longman, 1971)

Field, E. M. *The Child and his Book: Some Account of the History and Progress of Children's Literature in England* (London: Wells, Gardner and Darton, 1891)

Fox, G. and G. Hammond (eds). *Responses to Children's Literature*, proceedings of the fourth symposium of the International Research Society for Children's Literature (London: Saur, 1978)

Gardner, M. (ed). *The Annotated Alice* (Harmondsworth: Penguin, 1965)

Green, R. L. *Tellers of Tales, Children's Books and their Authors from 1800–1968* (Norwich: Kaye and Ward, 1969)

Greenland, C. 'Modes and Modules', *Times Literary Supplement*, 23 July 1982

Hildick, W. *Children and Fiction, a critical study in depth of the artistic and psychological factors involved in writing fiction for and about children* (1970) (London: Evans, revised edn, 1974)

Hunt, P. 'Critical Method for Children's Literature: A Booklist by Peter Hunt', *Signal*, 19 (January 1976) pp. 12–21

Hunt, P. 'Criticism and Children's Literature', *Signal* (15 September 1974) pp. 117–30

Hunt, P. 'The Mayne Game: An Experiment in Response', *Signal*, 28 (January 1979) pp. 9–25

Karavasil, Josephine. 'A Psychological Friend', *Times Literary Supplement*, 23 July 1982

Kirkpatrick, D. (ed). *Twentieth-Century Children's Writers* (London: Macmillan, 1978)

Meek, Margaret. 'The Disappearing Child', *Times Literary Supplement*, 7 April 1978(a)

Meek, Margaret. 'A View from the Steeple', *Times Literary Supplement*, 29 September 1978(b)

Meek, Margaret. 'Questions of Response', *Signal*, 31 (January 1980) pp. 29–35

Meek, Margaret. 'The Telling of Stories', *Times Literary Supplement*, 23 July 1982

Muir, P. *English Children's Books 1600–1900* (London: Batsford, 1954)

Orwell, G. 'Boys' Weeklies', in *Inside the Whale and Other Essays* (London: Gollancz, 1940)

Paton Walsh, Jill. 'The Devil and the Deep Blue Sea', *New Statesman*, 28 November 1980

Philip, N. *A Fine Anger. A Critical Introduction to the Work of Alan Garner* (London: Collins, 1981)

Phillips, R. *Aspects of Alice* (London: Gollancz, 1972)

Rees, D. 'Beyond Childhood', *Times Literary Supplement*, 23 July 1982

Salmon, E. *Juvenile Literature as It Is* (London: Drane, 1888)

Soriano, M. 'Cautionary Tales', interview with Marc Soriano by Michel Sailhan, *Guardian*, 24 January 1982

Soriano, M. *Le dossier Charles Perrault* (Paris: Hachette, 1972)

Stones, Rosemary. 'To the Salt Mines', *New Statesman*, 21 November 1980

Tolkien, J. R. R. 'On Fairy-stories' (1938) *Essays presented to Charles Williams* (London: Oxford University Press, 1947)

Townsend, J. R. *A Sense of Story, Essays on Contemporary Writers for Children* (London: Longman, 1971)

Townsend, J. R. 'Standards of Criticism for Children's Literature', *Signal*, 14 (May 1974) pp. 91–105

Townsend, J. R. *Written for Children, an Outline of English Children's Literature* (London: Garnet Miller, 1965)

Trease, G. *Tales out of School* (1949) (London: Heinemann, 1964)

Westall, R. 'How Real Do You Want Your Realism?', *Signal*, 28 (January 1979) pp. 34–46

Yonge, Charlotte M. 'Children's Books of the Last Century', *Macmillan's Magazine*, July–September 1869, reprinted *Signal*, 2–4 (May 1970–June 1971)

Yonge, Charlotte M. *What Books to Lend and What to Give* (London: National Society's Depository, 1887)

'Children's Books', *The Quarterly Review*, LXXIV, 174 (1844) pp. 1–26

'Children's Literature', *The London Review*, 26 (January 1860) pp. 469–500

'Literature of Childhood', *The London and Westminster Review*, XXXIII (1840) pp. 137–62

'Race, Sex and Class in Children's Books', *New Statesman*, 14 November–19 December 1980

EDUCATIONAL, LITERARY, THEATRICAL AND SOCIAL HISTORY OF CHILDHOOD

Appignanesi, R. 'Some Thoughts on Freud's Discovery of Childhood', in *Changing Childhood*, ed. Martin Hoyle (London: Readers and Writers Publishing Cooperative, 1979) pp 185–200

Ariès, P. *L'enfant et la vie familiale sous l'ancien régime* (Paris: Plon, 1960); *Centuries of Childhood*, trs. Robert Baldick (London: Jonathan Cape, 1962)

Armstrong, W. A. 'The Nineteenth-century Matinee', *Theatre Notebook*, 14, 2 (Winter 1959) pp. 56–9

Arnold, M. *Culture and Anarchy* (London: Smith Elder, 1869)

Arnold, M. *A French Eton, or, Middle Class Education and the State* (London: Macmillan, 1864)

Arnold, M. *Reports on the Elementary Schools 1852–1882*, ed. Sir Francis Sandford (London: Macmillan, 1899)

Athenaeum, the, the journal of English and Foreign Literature, Science, Fine Arts, Music and the Drama, 1–4737 (January 1828–February 1921)

Author, the, the organ of the Society of Authors, 1899–1913

Balibar, René with the collaboration of G. Merlin and G. Tret, *Les Francais Fictifs* (Paris: Hachette, 1974)

Board of Education. *Suggestions for the Consideration of Teachers and Others Concerned in the Work of Public Elementary Schools* (London: Board of Education, Circular 808, 1912)

Board of Education. *The Teaching of English in Secondary Schools* (London: Board of Education, Circular 753, 1910)

Boas, G. *The Cult of Childhood* (London: The Warburg Institute, 1966)

Bookman, the, a monthly journal for bookreaders, bookbuyers and booksellers, 1–87 (October 1891–December 1934)

Book Monthly, the, an illustrated record guide and magazine for booksellers, librarians and publishers, for bookbuyers, readers and writers, 1–15 (October 1903–June 1920)

Booth, M. R. *Victorian Spectacular Theatre 1850–1910* (London: Routledge and Kegan Paul, 1981)

Bullock A. *A Language for Life*, report of the Committee of Inquiry appointed by

the Secretary of State for Education and Science under the chairmanship of Sir
Alan Bullock (London: HMSO, 1974)

Chambers Narrative Readers, 5 vols (London and Edinburgh: W. and R. Chambers,
1906–14)

Chambers Narrative Series of Standard Reading Books, 6 vols (London and Edinburgh:
W. and R. Chambers, 1863)

Crozier, B. 'Notions of Childhood in London Theatre 1880–1905', unpublished
PhD thesis, Cambridge University, 1981

Cruse, Amy. *The Victorians and their Books* (London: Allen and Unwin, 1935)

Darwin, B. *The English Public School* (London: Longmans and Green, 1929)

Davin, Anna. 'Imperialism and Motherhood', *History Workshop*, 5 (Spring 1978)
pp. 9–65

Disher, M. W. *Clowns and Pantomimes* (London: Constable, 1925)

Farjeon, Eleanor. *A Nursery in the Nineties* (London: Gollancz, 1935)

Ganzel, D. 'Patent Wrongs and Patent Theatres: Drama and the Law in the
Early Nineteenth Century', *PMLA*, 76, 4 part I (September 1961)

Gernsheim, H. (ed). *Lewis Carroll, Victorian Photographer* (London: Max Parrish,
1949)

Gorham, Deborah. 'The "Maiden Tribute of Modern Babylon" Re-examined:
Child Prostitution and the Idea of Childhood in Late-Victorian England',
Victorian Studies (Spring 1978) pp. 353–79

Greater London Council Record Office and Library (SBL/1350), *Final Report of the School
Board for London 1870–1904*, Part I: *Books and Apparatus*, pp. 147–50

Greater London Council Record Office and Library (SBL/188), *Minutes of the Special
Committee on the Selection of School Books*, 1899–1901

*Greater London Record Office and Library, School Board for London, Minutes of
Proceedings*, 1899–1902

*Greater London Council Record Office and Library, London County Council Education
Committee Minutes*, 1904–1915

Green Room Book, the, or, Who's Who on the Stage, 1906–

Guthkelch, A. (ed). *English Texts for Secondary Schools* (London: Bell, 1907)

Guttsman, W. L. 'Aristocracy and Middle Class in the British Political Elite
1886–1916', *The British Journal of Sociology*, 5, 1 (March 1954) pp. 12–32

Halévy, E. *Histoire du peuple anglais au XIXe siècle*, 5 vols (Paris: Hachette,
1912–32), *Epilogue 1895–1914*, 4 (1), *Les Impérialistes au pouvoir 1895–1905*,
1926

Hollingsworth, B. 'The Mother Tongue and Public Schools in the 1860s', *British
Journal of Educational Studies*, 22, 3 (October 1974) pp. 312–24

Laporte, Dominique. 'L'histoire de l'éducation', *Ornicar*, periodical of the
Champ freudien (Paris: Le graphe) 2 (March 1975) pp. 41–53

Leavis, F. R. *The Great Tradition* (London: Chatto and Windus, 1948)

Leavis, F. R. *Mass Civilisation and Minority Culture* (Cambridge: Gordon Fraser,
1930)

Linklater, M. ' "Victorian" Photos Faked', *Sunday Times*, 19 November 1978

Longman's British Empire Readers, 11 vols (London: Longmans, 1905)

Mack, E. C. *Public Schools and British Opinion since 1860* (London: Methuen, 1941)

Marcus, S. *The Other Victorians. A Study of Sexuality and Pornography in mid-
Nineteenth-century England* (London: Weidenfeld and Nicolson, 1966)

Middleton, N. 'The Education Act of 1870 as the Start of the Modern

Conception of the Child', *British Journal of Educational Studies*, 18, 2 (June 1970) pp. 166–79

Mulhern, F. *The Moment of Scrutiny* (London: New Left Books, 1979)

Musgrave, P. W. 'The Relationship between the Family and Education in England: a Sociological Account', *British Journal of Educational Studies*, 19, 1 (February 1971) pp. 17–31

Newsome, D. *Godliness and Good Learning. Four Studies on a Victorian Ideal* (London: Murray, 1961)

Ovenden, G. *Victorian Children* (London: Academy Editions, 1972)

Pascoe, C. E. (ed). *Everyday Life in Our Public Schools* (London: Griffith and Farran, 1881)

Pitcairn, E. H. (ed). *Unwritten Laws and Ideals of Active Careers* (London: Smith Elder, 1899)

The Public Schools from Within, a collection of essays on public school education written chiefly by Schoolmasters (London: Low and Marston, 1906)

Publisher's Circular, the, and Bookseller's Record of British and Foreign literature, 1, 1, – 173, 4846 (October 1837–May 1959)

Rogers, A. 'Churches and Children – a Study in the Controversy over the 1902 Educational Act', *British Journal of Educational Studies*, 8, 1 (November 1959) pp. 29–51

Settle, A. T. and Baber, F. H. *The Law of Public Entertainments* (London: Sweet and Maxwell, 1915)

Simon, B. *Studies in the History of Education*, vol. 1, 1780–1870 (London: Lawrence and Wishart, 1960)

Sims, G. R. *Without the Limelight* (London: Chatto and Windus, 1900)

Speaight, G. 'Pantomime', *Theatre Notebook*, 5, 2 (January–March 1951) pp. 38–9

Stedman Jones, G. *Outcast London* (Oxford: Clarendon Press, 1971)

Theatre Magazine, the, (*The Book of the Play*), 1(1–8) (1906–7)

Tillotson, Kathleen. *Novels of the 1840s* (London: Oxford University Press, 1954)

Walkowitz, Judith. *Prostitution and Victorian Society, Women, Class and the State* (New York: Cambridge University Press, 1980)

Wilkinson, R. *The Prefects, British Leadership and the Public School Tradition* (London: Oxford University Press, 1964)

Williams, R. *The Long Revolution* (London: Chatto and Windus, 1961)

Wilson, A. E. *Christmas Pantomime, the Story of an English Institution* (London: Allen and Unwin, 1934)

Wilson, A. E. *Half a Century of Entertainment*, illustrations from the Raymond Mander, Joe Mitchenson Collection (London: Yates, 1951)

Wilson, A. E. *Penny Plain, Two Pence Coloured: a History of the Juvenile Drama* (London: G. G. Harrap, 1932)

Wilson, R. *Macmillan's Sentence Building*, a graduated course of lessons in synthetic English, 14 vols (London: Macmillan, 1914(a))

Wilson, R. *The Progress to Literature*, 5 vols (London: Macmillan, 1914(b))

Woodruff, P. *The Men who Ruled India*, vol. II, *The Guardians* (London: Jonathan Cape, 1954)

Wyld, H. C. *The Place of the Mother Tongue in the National Education* (London: John Murray, 1906)

PSYCHOANALYSIS

Baum, A. L. 'Carroll's *Alices*: The Semiotics of Paradox', *American Imago*, 34, 1 (Spring 1977) pp. 86–108

Bettelheim, B. and Zelan, Karen. *On Learning to Read, The Child's Fascination with Meaning* (New York: Knopf, 1981)

Bettelheim, B. *The Uses of Enchantment, The Meaning and Importance of Fairy Tales* (London: Thames and Hudson, 1976)

Bonaparte, Marie. *Edgar Poe, sa vie, son oeuvre* (Paris: Presses Universitaires de France, 1958)

Ferenczi, S. 'Confusion of Tongues between Adults and the Child' (1933), *Final Contributions to the Problems and Methods of Psychoanalysis*, ed. Michael Balint, trs. E. Mosbacher (London: Hogarth, 1955)

Freud, S. *Analysis of a Phobia in a Five-Year-Old Boy* ('Little Hans') (SE, x, 1909) pp. 1–149 (PF, 8)

Freud, S. 'Family Romances' (SE, ix (1908) 1909) pp. 237–41 (PF, 7)

Freud, S. *From the History of an Infantile Neurosis* ('The Wolf Man') (SE, xvii (1914) 1918) pp. 3–123 (PF, 9))

Freud, S. 'The Infantile Genital Organisation: an Interpolation into the Theory of Sexuality' (SE, xix, 1923) pp. 141–5 (PF, 7)

Freud, S. *The Interpretation of Dreams* (SE, iv–v, 1900) (PF, 4)

Freud, S. *Moses and Monotheism* (SE, xxiii (1934–8) 1939) pp. 3–137

Freud, S. 'Screen Memories' (SE, iii, 1899) pp. 301–22

Freud, S. 'On the Sexual Theories of Children' (SE, ix, 1908) pp. 205–26 (PF, 7)

Freud, S. *Three Essays on the Theory of Sexuality* (SE, vii, 1905) pp. 123–245 (PF, 7)

Green, A. *Un Oeil en trop* (Paris: Minuit, 1969). *The Tragic Effect; Oedipus Complex and Tragedy*, trs. Alan Sheridan (Cambridge University Press, 1979)

Greenacre, Phyllis. ' "It's my own invention": a Special Screen Memory of Mr. Lewis Carroll, its Form and its History', *Psychoanalytic Quarterly*, 24 (1955) pp. 200–44

Grotjahn, M. 'About the Symbolisation of Alice's Adventures in Wonderland', *American Imago*, 4 (1947) pp. 32–41

Grotjahn, M. '*Alice in Wonderland* and the Joy of Regression', in *Beyond Laughter* (New York: McGraw-Hill, 1957)

Grotjahn, M. 'The Defenses Against Creative Anxiety in The Life and Work of James Barrie', *American Imago*, 14 (1957) pp. 143–8

Jung, C. G. *The Archetypes and the Collective Unconscious*, Collected Works, 9 (1) (London: Routledge and Kegan Paul, 1959)

Karpe, Marietta. 'The Origins of Peter Pan', *The Psychoanalytic Review*, 43 (1956) pp. 104–10

Keller, Evelyn. 'Lewis Carroll: A Study of Mathematical Inhibition', *Journal of the American Psychoanalytic Association*, 28, 1 (1980) pp. 133–60

Lacan, J. 'L'instance de la lettre dans l'inconscient ou la raison depuis Freud' (1957), *Ecrits* (Paris: Seuil, 1966) pp. 492–528; 'The Agency of the Letter in the Unconscious or Reason since Freud', *Ecrits: a Selection*, trs. Alan Sheridan (London: Tavistock, 1977) pp. 146–78

Lacan, J. 'Le séminaire sur "la lettre volée" ' (1957), *Ecrits*; 'Seminar on "The Purloined Letter" ', trs. and ed. J. Mehlman, in *The French Freud*, Yale French Studies, 48 (1972) pp. 38–72

Lacan, J. 'Le stade du miroir' (1936), *Ecrits*, pp. 93–100; 'The Mirror Stage', *Ecrits: a Selection*, pp. 1–7

Meisel, F. L. 'The Myth of Peter Pan', *The Psychoanalytic Study of the Child*, 32 (1977) pp. 545–63

Peller, Lilli. 'Daydreams and Children's Favourite Books', *The Psychoanalytic Study of the Child*. 14 (1956) pp. 414–33

Pollock, G. H. 'On Siblings, Childhood Sibling Loss and Creativity', *Annual of Psychoanalysis*, 6 (1978) pp. 443–81

Schilder, P. 'Psychoanalytic Remarks on *Alice in Wonderland* and Lewis Carroll', *Journal of Nervous and Mental Diseases*, 87, 2 (February 1938) pp. 159–68

Skinner, J. 'James M. Barrie or The Boy Who Wouldn't Grow Up', *American Imago*, 14 (1957) pp. 111–41

Skinner, J. 'Lewis Carroll's Adventures in Wonderland', *American Imago*, 4 (1947) pp. 3–31

Solomon, J. C. 'Alice and the Red King: The Psychoanalytic View of Existence', *International Journal of Psychoanalysis*, 44 (1963) pp. 63–73

Winnicot, D. W. *Playing and Reality* (London: Tavistock, 1971)

OTHER WRITINGS

d'Aulnoy, Mme. *L'oiseau bleu et autres contes* (1696–99) (Paris: Bourrelier, 1953)

Bechstein, L. *The Old Story-Teller, Popular German Stories* (London: Addey, 1854)

Benveniste, E. 'La nature des pronoms' (1956) in *Problèmes de linguistique générale* (Paris: Gallimard 1966) pp. 251–7; 'The Nature of Pronouns', trs. M. E. Meek *Problems in General Linguistics* (Florida: University of Miami Press, 1971)

Benveniste, E. 'Nature du signe linguistique' (1939) in *Problèmes*, pp. 49–55; 'The Nature of the Linguistic Sign', trs. *Problems*, pp. 43–8

Benveniste, E. 'De la subjectivité dans le langage' (1958), in *Problèmes*, pp. 258–66; 'Subjectivity in Language', trs. *Problems*, pp. 223–30

Dasent, G. *Popular Tales from the Norse* with an introductory essay on the origin and diffusion of popular tales (Edinburgh: Edmonston and Douglas, 1859)

Defoe, D. *The Life and Strange Surprising Adventures of Robinson Crusoe* (London: W. Taylor, 1719)

Derrida, J. *De la grammatologie* (Paris: Minuit, 1967); *Of Grammatology*, trs. Guyatri Spivak (London and Baltimore: Johns Hopkins, 1974)

Locke, John. *An Essay concerning Human Understanding* 4th edn (London: A. J. Churchill and S. Manship, 1700)

Locke, J. *Some Thoughts Concerning Education* (London: Churchill, 1693)

Matthews, G. *Philosophy and the Young Child* (London: Harvard, 1980)

Mauss, M. 'Essai sur le don: forme archaïque de l'échange' *Année Sociologique*, I (1925) pp. 30–186, trs. I. Cunnison, *The Gift: Form and Function of Exchange in Archaic Societies* (London: Cohen and West, 1954)

Melly, G. and J. R. Glaves-Smith. *A Child of Six Could Do It!* Cartoons about Modern Art (London: Tate Gallery, 1973)

Perrault, C. *Contes* (1697) (Paris: Garnier, 1967)

Planché, J. R. *Four and Twenty Fairy Tales* selected from those of Perrault and other popular writers (London: Routledge, 1858)

Rousseau, J. J. *A Discourse upon the Origin and Foundation of the Inequality among Mankind* (1754) (London: Dodsley, 1761)

Rousseau, J. J. *Emile* (La Haye: Neaulme, 1762); *Emilius or Sophia*, trs. Nugent (London: Nourse and Vaillant, 1763)

Rousseau, J. J. *Essai sur l'origine des langues*, facsimile of 1781 edition (Paris: du Graphe, 1969)

de Saussure, F. *Cours de linguistique générale* (1915) (Paris: Payot, 1972); *Course in General Linguistics*, trs. Wade Baskin (revised ed.) (London: Fontana, 1974)

Tolkien, J. R. R. *The Lord of the Rings* (1954–5) (London: Allen and Unwin, 1968)

Index

Lightning Source UK Ltd.
Milton Keynes UK
UKOW051958150612

194488UK00001B/2/A